T0323234

UNDERSTANDING RESEARCH IN THE DIGITAL AGE

Sara Miller McCune founded SAGE Publishing in 1965 to support the dissemination of usable knowledge and educate a global community. SAGE publishes more than 1000 journals and over 800 new books each year, spanning a wide range of subject areas. Our growing selection of library products includes archives, data, case studies and video. SAGE remains majority owned by our founder and after her lifetime will become owned by a charitable trust that secures the company's continued independence.

Los Angeles | London | New Delhi | Singapore | Washington DC | Melbourne

UNDERSTANDING RESEARCH IN THE DIGITAL AGE

Sarah Quinton
Nina Reynolds

Los Angeles | London | New Delhi
Singapore | Washington DC | Melbourne

Los Angeles | London | New Delhi
Singapore | Washington DC | Melbourne

SAGE Publications Ltd
1 Oliver's Yard
55 City Road
London EC1Y 1SP

SAGE Publications Inc.
2455 Teller Road
Thousand Oaks, California 91320

SAGE Publications India Pvt Ltd
B 1/I 1 Mohan Cooperative Industrial Area
Mathura Road
New Delhi 110 044

SAGE Publications Asia-Pacific Pte Ltd
3 Church Street
#10-04 Samsung Hub
Singapore 049483

Editor: Matthew Waters
Editorial assistant: Jasleen Kaur
Production editor: Nicola Carrier
Copyeditor: Gemma Marren
Proofreader: Thea Watson
Indexer: Silvia Benvenuto
Marketing manager: Alison Borg
Cover design: Sheila Tong
Typeset by: C&M Digitals (P) Ltd, Chennai, India
Printed in the UK

Library of Congress Control Number: 2017955498

British Library Cataloguing in Publication data

A catalogue record for this book is available from
the British Library

ISBN 978-1-4739-7881-2
ISBN 978-1-4739-7882-9 (pbk)

At SAGE we take sustainability seriously. Most of our products are printed in the UK using FSC papers and boards.
When we print overseas we ensure sustainable papers are used as measured by the PREPS grading system.
We undertake an annual audit to monitor our sustainability.

From both NR and SQ – to all our past and present research students who have taught us as much as we have taught them about research.

From NR – to AD, AS and BS with gratitude for providing a solid academic grounding.

From SQ – to RPF, ORQ, ESQ and JNT with love.

CONTENTS

LIST OF FIGURES

LIST OF TABLES

ACKNOWLEDGEMENTS

In writing this book we acknowledge the influence of seminal authors and thinkers on this subject such as Robert Kozinets, John Suler, danah boyd and the contributors to Digital Research Confidential, as well institutions such as The Oxford Internet Institute, The Academy of Social Sciences and the Association of Internet Researchers. Our appreciation is also extended to Matthew Waters at Sage who enthused about the text from the beginning, and the rest of the Sage team who have seen this book through to completion. We are also grateful to Emma Coles for once again turning scribbles into professional graphics and to Sarah Glozer for her helpful comments on our first draft. Completing this book has been made easier by our colleagues whose positivity is much appreciated, specifically our thanks to Ana Canhoto, Peter Lugosi and Karen Handley, as well as Lois Burgess, Rodney Clarke, Lee Moerman, Celeste Rossetto and Ann Rogerson. Our appreciation is extended to Dr Harald Mayer from the Digital Space Lab who created the NodeXL semantic network map illustration Figure 1.2.

ABOUT THE AUTHORS

Sarah Quinton is a researcher fascinated by how digitalisation is changing society and how we as researchers explore that changed society. As an academic Sarah teaches research methods with a particular focus on the breadth and ethical implications of digital research possibilities and she spends much time encouraging her Masters' and PhD students to consider the opportunities and complexities of digital research. Previous writing for Sage includes a text book *Postgraduate research in business: a critical guide*. Sarah's research centres around how and why digital technologies are shaping the world of consumption, small business strategy, and citizen behaviour. Her work has been published in multiple international journals including *Industrial Marketing Management, Journal of Strategic Marketing, Journal of Marketing Management, International Journal of Management Reviews*. Sarah currently holds the post of Chair of Research Ethics at Oxford Brookes University.

Nina Reynolds is a Professor of Marketing at the University of Wollongong's School of Management, Operations & Marketing (Australia). She has a long established research stream that focuses on research methods, starting with her MPhil and PhD research projects. This is reflected in her contribution to both qualifying (Master/Doctoral) and non-qualifying research methods education within and across institutions. She is currently supervising a number of research students that are facing the problems associated with research in the digital age. As well as her methodological research stream, her other research interests currently focus on understanding how consumers might develop or increase their wellbeing through consumption, and how transformative services realise positive outcomes. While this is her first text, her methodological research has been published in a number of journals including *Journal of International Business Studies, Journal of Service Research, European Journal of Marketing, International Marketing Review*, and the *International Journal of Market Research*.

PREFACE

This book is the result of a collaboration between two authors who met at an academic conference where one attended the presentation of the other. This led to face-to-face discussions about how digital research could be described and explained. That meeting combined with questions by students, colleagues and from ourselves as researchers over the complexities of research in the digital environment formulated the germ of this book. So in an effort to unpick, explain and make sense of the emerging digital world in which social scientists are now researching we have written this book. We intend that the text and included frameworks will act as a useful guide to understanding digital research from both a conceptual and a practical perspective.

This text, unlike others, does not tie itself to any tool or technique but rather encourages researchers to ask more fundamental questions about the phenomenon they are researching and how to best research those phenomena within the digital context. This book brings to the fore the big questions about digital research and how these questions might apply to our own research. Our text illustrates that the digital age is transforming social science research and by doing so re-evaluates established thinking about the contemporary research environment.

While this text exists in a material sense we are well aware of the shifting and changing digital sands about which we have written, indeed you might be reading this on screen as an e-book, or in the future as an interactive real-time Bot facilitated discussion. To this end we have avoided explicit inclusion of specific software, which may well have disappeared or become obsolete by the time of publication. Instead we offer general social science examples that are contemporary and wide ranging in order to bring to life our underpinning discussions. We have divided the text into three main parts dealing with: the re-conceptualisation of digital research, followed by assessing digital data, and moving onto the practicalities of doing digital research. As we were writing we found that certain ideas such as temporality and the human/technology interface outgrew our original and individual thinking owing to their complexity. Thus certain topics have been given pre-eminence over others and for this we make no apologies.

Broadly speaking we ground the book in two core dimensions of digital research. First, the social science phenomenon being investigated and second, the methods that may be used to research such phenomena. As we created the text three core threads developed: ethics, expectations and expertise. We think that the increasing complexity of researching in the digital environment requires us as researchers to think in a more interconnected way about these three aspects. For example, working with digital data necessitates reflection on the ethics surrounding ownership, sharing and use of digital data, which is connected to the expectations of the researcher, the participant and the reader, which is in turn connected to the expertise required of the researcher to successfully navigate those data. Owing to our different research perspectives (one author takes a deductive stance and the other author is of a more inductive persuasion), during the course of writing we challenged each other's approaches and assumptions about research in the digital context. As a result we feel that this text will be valuable to researchers who take either perspective.

Understanding Research in the Digital Age is targeted towards postgraduate social science research students, doctoral students and their supervisory teams, and experienced researchers who may be embarking on digital research. This text may also be useful for tutors in research methods and will help clarify certain digital research questions for social scientists.

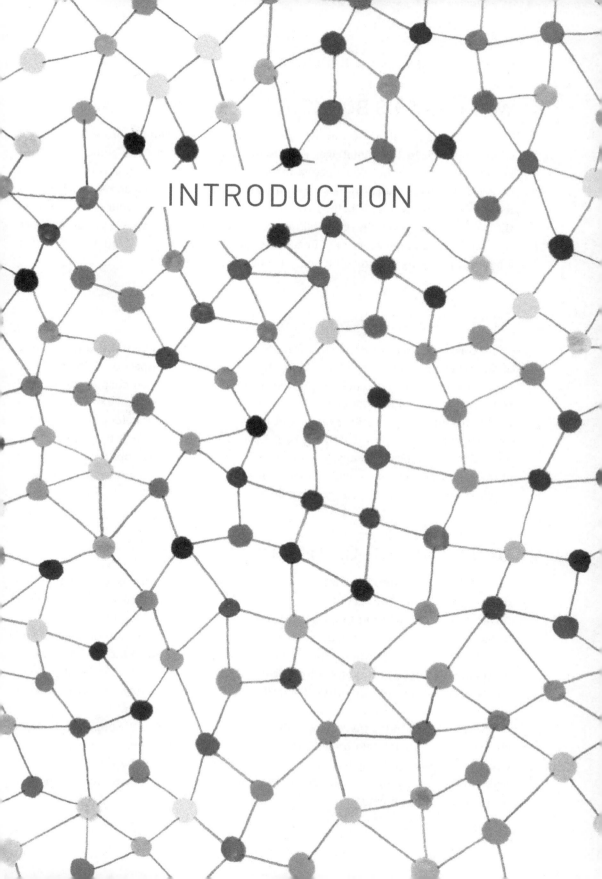

INTRODUCTION

WHY USE THIS BOOK?

This book aims to guide you through the issues, challenges and opportunities of social science research in the digital age. The discussions, frameworks and guidelines in this book will help you to develop a better understanding of how the digital context impacts on social science research in general, and your research in particular. Our goal for our readers is that we will have helped you to consider and reconsider your assumptions of the possibilities and pitfalls of digital research and that this will enable you to enhance the robustness and relevance of your subsequent research. This book can also be used as a basis for justifying your methodological approach.

HOW TO USE THIS BOOK

While this book can be read from cover to cover it is highly likely that it will be dipped into as and when you feel the need for clarification on a particular aspect of digital research. While we may make references to previous or other chapters, each chapter can be read individually as a standalone piece. You could use this book as a source of resources for further reading, of illustrative examples or to help you build your defence for a doctoral viva. The frameworks provided by the book have been designed so that they can easily be applied by researchers investigating a wide range of social science topics. The questions at the end of each chapter could be used within a study group scenario to aid discussions that you might have with your peers on digital research.

ORGANISATION OF THIS BOOK

This book is broken into three main parts. The focus of the first part is reconceptualising digital research. Here we set out to explore how the digital environment is transforming social science research and examine why reviewing current research methods thinking is necessary. We use the distinction between digital as the phenomenon of research and digital as the method/instrument of research, to begin to break down the aspects of digital research. This part also introduces three themes that are returned to throughout the book – ethics, expectations and expertise. The ordering of these three themes is deliberate as good ethical practice is the cornerstone of credible academic research.

The second part of the book assesses digital data by considering the opportunities and challenges that digital data present. Here we explore the characteristics of digital data, temporality issues in digital research and different data sources, along with the processes required to conduct digital research and the interface between humans and technology in the digital environment.

The third part of the book explores the practicalities of how to conduct digital research. Here we offer examples and suggestions to strengthen the implementation of any digital research you might undertake, before returning to the bigger picture of the current research environment. The final chapter returns to the three themes of ethics, expectations and expertise and shows how those themes interconnect in a digital research project, as well as revisiting how digital as a phenomenon and digital as a method/instrument may manifest in digital social science research.

CHAPTER STRUCTURE OF THIS BOOK

Each chapter commences with bullet points to enable you the reader to identify the key areas to be covered, and includes consideration of how the topics covered are influenced by or impact on the three main themes of ethics, expectations and expertise. At the end of each chapter you will find questions to reflect on, as well as a list of further reading that delves into greater detail on the topics covered in the chapter.

PART 1

A Justification and Reconceptualisation of Digital Research

In this part we consider how social science research in the digital age can be conceptualised. We look at both the macro-level conceptualisation of digital research, as well as micro-level issues for individual research projects. In Chapter 1 we identify the importance of recognising that the digital environment impacts on social science phenomena, presenting us with opportunities for research, as well as providing a method or instrument through which research can be undertaken. This chapter also discusses how digital phenomena and/or methods can productively be combined with more established methods and/or known phenomena to produce new insights. Finally in Chapter 1, we outline some of the broad issues for digital researchers to consider and outline the structure of the book.

Chapter 2 takes a narrower perspective, focusing on the impact of the digital environment on research and the research projects we undertake. It starts by considering how working in the digital context may need to change the heuristics we use to think about research. The dynamic nature of the digital environment requires us to contextualise our research within the socio-technological context. We present some questions that will help digital researchers consider both how their research is broadly contextualised, as well as how their research design might need to consider socio-cultural and technological factors.

1
DIGITAL RESEARCH AS A PHENOMENON AND A METHOD

In this chapter we will:

- identify what is digital research
- explain why it matters
- outline the structure of the book.

INTRODUCTION AND SCOPE

As researchers, we can take an optimistic and open, or pessimistic and closed, stance on the use and application of digital technologies for research (Marres, 2012). We can choose to see new technologies as opening up new possibilities of discovery or we can choose to see research and the development of insight as being endangered by a technological shift over which researchers are powerless; a new world where human involvement is lost and research is conducted, analysed and results implemented by 'smart' connected technology. Whichever perspective you hold, or perhaps you are agnostic in your views, this text aims to clarify understanding of digital research across the social sciences to inform post-graduate, doctoral and post-doctoral researchers about the opportunities and issues surrounding digital research while at the same time empowering us to make informed choices.

The digital landscape has both extended existing human behaviours and introduced new ones, as well as interweaving the two (Pink et al., 2016). For researchers it has thus altered what (phenomena) and how (methods) we research. The internet and digital technologies are enabling advances and contributions to scholarship across all disciplines. The creativity afforded by the new digitalised environment and the disruption to some of our established notions of knowledge and research practices offer potential new ways to envisage and conduct research (Knox and Walford, 2016). This book intends first to conceptualise digital research and then to provide questions and, we hope, some answers to researchers wishing to incorporate digital research in their investigations.

Digital technologies continue to have social implications in their effect on individuals and groups, as an enabler or otherwise (Belk, 2013). All social science subjects are affected by the digitalisation of society to some extent, from politics and citizen journalism, through geography and the mapping of movements, and healthcare and the monitoring of people's wellbeing, to business and the real time reporting of e-commerce sales. Following the definition by the Economic and Social Research Council (ESRC) we are including the following subjects within our framing of social science: development studies, human geography and planning, economics, education, social anthropology, linguistics, law, international relations and politics, psychology, management and business, social statistics and computing, and social policy (www.esrc.ac.uk/about-us/what-is-social-science/social-science-disciplines/). Digital research has the potential to develop new knowledge, enhance scholarly practice, encourage participation in research, and extend the reach and impact of research findings to new as well as existing audiences, yet it can also provide a daunting array of possibilities that can be difficult to make sense of.

As researchers we all work within personal, disciplinary, institutional and political constraints of varying types. Embarking on digital research will, potentially, place a researcher on less stable ground owing to the perceived newness of the terrain. This may cause doubt in the mind of the researcher. Doubts may also be manifested as scepticism or uncertainty on the part of a doctoral supervisory team or a university ethics review board. Research in previously uncharted territory is exciting, and learning to defend the choices made will help in the robustness of the research undertaken, but it can also be time consuming. Developing agility and flexibility as a digital researcher is necessary to manage research in the digital environment, but this agility can appear to conflict with the stable traditions of academic research. We suggest that anyone considering digital research should identify any constraints that may limit their ability to successfully undertake digital research. Researchers need, for example, to consider whether their technological skills are appropriate for the research they intend to undertake, and the extent to which their pre-existing knowledge concerning the digital context is relevant to a particular research problem. Disciplinary, institutional and organisational preferences should be acknowledged as well as the prevailing political landscape. It is currently popular to examine the Internet of Things (IoT) within a business perspective, visualising mass movement of people from human geography and the use of technology in the automation and subsequent change in the labour market from a political standpoint. For doctoral students, identifying supervisors who are open minded is a good starting point. For more established researchers, identifying research colleagues who are not risk adverse would be beneficial.

A critical issue to be cognisant of is that digital data are not politically, or socio-culturally neutral. Data are generated for a purpose; with codes used to create data sets and algorithms designed as a result of questions asked, or a commercial problem being solved. Google search results are not complete and unfiltered; using the API (Application Programming Interface) for a social media platform does not provide us with access to all the relevant content. Although it could be argued that non-digital data also have a political dimension, the lack of transparency in the digital data domain raises the level of uncertainty over the original purpose, intent and authenticity. A very useful starting point in understanding the development of digital research and also big data research is Youtie et al.'s (2017) paper charting early social science research in this sphere.

WHAT DO WE MEAN BY DIGITAL RESEARCH?

Digital research is not restricted to particular ontological or epistemological perspectives. Researchers using digital research methods or exploring digital phenomena may believe there is a single, knowable truth, or believe that there is no single truth that can be discerned. They may work towards uncovering a truth or explore how we construct our world. Whichever position we adopt does not preclude researching digital phenomena, impact on the usefulness of digital research as a method, or constrain our exploration of the digital research domain, though it obviously impacts on the particular methods we choose and the particular questions we explore. This book does not adopt a particular ontological or epistemological position as these are explored elsewhere (see, for example, Knox and Walford, 2016; Lankshear, 2003), rather it attempts to understand digital research and how it relates to the choices we all need to consider as researchers. Indeed one of the two authors of this book undertakes research at the more positivist end of the spectrum, while the other takes a more interpretivist approach to research.

Digital media, for the purposes of this book, encompasses all computer mediated internet and digitally enabled media through which data may be collected, shared and/or analysed, including, for example, blogs, online forums, QR codes, online questionnaires, emails, Skype interviewing, YouTube material, Instagram images, Twitter content, geo-location and internet navigation. Readers can see from this extensive, but not exhaustive, list that social media is included and as such we extend Scolari's notion of 'digital media' as an umbrella term for the digital technology-based environment that allows '*networking, multimedia, and collaborative and interactive communications*' (Scolari, 2009: 946, italic added).

Generally with the use of digital technology for research, emphasis has been placed on the use of digital communication tools to collect data and then as platforms on which to disseminate research findings. Some limited attention has been paid to the tools for analysis of digital data such as ATLAS.ti or NVivo and the development of open source analytical software, e.g. NodeXL, although this is highly limited owing to the potential commercial value to be made from digital data analysis. Increasingly large commercial firms are creating proprietorial tools for analysis of digital data (IBM, Microsoft, Google), thereby excluding all but a tiny number of selected academic researchers from accessing and exploring certain types of digital data. A concern has been raised in the academic community over the shrinking of access to both digital data and the tools with which to explore the data (Wessels et al., 2014).

Although we are proponents of engaging with digital technologies and digital research we are also aware that thinking is required about where the human/technology divide resides in research. One question to consider is which aspects of research should be trusted to automation. As computing power and data processing speed continues to accelerate we need to remember the value of sense making by humans and the connections that may be made by people acting as researchers rather than computer code and algorithms. Consider, for example, the implications of Facebook algorithms re-presenting us with our historic posts (Griffin, 2015). An algorithm that cannot distinguish between positive and negative events could be potentially harmful and this has been recognised, at least implicitly, by some social networking sites. Broad thinking about the consequences of automation needs to consider the challenges as well as the huge opportunities that automation might bring.

A second question to consider concerns research practices themselves. We should reflect on which elements of pre-digital research practice should be retained and which have become obsolete. 'Good' research requires us to understand the context in which we are undertaking research, and how that context impacts on our ability to 'produce' knowledge. A deep understanding of the digital context is problematic due to the dynamic nature of that environment. This means that we, as digital researchers, have to consciously maintain a questioning stance concerning, for instance, why we are asking the questions we ask, what we choose to read and how we interpret it, the choices we make concerning how we examine our research questions, and the implications of our methods of investigation on the knowledge we produce. Striving for good practice in research remains appropriate and critical reflection on the part of the researcher is still paramount.

As digital research develops as an area of research across the social sciences, different perspectives from different disciplines should be included wherever possible. Even within the social sciences, how digital is 'seen' and operationalised across subjects such as sociology, education, criminology and business and management will be different. A big digital research question that applies across all social science disciplines is the extent to which the digital context impacts on the theories and concepts of the discipline. Digital research may expose unconscious theoretical assumptions we have been making, help clarify conflicting findings by revealing a new conceptual element in a theory, or may demonstrate the limitations of a theory by showing how it is unsuited to explaining the relevant phenomenon in the digital context. As the digital environment becomes more pervasive, we have to ask whether the digital context represents a fundamental shift in how a discipline's theories and concepts are understood, or whether the digital environment is merely a context, however important that context might be.

Here, we can and should learn from other subject areas, possibly by exploring how other researchers have dealt with digital methodological issues or by looking at how fellow researchers have framed their questioning of the digital landscape. Moving forward, achieving a critical mass of cross-disciplinary researchers engaged in digital research will contribute significantly to digital knowledge development. Subject knowledge development may also be achieved by taking a more open approach to methodological standpoints, possibly moving away from entrenched views on the 'value' of either quantitative or qualitative approaches to research towards more mixed methods approaches that acknowledge the insight that can be derived by considering a problem from multiple perspectives.

DIGITAL AS A PHENOMENON AND/OR DIGITAL AS A METHOD/INSTRUMENT

This book explores digital research both as a phenomenon and as an instrument of research. That is research about the digital domain and its characteristics (*phenomenon*), as well as research that uses the digital domain as a source of and means to access information (*method/instrument*).

Digital as a phenomenon: Digital phenomena are unable to exist without the digital environment; they are dependent on some characteristic of the digital environment. Consequently, research questions where the digital domain is the phenomenon of interest would not exist if the digital domain did not exist. For example, psychologists wanting to explore the impact of the disconnection between an individual's physical and digital identities can only do this because the characteristics of the digital environment allow that disconnection to occur. Digital researchers might examine how the ability of an individual to anonymously explore identity options impacts on mental health where the digital environment means that characteristics do not have to be assumed either permanently or publicly. For example, avatars created by individuals when part of a virtual world. As a set of social phenomena and object of research, the digitalised world offers huge scope for research across subject areas (Meyer and Schroeder, 2015). Considering the digital domain as the phenomenon of research has opened up or created new topics that can be considered, as well as changing the emphasis of those topics. Research topics that have emerged through the advent of digitalisation include, but are not limited to: technology adoption, network formation and behaviours, and exploration of identities. In addition, new discipline areas have been forged, such as Webscience, and human and social computing. Pursuant to this, a new industry has built up around the digital phenomenon: digital labs, digital consultants, social media tracking firms, digital analytics and social computing specialists are now involved in the production of knowledge from digital data. How individuals and groups digitally interact with each other, with governments, with businesses, in addition to a new global industry of those involved assisting in the design, collection and analysis of digital research, are all phenomena that require the digital domain to exist.

Digital as a method/instrument: In contrast to digital as a phenomenon, digital as a research instrument considers all those aspects of the digital context that relate to our ability to access information. Digital research may be used to label research that uses digital means to source data, or to access particular participants. Here the digital domain is the method or instrument of research which facilitates access to information that will help the researcher address the questions that concern them, even though these questions are not necessarily specific to the digital environment. Some of these methods may appear to transfer almost directly from the non-digital domain (e.g., from offline to online questionnaires) and appear to be straightforward. However, others cannot feasibly be executed without the aid of digital tools. So digital research can change how existing research tools and techniques are used, as well as provide researchers with a new toolkit for research using methods that previously did not exist. Digital as an instrument of research also includes consideration of the value we place on different types of information, what we consider as appropriate 'data' and how we access information. The disruption caused by the digital environment exposes how some of these methodological questions are submerged within disciplinary value systems and traditions, and can lead to re-examination of ontological and epistemological positions (Knox and Walford, 2016).

Examination of the digital context as both phenomena and instrument of research exposes the fluidity of digital research and can clarify some of the complexities over whether the researcher's focus lies in the phenomenon, the instrument, or across both. The extent of crossover needs to be understood within the context of specific research projects. For instance, research that helps us understand how people communicate online treats the digital domain as the object or phenomenon of study. However, understanding how people communicate online also can help us to understand the digital domain as a method of study (i.e., digital as a research instrument). Equally, using online material such as user generated videos to understand consumers' relationships with brands (i.e., digital research instrument), can lead to broader questions related to how people construct their online identity where the digital domain is the phenomenon researched.

Combining the two elements of research (phenomenon/question and instrument/method) leads to four broad classifications based on the focus of the research question (Figure 1.1). As researchers in the social sciences investigate many different questions using a variety of established methods this simple, but useful, 2x2 matrix illustrates the ways in which the digital domain can contribute to social science research. The first axis is concerned with the type of phenomenon being investigated, the second axis with the methods used to undertake research. Emerging phenomena and methods are those phenomena and methods that are dependent on the existence of the digital environment – if the digital environment had not been invented and developed, these phenomena and methods would not exist. For example, studying the impact of online friendships on mental health by studying social media interactions would be an emerging phenomenon investigated using an emerging method. In contrast, established phenomena and methods are those that exist independently of the digital environment. So studying the impact of participating in exercise classes on friendship formation through participant observation would be classed as an established phenomenon studied using an established method.

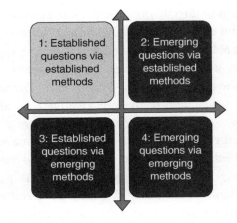

Figure 1.1 Matrix of research questions and methods for the digital age

Three points are important to note here. The first is that the choice of appropriate terms to indicate whether the phenomenon or instrument is either digital or non-digital, either new or old, either virtual or real, indicates unconscious, or possibly even conscious, beliefs (Suler, 2016). Using digital/non-digital preferences digital, as 'non-' signals an absence of an attribute, not a description of an attribute possessed by the other context. In the western socio-cultural context where value is placed on novelty and youth, new is preferable to old in most circumstances. In contrast, virtual implies something less than real, consequently indicating that 'real' has more value. As such, in an attempt to avoid potentially value-ladened terms, in Figure 1.1 we refer to the digital/virtual as 'emerging' and the non-digital/real as 'established'.

The second point to note is that it must be acknowledged that the choice between digital/virtual and non-digital/real presents a duality that does not hold at the level of the lives we live (Knox and Walford, 2016; Molesworth and Denegri-Knott, 2013). The real and the digital are intertwined in everyday lives. So while a specific phenomenon or instrument may be confined to one sphere, the phenomenon/instrument operates in a broader socio-technological context that is not confined in the same way; the world of the social sciences is neither confined to the real world, nor solely expressed in the digital.

The third and final point to note is that one quadrant will not be considered in this text: the first quadrant detailing, 'established questions via established methods'. This quadrant would include studies such as a research study concerning voter intentions using face-to-face focus groups. This type of research study does not fall within the scope of a book that specifically seeks to understand the digital research environment.

Emerging questions, established methods

The second quadrant examines emerging questions via established methods and considers how the digital environment has presented researchers with phenomena that were not previously the focus of research. These phenomena include human behaviours that are extended by the characteristics of the digital environment. For example, a human behaviour that has been changed by the digital environment is how we communicate with others. The digital environment has greatly enhanced people's ability to interact with larger numbers of people at once (e.g., status updates on social media sites, tweets), as well as how we keep in contact with intimate others (e.g., text messages, electronic monitoring of children). This leads to questions concerned with how people communicate. However, these questions do not need to be researched using digital methods. Researchers can assemble a face-to-face focus group or develop a telephone survey that asks individuals questions about their digital communication (although taking this type of approach may limit the insight developed). Thus, these digital communication behaviours can be researched using established research methods.

Emerging questions can also be concerned with phenomena that only occur within, or because of, the digital environment. These include both digital phenomena and phenomena that are social in nature. An example of a digital phenomenon is that digitalisation has led to personalisation that occurs both to and by the individual: websites employ proprietary algorithms that are hidden from the individual yet impact on their digital experience, and individuals are able to use customisable options in the digital environment that make their digital experience different from other people's experiences, for example, mobile phone options. Once again, these phenomena could be investigated using established methods, for example, awareness of and attitudes towards different facets of personalisation could be investigated through a mail survey. An example of a new social phenomenon that has appeared as a result of the digital environment is flash mobs. Flash mobs comprise groups of individuals 'invited' via social media or shared-message to an activity or event, such as a short term sale or an outdoor performance (see, for example, www.youtube.com/watch?v=bQLCZOG202k). These events rely on the characteristic of the digital environment that enables communication with a number of relative strangers. Yet flash mobs extend human behaviour as they present a particular way of connecting with those strangers in the physical/material world, even if that connection is transitory. These digital phenomena can, nonetheless, be researched using established research methods. For example, personal interviews could be used to examine what motivates flash mob participants. Interviewing online gamers face-to-face provides another example of an established research method that could be used to investigate a digital phenomenon.

Established questions, emerging methods

The third quadrant considers established questions using emerging research methods. The digital/virtual aspect of the research may be the location, or the means, of accessing the research data. That is, while the question asked and/or the phenomenon investigated may not be digitally focused, the methods used to access research data, and/or the data accessed, are digital. For example, political scientists have long been interested in citizens' opinions about political parties, policies and politicians. Non-digital methods could be used to access these opinions (e.g., focus groups and questionnaires), however, so could digital methods. Digital data, such as tweets and posts about political parties or political blogs, could be used to understand citizens' opinions about political parties. Alternatively, digital methods, such as online surveys, could be employed by the researchers to access the relevant information. The digital environment has, as such, changed the information that is available about the known phenomenon and the way in which that information is accessed. While some of these digital methods are clearly extensions of previously established methods (e.g., online questionnaires), the unique characteristics of the digital environment have uncovered new questions related to their use.

New methods of data collection have also emerged in the digital context. These methods use the characteristics of the digital environment, particularly its ability to store and process large volumes of data, to allow the researcher to access relevant data. For instance, being able to efficiently process large volumes of data allows social media data mining and 'scraping' where software automatically extracts specified data from multiple web sources, as well as usability testing where multiple variations in a website design are automatically tested against each other to determine which performs best. The opportunity provided by the digital environment to communicate data in ways previously not possible also enables the researcher to provide new types of information such as data visualisation (see Figure 1.2). A number of examples of data visualisation can be seen in the TED talks by McCandless (2010) and Rosling (2006). McCandless (2010) uses both scraping and data visualisation to understand military power, reported social fear and the impact of volcanic eruptions on carbon 'emissions', while Rosling (2006) shows how data can be displayed dynamically to illustrate changes over time. Other digital sources such as personal blogs can be related to non-digital data sources (e.g., editorials in newspapers). However, differences in their socio-cultural contextualisation (e.g., individual opinions versus owner-constrained viewpoints) mean that their analysis differs from their more established counterparts. Sources of data, such as tweets, posts and blogs, that did not exist prior to the digitalisation of communication, together with novel data collection and analysis tools, enable us to rethink how we turn raw data into useable information to create knowledge. The opportunities afforded by digital methods, however, also challenge us as we need to ensure we present a fair representation of the data that are available.

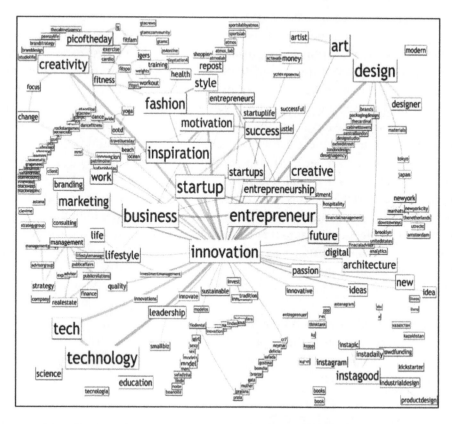

Figure 1.2 Visualisation of social media research data: An example of a semantic network map of the sharing of the concept of innovation via Twitter through #innovation hashtags

Emerging questions, emerging methods

The fourth quadrant incorporates both digital questions and digital methods. As well as including research that considers digital phenomena that are investigated using digital methods and digital data, this quadrant includes questions about the digital methods themselves. Examples of digital questions that can be researched through digital methods include examining people's website navigation behaviour using webpage analytics, considering the effectiveness of internet brand advertising by looking at the conversion rate achieved, investigating the return on email campaigns via analysis of purchase data in Customer Relationship Management (CRM) systems, and exploring the role of blended learning in the rehabilitation of young offenders using Skype interviews.

Digital research methods are themselves a new phenomenon and deserve investigation. As researchers we need to reflect and examine digital research methods in order to understand the opportunities they present, the challenges inherent in their use, and how to demonstrate their rigour, value and purpose with respect to developing knowledge. Authors such as Hine, Kozinets and Poynter have developed and/or examined a variety of digital research methods (including data sources, means to access data, and analysis and presentation of data) and have provided sound rationales for their appropriate use. Nevertheless, as technology develops, methodological research that looks at understanding how these developments impact on social science research will need to continue. What, for example, is the impact of 'the internet of things' on social science researchers?

Of the four quadrants, the emerging questions, emerging methods quadrant is the furthest from the well-understood opportunities and challenges encountered when undertaking research into established phenomenon using established methods. As a result, research undertaken in this quadrant requires the most explanation for those who are not researching in the digital space. The research opportunities found in this type of research are great precisely because they are novel. However, the challenges presented are correspondingly complex as they may require us, as digital researchers, to justify both the importance of the phenomenon of interest and the veracity of the method proposed to investigate that phenomenon. Nevertheless, research on emerging phenomenon using emerging research methods can provide valuable insights in the social sciences.

We hope that explicitly identifying the focus of the research question (i.e., phenomenon), and the tools and techniques of research (i.e., methods/instruments of research), will help you to separate out the opportunities and issues associated with each when undertaking digital research.

THE CONSEQUENCES OF THE DIGITAL ENVIRONMENT FOR DIGITAL RESEARCH

The established norms of research contain ideological boundaries (i.e., conditions that are accepted as the natural order of things, unstated assumptions) that help to scope and limit research projects, methods and analysis. For example, in relation to exploratory research objectives, established research norms maintain that collecting large volumes of qualitative data is wasteful of resources and unnecessary to achieve the research objectives, and that quantitative data sets are not generally suitable for this type of research. The advent and adoption of digital technologies in our lives has changed the environmental conditions in which research now operates. These changes in environmental conditions in the digital context include:

- the ability to automatically record digital data – these data range from navigation behaviours and transaction data to comments, videos and images
- the capacity to store digital data cheaply – for example, via the use of data warehousing creating vast archives of data
- the processing power to be able to search large volumes of data effectively and efficiently as typified by search engines that operate across the digital environment (e.g., Google) as well as those that operate with particular platforms (e.g., website search facilities)

- the processing power to analyse large volumes of data, which is illustrated by the increased use of data mining
- the removal of geographic and/or temporal barriers to first asynchronous (e.g., email) and then synchronous (e.g., Skype) communication
- the ability to separate physical/material identity from the digital representation of self; this can range from, for example, creating fantastical avatars when interacting in virtual worlds such as Second Life, through separating different aspects of self on social networking sites such as Facebook, to hiding one's identity when taking part on discussion boards.

Underlying environmental conditions that were taken for granted as 'natural' and led to the established research norms, for example, isolating a participant from distractions while they are completing a questionnaire on healthy eating, have now changed to such an extent that we need to reappraise and question the usefulness of those established research norms and boundaries. The use of these boundaries assisted researchers by providing methodological heuristics that facilitated their research decision-making. These heuristics no longer account for the conditions in the current environment and are no longer congruent with the prevailing research landscape that we find ourselves in. For example, digital technologies now allow us to explore large datasets where previously we did not possess the computing processing capacity to do so. Thus, we need to revisit and reassess the usefulness of these 'natural' research norms and boundaries, and pursuant to this, question the validity of those norms and boundaries in digital research methods.

Nevertheless, the fast pace and evolutionary nature of the digital landscape, and the need for researchers to remain current in that environment, may mean that new research methods' heuristics cannot be formed. That is, the digital environment may not remain stable for long enough for us to establish unquestioned research norms and/or boundaries. Whether change is due to new platforms, or modifications to existing platforms, the stability needs to be established rather than assumed. In addition, changes in the digital landscape, with their inevitable impact on human behaviour, may lead to issues with how we assess the immediacy and currency of data for research purposes. Simply put, data may now age faster as new technologies impact on our behaviour, though how much this might impact on the research insight gained related to a particular phenomenon needs to be evaluated on a case-by-case basis. Again, these changes may necessitate us engaging reflexively with our digital research methods to continuously review, reflect and adapt as a standard element of every research project in order to ensure that our research practice, and the subsequent findings from those projects, remains relevant.

Overall, the dynamic nature of the norms and boundaries in digital research means that, as researchers, we need to emphasise the robustness and relevance of our research methods in relation to our specific research question(s). Throughout our research project, the purpose of the research (i.e., research question) should be revisited to contextualise the research appropriately within the digital landscape. In the ever-changing digital landscape, it is more important than ever for us to anchor our methodological decisions on the research questions we are asking. These questions should act as a guiding light for the iterative development of our digital research projects. This will necessitate the researcher becoming increasingly reflexive and self-questioning about their methodological decisions and the impact of those decisions on the veracity of their findings. This text aims to help in that reflexivity by highlighting the key opportunities and challenges faced by social science researchers in the digital age.

UNDERSTANDING DIGITAL RESEARCH

As researchers ourselves, as well as PhD supervisors and teachers, we felt there was a knowledge gap in the critical understanding of the relevance and value of digital research in the social sciences. So in order to help other researchers and students we wanted to provide a framework in which digital research could be better understood. By creating questions and justifications in this book, we intend to offer frameworks for understanding digital research, and suggestions for defending the adoption of digital research, which can be used when presenting research in both written and verbal formats. As this book aims to help you develop an understanding of the broader issues related to digital research, our focus is not on whether a particular research tool or technique is appropriate for a specific research project, or on whether a specific topic is worth investigating, rather our focus is on exploring the issues that underlie how these assessments are made. That is, we aim to provide a basis on which researchers can make project specific assessments for themselves.

This book will explore the underlying assumptions behind the heuristics associated with research methods, and consider how the characteristics of the digital environment impact on them. We investigate the key debates concerning digital research across a range of methodological areas. Throughout the book we consider how research in the digital domain challenges our interpretation of ethical principles, changes our relationship with our research participants, and requires us to re-evaluate how we assess research quality. Each of these areas interact with specific, key characteristics of the digital environment, such as the volume of available data, the myriad sources of data, the level of interactivity of actors in data, possible automation within digital data, and the transparency or lack of it.

Understanding digital research requires us to continuously (re)assess three areas:

1. *Ethics* and how we maintain ethical standards.
2. *Expectations* that we have concerning the digital context and the research we are undertaking.
3. *Expertise* requirements for the research we wish to undertake and how we demonstrate that we are accurately representing our research topic.

Ethics

Our understanding of how ethical research is practised needs to consider the particular research context when working in the dynamic digital environment. Questions that might be straightforward in the non-digital context become more complex in a dynamic socio-technological context. For example, what is considered public/private in non-digital research is well thought through, and has well-established research practices to ensure participants are protected. Indeed, many aspects of the digital environment complicate ethics questions and decisions that are well-understood in the non-digital context, and these issues will be considered throughout the book.

Our approach, like other authors (Mckee and Porter, 2009), important research bodies such as Research Councils UK (RCUK: www.rcuk.ac.uk/) and the ESRC (www.esrc.ac.uk/), and research ethics committees of universities, is that the first principle of research ethics is to do no harm to those participating in research and to do no harm to those who are researching. In digitised societies this can become more complex than previously considered. Digital researchers may need to start by unpicking what is meant by 'harm' in an environment where data are plentiful, automatically retained and easily searchable, where anonymity is easily established and retained in some circumstances (e.g., through usernames unconnected to the individual's offline identity), but difficult to maintain in others (e.g., where search capacity allows anyone to associate reported quotes with specific digital identities), and where the socio-cultural norms question traditional ideas of 'privacy' (Zwitter, 2014).

Research within the digital environment resurfaces previously 'resolved' ethical questions for the researcher. Questions surrounding the level of informed consent, an established requirement of offline research, arise in a research environment where researchers use 'raw' data that are historic and are produced by individuals who have hidden their offline identity. Thus established ideas around protecting individuals may now need reconsidering to incorporate the protection of groups or online communities. Privacy issues, such as what is considered 'public' in the digital environment, also need to be considered, as does how researchers consider unintended consequences of combining different data sources for privacy (i.e., while individual databases might be anonymised, combining multiple databases might enable individuals to be identified).

Along with the ethics associated with research issues for participants and researchers, we also have to consider our responsibility as producers of knowledge to the users of that knowledge. Maintaining the integrity of our research findings is critical for researchers. We base our reputations on fairly representing the phenomenon we study, and explicitly considering how well we are achieving this by acknowledging the limitations of what we know and can achieve in the digital context is necessary precisely because of the dynamic nature of the digital environment. We cannot expect our research users to unpick the time and place of each piece of research in order to assess what can be reasonably known.

Expectations

Our expectations as social science researchers are also challenged by the characteristics of the digital environment. The digital context challenges many research norms, raising questions such as: What are our expectations as researchers concerning the longevity of our research? To what extent do we need to consider our participants' socio-cultural context when developing our research? What is the role of the research participant? For example, the digital environmental characteristics of connectivity and interactivity have facilitated opportunities for co-production and/or co-creation of research that have previously not been easily accessible or even possible. Instances of this include participative research through citizens using mobile phone devices to document events or assessing images to assist in big data analysis. Some authors suggest that digitalisation has, in part, democratised research in enabling co-created citizen science projects, which develop collaborative knowledge through a rigorous and more transparent and thus ethical research approach (Halfpenny and Proctor, 2015). Conversely, other aspects of digitalisation, such as algorithms, navigation data and shopping cart analysis, take control away from the researcher, the participant, or both. This automation of research distances the participant and/or the researcher from elements of the research process and leads to fewer opportunities for co-production/co-creation of research.

Expertise

Our expectations of the digital environment are mirrored in the expertise requirements that digital research places on us as researchers. Broadly, we need to consider how the digital context impacts on the skills and capabilities that are needed to produce the research. More specific questions might include: How realistic is it to expect one individual to undertake digital research? To what extent do our disciplinary research norms equip us to engage with research in the digital environment? Questions concerning expertise also include consideration of our ability to assess the rigour of research and its relevance. Here we have to be able to demonstrate the usefulness of digital methods and the importance of understanding digital phenomenon. Essentially, we have to develop a deeper understanding of how the method we use impacts on the knowledge we can develop.

Research heuristics have already been developed for more established research methods where underlying assumptions have been identified. We need to consider how, indeed if, the characteristics of the digital environment negate these heuristics. We are all aware, for instance, that quantitative methods are judged on their replicability and the generalisability of their results. Quantitative researchers rely on strict sampling processes and clearly planned and executed research design in an attempt to show how humans *generally* behave under clearly specified conditions. In contrast, qualitative methods are judged on how well they address the specific context, and the authenticity, credibility, etc., of their findings. Qualitative researchers are interested in unpicking differences in context or individuals and fully understanding that context. So what are the equivalent research heuristics we need to develop to be able to robustly assess the quality of our digital research? Will the dynamic nature of the digital environment make general 'heuristics' too rigid to be useful? What criteria do we need to apply to assess the 'quality' of digital methods, and how do these criteria impact on our understanding of the phenomenon (both digital and not) of interest to the researcher?

CHAPTER SUMMARY AND BOOK STRUCTURE

This chapter has clarified our understanding of the domain of digital research in terms of both digital phenomenon and digital methods. A simple two dimensional matrix has been presented and explored concerning the inter-relatedness of established/emerging phenomenon and established/emerging methods. This framework can be used to identify where the digital environment might impact on any particular research project. This chapter has also outlined three underlying issues that impact on different aspects of digital research – the 3 Es of ethics, expectations and expertise. These three issues will be returned to throughout this text as we summarise the chapters that deal with specific aspects of digital research (Chapters 2–6) both to help ground our discussions and to facilitate researchers to produce more rigorous and credible digital research.

Following this introductory chapter, we start by looking at how we can unpack the relationship between the research questions we ask as digital researchers and the characteristics of the digital environment. Next we consider how the digital context impacts on data through the explosion of different data formats that we can access as researchers, the influence of temporality on digital research, and how we might identify potential data sources. The process of data collection and the complexity within the human/technology interface in research is then considered before moving forward towards integration of the key ideas of the book into practical application for digital researchers. We conclude by drawing together the blurred boundaries and uncertain territory of the new digital research landscape.

The chapters in this book consequently address aspects of research that are of interest to us all as researchers. The impact of the digital environment on methodological topics is considered separately, and key questions for researchers to address are identified in each chapter. Specifically, this book:

- considers how the digital environment exposes as simplistic the established norms and boundaries surrounding the qualitative/quantitative classification of research and leads to the requirement for a more nuanced view of research classifications

- explores the huge variety of data formats that are available in the digital space and the issues that arise when unfamiliar data sources are used and/or multiple data formats are combined to address a problem
- reflects on the issues that arise when attempting to identify suitable sources of data, thinking about whether we are interested in the individuals themselves, or their digital manifestation (footprint or shadow), whether we are interested in the (multiple) singular instances of that data source, a collective, or the interactions associated with singular entities or groups
- evaluates temporality in relation to time and speed of data collection, and how the ability of researchers to extract data at different times and with varying depth impacts on the characteristics of our findings and the decisions we have to make
- investigates how the digital domain has changed how research is designed, and what this means to us as researchers of and in the digital environment.

Finally, it is worth acknowledging what this book does not claim to do. This text is not a 'how to do' research in or on the digital domain. Texts and online resources including YouTube video tutorials advising on specific software for text mining or python coding for social media analysis etc. are already plentiful. In addition, most universities have in-house training courses for common analytical tools that can be used in digital research, for example, NVivo. Rather this book will provide sufficient information for digital researchers to be able to explicitly question their own decisions about digital research and justify the choices made to such a degree that they will be able to form persuasive arguments for any assessment of their research, including a doctoral viva.

Questions

1. To what extent do you think your research is concerned with digital as a phenomenon?
2. To what extent do you think your research is concerned with digital as a source and/or a means of accessing data?
3. When thinking about your research topic, how open or closed do other researchers appear to be about the use of digital methods?
4. When thinking about the reader of your research, how much do you think they will need to be convinced of the opportunities presented by digital research?

FURTHER READING

Lupton, D. (2015). *Digital Sociology*. London: Routledge.

Pont, S. (2013). *The Digital State*. London: Kogan Page.

Youtie, J., Porter, A.L. and Huang, Y. (2017). Early social science research about Big Data. *Science and Public Policy*, 44 (1), 64–74.

REFERENCES

Belk, R.W. (2013). Extended self in a digital world. *Journal of Consumer Research, 40* (3), 477–500.

Griffin, A. (2015). Users can pick a date or a person that is associated with sad memories, and have them hidden. *The Independent*, Wednesday 14 October 2015. Available from www.independent.co.uk/life-style/gadgets-and-tech/news/facebook-s-on-this-day-tool-introduces-option-to-hide-bad-memories-stopping-notifications-about-exes-a6693296.html (accessed 14 April 2017).

Halfpenny, P. and Proctor, R. (2015). *Innovations in Digital Research Methods*. London: Sage.

Knox, H. and Walford, A. (2016). Is there an ontological to the digital? Theorizing the contemporary. *Cultural Anthropology*. Available from https://culanth.org/fieldsights/818-is-there-an-ontology-to-the-digital (accessed 19 December 2016).

Lankshear, C. (2003). The challenge of digital epistemologies. *Education, Communication & Information, 3* (2), 167–186. http://dx.doi.org/10.1080/14636310303144 (accessed 12 December 2017).

Marres, N. (2012). The redistribution of methods: On intervention in digital social research, broadly conceived. *The Sociological Review, 60* (51), 139–165.

McCandless, D. (2010). The beauty of data visualization. TEDGlobal. Available from www.ted.com/talks/david_mccandless_the_beauty_of_data_visualization (accessed 23 January 2017).

Mckee, H.A. and Porter, J.E. (2009). *The Ethics of Internet Research: A Rhetorical Case Based Process*. New York: Peter Lang Publishing Inc.

Meyer, E.T. and Schroeder, R. (2015). *Knowledge Machines: Digital Transformations of the Sciences and Humanities*. Cambridge, MA: MIT Press.

Molesworth, M. and Denegri-Knott, J. (2013). Digital virtual consumption as a transformative space. In R.W. Belk and R. Llamas (eds), *The Routledge Companion to Digital Consumption*. Abingdon: Routledge, pp. 223–234.

Pink, S., Ruckenstein, M., Willim, R., Ardevol, E., Berg, M., Duque, M., Fors, V., Lanzeni, D., Lapenta, F. and Lupton, D. (2016). Data ethnographies 5: Broken data. *Data Ethnographies*. Available from: https://dataethnographies.com/paper-v-broken-data/ (accessed 12 December 2016).

Rosling, H. (2006). The best stats you've ever seen. TED2006. Available from: www.ted.com/talks/hans_rosling_shows_the_best_stats_you_ve_ever_seen (accessed 23 January 2017).

Scolari, C.A. (2009). Mapping conversations about new media: The theoretical field of digital communication. *New Media & Society, 11* (6), 943–964.

Suler, J.R. (2016). *Psychology of the Digital Age: Human Become Electric*. New York: Cambridge University Press.

Wessels, B., Finn, R.L., Linde, P., Mazzetti, P., Nativi, S., Riley, S. and Wyatt, S. (2014). Issues in the development of open access to research data. *Prometheus, 32* (1), 49–66.

Youtie, J., Porter, A.L. and Huang, Y. (2017). Early social science research about Big Data. *Science and Public Policy, 44* (1), 64–74.

Zwitter, A. (2014). Big data ethics. *Big Data & Society*, July–Dec, 1–6. DOI: 10.1177/2053951714559253

2

THE CHANGING
RESEARCH LANDSCAPE

In this chapter we will:

- outline the ways in which research boundaries are becoming increasingly blurred
- describe macro-level reflections for digital researchers
- describe micro-level reflections for digital researchers
- emphasise the central role of contextuality in digital research decisions.

INTRODUCTION

This chapter opens with a discussion of how the well-established characteristics, strengths and weaknesses of different types of research methods (e.g., qualitative/ quantitative) are blurred in the digital environment. It explores how the digital era is now influencing our understanding of broad classes of research techniques and raises questions concerning the boundaries of traditional 'classifications' of research methods. This leads to questions concerning whether the established 'boundaries' used to classify research (e.g., qualitative/quantitative) remain as useful in the digital research environment. The theme of blurred boundaries is revisited throughout the book. How place and space are blurred by the digital environment removing temporal boundaries is a theme considered in Chapter 4, how the digital context impacts on the roles of the participant and the researcher is covered in Chapter 5, while how notions of public and private are impacted by socio-technological norms can be found in Chapter 6.

How, then, can digital researchers understand and justify their research choices when established ideas are morphing and the environment they work in is dynamic? Whether it is the choice of research topic or specific research methods used, the blurring of boundaries reduces the usefulness of the established research heuristics that are used to make research design choices. Consequently, as digital researchers we need to return to examining our underlying research assumptions. To facilitate this exercise, this chapter unpacks the applicability of the established research heuristics in the digital environment, examines some of the macro-level questions related to what we are aiming to achieve with our research as well as considering questions that will help us to understand how our choices fit into the current socio-technological context. This chapter also explores the micro-level questions related to our digital research design choices, as well as considering the relevance of contextuality to digital research.

ESTABLISHED RESEARCH HEURISTICS IN THE DIGITAL ENVIRONMENT

Classifying research can be helpful in putting boundaries around ideas and creating structures to work within both in terms of how we as researchers might implement our research ideas, and how we might maximise the potential of our research outputs. Some critics of categorisation consider boundaries to represent false parameters, which impose self-limiting results and shorten the research horizons of what might be possible. Nevertheless, many research methods texts categorise the tools and techniques they describe to enable clear description of their strengths and weaknesses, as well as to facilitate understanding. As researchers often focus on the theoretical and conceptual elements of their work, rather than developing an in-depth and nuanced understanding of the research methods they are using, implicit associations can develop.

A well-established and pervasive classification for research methods is qualitative or quantitative. Classifying research into qualitative and quantitative essentially provides us with an easily accessible shorthand that allows us to determine which types of research methods are more suitable for the research question we are asking. The classification allows us to access the qualities of the available types of research with respect to their suitability for our research question (Table 2.1). That is, whether the design is suitable for achieving the research objectives; whether the methods and analysis could

Table 2.1 Established norms of qualitative and quantitative research

	Qualitative	Quantitative
Research type	Exploratory	Descriptive or causal
Dominant paradigm	Interpretivist	Positivist
Research questions	Fluid: modification can occur throughout the research process	Static: fixed prior to data collection
Data format	Unstructured words/text	Structured numeric representations
Methods	Interviews, focus groups	Surveys, experiments
Determination of findings	Understanding developed through immersion in the data	Meaning extracted through interpreting statistical analysis
Data characteristics	Rich, in-depth, contextualised	Aggregated, decontextualised, generalisable
Data quality expectations	Consistency, authenticity, credibility and reflexivity	Reliability and validity
Strengths	Ecological validity Deep understanding/nuanced	Generalisability across groups Predictions/forecasting
Weaknesses	Lacks breadth Context specific	Lacks depth/nuances Decontextualised

be justified as appropriate; if the sample was collected in a way that adds to, rather than detracts from, the 'quality' of the data. Qualitative research is, as such, understood to be less structured and more exploratory in nature. It is, generally, focused on words rather than numbers, and is used to explore research questions that are fluid rather than fixed. In contrast, quantitative research is associated with structured designs and data. It attempts to provide conclusive answers to descriptive or causal questions through the use of numbers to test research hypotheses. These research questions are fixed prior to data collection.

The division between qualitative and quantitative research developed partially because research was constrained by the ways in which we could communicate with people or observe events, as well as how we were able to analyse different data types. So how did resources previously constrain research? Looking at the resources required for survey research, historically researchers would have to either personally interview, telephone, or send a questionnaire out to participants individually. How many participants were obtainable depended on the method chosen, the time available to collect the data, and the number of people that could be recruited to act as interviewers. Generally speaking, the fewer resources there were available to the researcher, the longer it would take to collect the data. With survey research, the large volume of data was collected in a stand-ardised form that was designed to allow statistical analysis. In contrast with qualitative research, interviews would generate a large volume of data that the researcher would have to immerse themselves in, perhaps reading and re-reading the raw data to determine key themes. Overall, research in the pre-digital environment was essentially constrained by resources such that we could either access a large number of people/events with relatively shallow data, or get large volumes of data from a few people.

The data storage and processing characteristics of the digital environment mean that research in the digital environment does not face many of the constraints faced previously. In some cases this is because the data formats are new (Chapter 3), in others it is because familiar data formats are processed in a different way (Chapter 6). Text mining of social media, for example, structures words in a highly systemised way similar to the coding of quantitative data, yet questions addressed through data mining techniques can be unambiguously exploratory. In contrast to these historical constraints and boundaries on research, we can now design a digital questionnaire and make it available online at very low cost, and invitations to participate can be posted on multiple online forums. Consequently, the scaling issues associated with obtaining a large enough sample size for quantitative research are no longer constraints to us as digital researchers. A caveat worth noting though is that as the online environment becomes more popular for research so the response rate and completion rate of online surveys etc. continues to fall. In addition, qualitative analysis software can deal with volumes of text so large that previously, it would have been impossible to analyse manually.

Research in the digital environment is quite likely to take a multi-methods or mixed methods approach, combining elements of both qualitative and quantitative research to address a research problem (Cenni and Goethals, 2017; Hughes et al., 2017). Resource constraints no longer require digital researchers to make a choice between qualitative or quantitative research methods. The technological context has reduced the resources required to communicate with large numbers of participants (or examine of a large number of events), and to scrutinise large volumes of text. The digital environment has changed how we communicate, making reaching large numbers of participants more accessible. It has also, through the digital archiving of behaviours, made the storage of huge volumes of behavioural data possible – think, for example, of the data held by Google concerning our search behaviours, or the details held by online retailers concerning how we navigate through their websites when making a purchase. In addition, software developments mean that the qualitative analysis of large volumes of text is accessible. Digital research does not fit neatly into conventional classifications such as qualitative or quantitative, so the short-cuts used to understand the strengths and weaknesses of non-digital research cannot be accessed to understand the strengths and weaknesses of digital research. We are no longer constrained by the resource issues that historically led to the division of research into qualitative and quantitative.

Why we classify research is worth reflecting on here. What purpose does the classification of research serve? Classifying research helps us to identify general strengths and weaknesses of the research types. Classifying research according to the methods that are most appropriate for us to answer a particular question serves the purpose of enabling us to quickly identify the skills and resources we need to address our particular research problem, and provides us with arguments we could use to justify our research choices. As established classifications become less relevant, we need to rethink the 'boundaries' used to classify research. If our research classifications are not constrained by methods, then this leads to the question: *What is the most appropriate way to classify, and as such understand, our digital research?*

JUSTIFYING RESEARCH IN THE DIGITAL ENVIRONMENT

Breaking down how we think about our research can help us to identify potential issues we might encounter when doing our research, as well as pointing us towards the strengths of our research. There are a number of models of research that can help us to think about the research questions we are asking at a higher level. They make us consider macro-level questions such as how our approach to research impacts on what we will extract from our data (e.g., intellectual projects), and what type of knowledge we aim to produce (e.g., theory, research, practice) (Wallace and Wray, 2016). Models of research can also help us consider questions that are more micro-level, that is, focused on the place of our particular research project within the greater body of research that already exists (e.g., stages of research), and how the different elements of research – theory, methods and context – fit together to make a robust research project (McGrath and Brinberg, 1983). The high level of abstraction of these models means they continue to hold value in the digital research context. However, as they were designed to help us unpick research in a stable research environment where certain things are accepted as known (e.g., characteristics and value of qualitative and quantitative research), they need to be augmented with a clear understanding of the socio-technological context when used in a dynamic digital environment.

We, as digital researchers, need ways of unpicking the macro- and micro-level questions that surround digital research, and these questions need to be suitable for the dynamic and uncertain digital environment. At a macro-level, we need questions that allow us to unpick how underlying purposes, perspectives and approaches will impact on what we investigate and consider worth reporting on. Macro-level considerations are influenced by our socio-cultural, disciplinary and personal contexts as these all impact on our values, interests, knowledge and beliefs. So, for example, disciplines differ in their emphasis on groups (e.g., sociology) or individuals (e.g., psychology), the applicability of their results to practice (e.g., anthropology) or policy (e.g., public health), and the importance of the particular context (e.g., business/management in contrast to geography). There are also differences in how individuals, disciplines and/or institutions view digital phenomena (e.g., as 'just' another context, or as a new dimension of study) and in how open different audiences are to research that has considered digital phenomena, or has used digital methods.

At the individual (micro) level we have views concerning the value of different types of research, we may have developed particular research skills and interests, and we are influenced by our own values and the individuals and groups with whom we interact. As individuals we may be digital natives or technophobes, we may see the digital environment as progressive or harmful. While at the socio-cultural level we deal not only with culturally embedded assumptions and our social history, but also with specific socio-cultural historic events. (So, for example, while writing this I am thinking about the UK referendum result that has just been announced, and the implications of the vote to exit Europe for me, the UK and the other countries in the European Union. How, for example, will exiting the EU impact on roaming changes for mobile phones, or privacy laws? Will it change access to European data, and if so, how quickly?) Digital factors are also relevant for/to our socio-cultural environment. These might, for example, be reflected in privacy laws and our access to data about ourselves. These influences all impact on what we choose to research, what we want to achieve with our research, and how we approach our research. While the macro-level questions ask us to consider how the research we are doing fits into the broader socio-cultural and digital context we are living and working in, the micro-level questions are more specific to choices we make when developing our research design.

Macro-level areas for consideration

Considering the macro-influences that impact on our digital research choices will help us to develop robust research designs that:

- are more likely to produce value within our particular socio-cultural historic context
- identify potential pitfalls in the type of research we want to undertake and take those pitfalls into account
- explicitly consider and incorporate our research aims, and, as such, help us to achieve them.

So what are the macro-level issues that we can consider with respect to digital research? Macro-level issues are concerned with the higher-level goals concerning our research, and what we are trying to achieve. They help us to think about our research, and can alert us to gaps in our thinking. Nevertheless, we cannot simply answer each question independently, as different influences can interact with each other. Rather we need to consider our responses, and their impact on our research, holistically.

There are four macro-level questions that need to be addressed:

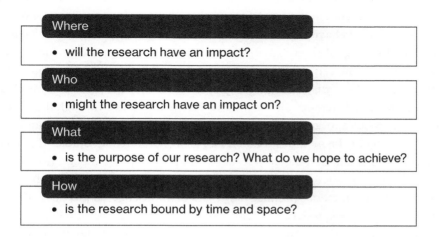

Where
- will the research have an impact?

Who
- might the research have an impact on?

What
- is the purpose of our research? What do we hope to achieve?

How
- is the research bound by time and space?

Where will the research have an impact?

In relation to the first question above, digital research can have an impact in the digital environment, in the non-digital environment, or across both. Looking back to the established/emerging matrix in Figure 1.1 (Chapter 1) provides a starting point for considering where the digital research is intended to have an impact. So, for example, if research deals with a digital phenomenon (e.g., examining trolling behaviours towards public figures) then its impact is likely to be confined to the digital environment, whether this impact is through individuals having a greater understanding of trolling, or government legislation concerning trolling. However, if the research is digital because it investigates a non-digital phenomenon through digital means, then the impact of the research may either be confined to the non-digital domain, or be seen in both the digital and non-digital domains. For example, digital researchers might use online surveys to examine how public figures cope with trolling behaviours and their recommendations could include guidelines for individuals concerning how to behave in the digital domain as well as recommendations for law makers concerning penalties for the perpetrators of trolling. Understanding where research could be applied helps us make decisions throughout a research project. Extending the previous example, it will help us at the beginning of our research to frame the research objectives we are interested in (e.g., focus on information that will help individual actions, or information that will provide evidence for policy changes), it will help us during our research to make research design decisions (e.g., what constitutes 'coping', how is trolling defined), and it will help us at the end of our research when choosing how to communicate the findings of our research (e.g., specific journals, popular outlets or a blog, a formal report submitted to legislators).

Considering where we intend research to have an impact also involves considering our research methods choices, as the method(s) used impacts on the type of knowledge produced. What evidence do we have, for example, that opinions expressed in the digital environment reflect behaviours in the non-digital environment? How valid are research findings based on digital (non-digital) data collection when applied in the non-digital (digital) context? How can we show that digital samples do not suffer from selection bias? How do we show that emerging digital methods can provide valid insights into general attitudes and behaviour? If the insights eventually gained through the use of digital research methods appear to contradict existing knowledge we need to consider more closely the impact of the methods used on knowledge production. Studies that compare the results of digital and non-digital research into the same phenomenon (e.g., influence of friendship groups) address this issue in a limited way. However, what these studies overlook is that new methods produce new types of knowledge, so just because the digital method does not (re)produce the knowledge found with its non-digital counterpart, it does not mean that the knowledge gained through the use of digital methods is not valid. It might be that the digital method produces a more accurate/authentic account of the phenomenon under study, or it might be that the characteristics that underpin the digital method access different aspects of the phenomenon being scrutinised. That is, the insights gained using the different methods might be complementary; not 'better', just different.

Unpacking the implications of using digital research methods (with a digital or non-digital phenomenon) needs to include some consideration of the relationship between the method of research and the type of knowledge that can be produced by or through the method used. Borrowing from the qualitative/quantitative distinction used within established research methods, as researchers we are aware of the type of knowledge produced by each. Thus, when we conduct qualitative research we are not aiming to produce generalisable knowledge that might be used by policy makers to make funding decisions, and when we conduct quantitative research we do not aim to produce in-depth knowledge that might be used in clinical practice. Particular research methods develop different types of knowledge that serve different purposes. So when considering how digital methods impact on knowledge, the questions then become 'what type of knowledge is produced by the digital research methods I have used?' and 'how does this knowledge differ (if at all) from the knowledge produced by the (non-digital) methods previously used to study this phenomenon?' As more research occurs through (and on) digital research we will accumulate greater understanding of the type of insights digital methods can provide.

Developing our conceptual understanding of digital methods and how different methods produce knowledge and provide insights into phenomena is critical to advancing digital research. Understanding the influence of methods is particularly important when we attempt to consider how insights from individual projects fit into accumulated disciplinary and/or context-related knowledge. For example, if digital research methods produce findings that counter findings from non-digital methods, then we need to reflect on whether these different findings are due to methodological, contextual or phenomenological differences between the new research and the research field.

Who might the research have an impact on?

As well as considering where our research will have an impact, we also need to consider who our research will have an impact on as identified in the second question; that is, who is the audience for the research. The purpose and scope of the research will influence the number of stakeholders with whom we wish to engage. There are four broad groups of stakeholders we will consider here: academics, practitioners, policy makers and the public. Each group will be interested in particular aspects of the research, and we may need to engage with them in different ways. These audiences are not confined to digital research, however, the digitalised environment now has a huge impact on how we interact with them.

A typical social science PhD may be self-funded, without an external organisation expecting results/insights to be delivered to them. However, some PhD studies may be funded by national governments, which are financially supporting a doctoral student or an industry group that is contributing towards the cost of a PhD. These groups of stakeholders may desire (or require) engagement at different stages of the research study. Externally funded research projects such as those supported by European funding, or the Research Council UK, will have specific and stated requirements as to who, when and in what form the research should be communicated back to these stakeholders. Overall, the amount, format and timing of dissemination of research should be clarified at the outset of the project.

Digitalisation has created opportunities for greater transparency and communication of research to multiple stakeholder groups, not only as the research is being conducted, but also as a means to disseminate findings of research. How research may be communicated digitally impacts who will be able to access the research, and as such, who the research impacts. Consideration should be given to digitally excluded members of the public, particularly if the outcomes of the research may have social or cultural impact, and alternative channels should be found such as locally organised face-to-face debriefing and feedback sessions. For example, for a research project that investigates citizen engagement with local government services, the results should not only be posted on the local government and research websites but offline dissemination should also be planned (e.g., posters, town-hall meetings and presentations, leaflets).

In order to maximise the impact of our research the dissemination of research findings requires planning as different groups will perceive different platforms as their norms for obtaining information. Policy makers may refer to research websites, practitioners across different professions may gather information via LinkedIn updates to their chosen groups or via webinars on newly created insights, academics may be more likely to read disciplinary relevant email updates, etc. So the digital media used to engage and communicate with our research stakeholders needs to be targeted wherever possible.

What is the purpose of our digital research?

While considering where the research is likely to have impact, and who relevant stakeholders are, is relatively straightforward, the third question of unpacking the underlying purpose of digital research, whether conducted through digital or non-digital research methods, is more involved. Drawing from Wallace and Wray's (2016) types of intellectual projects, digital research can aim to:

1. develop understanding of a digital, or non-digital, phenomenon
2. challenge understanding of a digital, or non-digital, phenomenon
3. aim to promote change in some practice (e.g., organisational practice, government policy), or some person (e.g., an individual's or group's behaviours or attitudes).

Researchers trying to develop understanding reflect on and question what is already known from an impartial standpoint (Wallace and Wray, 2016). The neutral stance adopted by researchers is nevertheless affected by subtle influences that derive from their socio-cultural, disciplinary and/or personal, as well as the digital, context. Research of this type is generally attempting to build on what already exists. Having considered existing knowledge it looks at how that work can be extended through, or developed in, the digital context. This may, for example, involve transferring concepts or methods from the non-digital to the digital arena. The underlying aim of this type of research is to build on existing knowledge. Consequently, this type of digital research does not question the overall validity of existing digital, or non-digital, research knowledge, rather it builds on existing knowledge or 'stands on the shoulders of giants' (Newton, 1676). For example, this approach to research could include testing existing theoretical understanding of word of mouth by applying it to electronic word of mouth communication using email, social media or online discussions. On the downside, research of this type can be quite incremental in the way it advances knowledge.

Digital researchers that challenge existing thought have already made a value judgement about existing knowledge – that is, they have decided that existing knowledge is lacking in some way (Wallace and Wray, 2016). This challenge might be concerned with how the existing research is understood in, or transferred across to, the digital environment, or it might be a more fundamental challenge to the underlying assumptions of the phenomenon. Digital researchers can challenge both the applicability/suitability of non-digital knowledge in the digital context through digital and non-digital methods, and, through digital research methods, the validity of non-digital knowledge itself. For example, we could take the pre-established concepts regarding word of mouth communication and through research, determine that these concepts are not entirely suitable for electronic word of mouth, that the ways of communication have in some way changed and that either previous work can be refuted or we may suggest new, more relevant theories on electronic word of mouth.

As researchers who challenge existing knowledge can take an inherently combative stance towards that knowledge, it is important that those researchers are aware of their own prejudices. As researchers, we need to consider the extent to which it is our socio-cultural, disciplinary and/or personal influences that lead us to take a negative stance towards existing knowledge or practice. Without an understanding of why we might believe the current knowledge is lacking, and an understanding of where that belief derives from, we are unlikely to be able to clearly articulate our beliefs. This type of research can be very insightful with respect to how context impacts on knowledge. However, there is a danger of discarding useful knowledge alongside outdated ideas, if we are not aware of our own prejudices.

Digital researchers who are looking to change some practice or some person may be aiming to prompt those changes either in the digital sphere, the non-digital sphere, or both.

This type of research is directly targeted at making some change in the world, not just at understanding it (Wallace and Wray, 2016). Changes that involve digital practices or people's digital behaviours would fall under the banner of this type of research – for example, research looking at how to maximise personal branding, or website usability studies would be relevant here. While this type of research is highly practical, it may not advance theoretical or methodological understanding of the phenomenon studied.

How is the research bound by time and space?

The fourth macro-level question brings to the fore the reality that digital research occurs in a dynamic, uncertain environment. New digital technologies are being developed and released at an increasing rate (e.g., virtual reality headsets, driverless cars), new data are produced so quickly that it is now impossible to keep up with it (e.g., several quintillions of data produced every day), and new practices continue to be adopted by digital users (e.g., the adoption of applications ('apps') to remotely run households). Researching in this environment requires us to pause and consider how the phenomena we are interested in are specific to the time and space we are considering. Effectively we need to consider whether what we are interested in is a fad or meme (e.g., cat selfies), a fashion (e.g., particular hashtags #throwbackThursday) or a trend (e.g., uptake of mobile commerce). We can do this by considering:

- the level of embeddedness of our topic in time, that is, the time period of the research
- the socio-cultural perspective we are taking (both in terms of ideology and value)
- the particular technology(ies) or platform(s) (place) where the phenomenon is manifested
- the digital and non-digital environmental space (or ecosystem) where the phenomenon is found.

How is digital research bound by time?

A feature of the digital environment is its immediacy. Individuals and organisations are able to react instantly to events and this can result in a 24/7, always on, expectation of interactions within the digital environment. Events in this digital environment can, nevertheless, have different temporal characteristics that we need to consider in relation to how they impact on our research. Temporality is so important to digital research that we have devoted a whole chapter to it (Chapter 4). In digital research, temporality can include whether activities are cyclical (e.g., holiday destination internet searches, seasonality of clothing purchases, the release of a new version of mobile phone software). Temporality can be important in relation to understanding unusual events (e.g., the 2013 Boston marathon bombing, the 2016 EU Brexit referendum, or an outbreak of a specific computer virus), and temporality can be considered in relation to how a particular phenomenon develops over a period of time (e.g., number of adopters of a technology, adoption of a particular type of behaviour). The first two aspects of temporality can originate from either inside or outside the digital environment, the third is related to developments in digital phenomena.

Some external environmental events can be anticipated, so we can plan for the digital phenomena that emerge from them. For instance, the cyclical nature of some website searches (e.g., flu vaccine availability), seasonal purchases (e.g., clothing choices), changes in services related to demographic trends (e.g., websites designed specifically for older users), and events such as elections (though not their outcomes), can all be predicted. The temporal characteristics of these events are due to broader environmental developments, but as their predictability makes them relatively easy to anticipate, we can incorporate them into our research designs. Other external environmental events cannot be predicted (e.g., an airplane disaster and the tweets associated with it, or understanding rioting by urban residents through digital postings on YouTube, Facebook, etc.). These events are unusual, occur in an ad-hoc manner, and represent rich opportunities for researchers to look at a specific digital phenomenon. Nevertheless, their unpredictability means that they usually need to be researched retrospectively.

Temporality can also be considered in relation to purely digital phenomena rather than broader environmental events. We might, for instance, be interested in considering how the time over which a particular technology has been available impacts on its use (e.g., changes in tweet content), or in comparing technological life cycles. For example, researching the patterns of technology adoption across cultures through looking at social networking sites such as Facebook and Weibo. A further element when considering temporality is that there may be interaction between events and the development stage of the digital phenomenon – for instance, the digital response to the Boston marathon bombings would have been different if it had happened five or ten years earlier as the communication platforms available evolved over that time period, resulting in a wider variety of media with which to use as a response mechanism. So some consideration may be needed concerning whether temporal factors related to the external environment interact with temporal factors in the digital environment.

Research is bound by time when time impacts on the usefulness of the research findings. Insights derived from researching one type of platform, for example, might become obsolete when a different type of platform emerges (e.g., Twitter changing communication behaviours). Findings based on data that have been impacted by unpredictable environmental events, or at a particular point in a cyclical phenomenon, might not be typical, reducing the value of those findings. These temporal factors have greater potential to impact on digital research due to the dynamic nature of the digital environment.

How is digital research bound by socio-cultural perspective?

The socio-cultural context of digital users, research participants and researchers can all impact on digital research. The questions we, as researchers, ask reflect the interests and concerns of our socio-cultural context (i.e., the reflections of our age, country, etc.) even if we are not aware of how those specific interests came about. For example, research on environmentally responsible behaviours occurs due to a general acceptance that people have an impact on planetary resources and climate patterns, as well as a responsibility to try to minimise that impact. What we consider important and/or interesting is dependent not just on our own skills, abilities and interests, but also on the interests of those around us – we do not work in a vacuum. What our participants choose to share or withhold is impacted by social norms, as is how digital users behave.

The socio-cultural environment reflects the ideology of the time and place – what is considered acceptable and ethical in terms of behaviour (e.g., slavery, racism, privacy), as well as what is acceptable in terms of research practice (e.g., deception, the notion of participants of research as 'subjects', researching the dark web – the part of the internet accessed only through certain networks, and which is not searchable by search engines. A wide variety of interactions take place on the dark web, such as illegal trading, and media exchange for those interested in pornography but also those people who wish to pursue legitimate but untracked interactions); both have ideological elements. The socio-cultural context shapes our values. For instance, whether we consider economic development more important than protecting the environment is not unrelated to how economically developed the country we live in is, and whether we consider relationships more important that individual success is, at least partially, culturally determined. As such, the socio-cultural environment provides an unconscious lens through which we problematise particular issues, interpret the digital context, and determine which research practices are acceptable. The more we are aware of how our socio-cultural environment impacts on our thinking, and on our research choices, the more we can consider how they interact.

How is digital research bound by technology/platform (place)?

The digital technologies used in the digital environment are not context-free, and various platforms exist that can be used for similar and different purposes (e.g., SnapChat versus Pinterest versus LinkedIn as described in Tuten and Solomon's (2018) social media zones). What we need to acknowledge here, as researchers, is that the technologies and platforms we select to study, that is the digital place we choose, can itself create boundary conditions that relate to what we will discover. For instance, if tweets are used as part of the research design, the message, until recently, was confined to 140 characters, though shortened hypertext links or ow.lys are often used to include further message content.

This limit constrains the data that are produced and subsequently collected, and would have knock-on effects to the insights that were drawn (e.g., depth of understanding of an issue). Other forms of data, such as a blog post, are less constrained.

As digital platforms differ from each other, certain platforms may have characteristics that make them more valuable as vehicles for collecting certain types of data or for providing insight into different types of behaviour. For example, complaint behaviour may be more effectively researched through investigating TripAdvisor review data than Facebook. Young people's perceptions about higher education may be more usefully explored through discussions on the Student Room website forum. Usage of urban outdoor spaces may be reviewed by town planners through the analysis of digitally recorded CCTV videos illustrating patterns of human movement. Thus media, technology and platform chosen should not only relate to the research objective but also how the resulting data will be bounded by the platforms chosen. The point here is not that one of these forms of data is generally 'better' than the other, but that it is important to ensure that we are aware of the limits of our potential data sources prior to data collection, and that we have asked whether our data will enable us to examine/explore our research question in sufficient depth.

As researchers, we also need to consider how the findings from one technology or platform can apply to another. Any unquestioning application of the findings of a study using one technology to another technology is false, just as we need to consider how a study undertaken in non-digital contexts (e.g., church communities) cannot automatically be applied to other non-digital contexts (e.g., addiction recovery communities). We cannot automatically assume that a model developed using one digital platform will be applicable to another (although it may be). For example, messages posted on Facebook cannot be considered as equivalent in format or in purpose as tweets on Twitter or pictures on Instagram, and models of digital communication networks developed on Facebook may not transfer to Twitter or Snapchat.

How is the research bound by the digital and non-digital space?

Individual technologies and platforms do not exist in isolation; they exist in a complex ecosystem with shared content, ownership structures and competing characteristics. That is, they exist in a technological space that itself exists alongside and interacts with a non-technological space. Technologies and platforms compete with each other for their 'share' of the digital user, but the share they gain does not just depend on their technical characteristics, but also on network effects (i.e., the number of relevant/current users they already have). Which technology individuals gravitate towards will depend on a number of complex non-digital and digital characteristics. For example, the Chinese government restricts access to some social networking sites (e.g., Facebook), so other choices have developed that cater to the needs of Chinese people (e.g., Weibo, RenRen and WeChat), and at the family level, a particular website might be blocked by parents to prevent access by children. Knowledge of the external factors that impact on technology/platform uptake informs us of potential bias in our sampling, or might prove a helpful pointer as to which particular research questions might not be answered via particular platforms.

While technologies/platforms all need to claim a share of the digital user to thrive, they might not need to compete directly. Technologies/platforms can also coexist independently alongside, or be complementary to, other technologies/platforms. Understanding whether one technology/platform competes with, co-exists with, or is complementary to another is important when selecting platforms for data analysis, and when we interpret our findings. An example of complementarity might be an individual using Facebook to keep in touch with a broad group of friends, WhatsApp to have conversations with a family group, and LinkedIn to maintain loose professional networks.

Micro-level areas for consideration

As with any research design, digital research needs to have a starting point. From within the digital environment this starting point could be an interesting digital phenomenon that has not been explored before, or we might be interested in looking at how we can develop a new digital theory, or extend a digital theory to another (digital) context. Alternatively starting from outside the digital domain, we might wonder how a non-digital phenomenon manifests in the digital domain, or be concerned with how pre-existing (non-digital) theory applies in the digital domain. Whatever our starting point, our research design will need to decide what and where/when we are considering, and how we will gain data in relation to that consideration. While these considerations will all impact on our research design, they can also prompt further research design questions. Drawing from McGrath and Brinberg (1983), four questions can help us consider how the different elements of the digital research design 'fit' with each other. These are:

What

- conceptualisations (theories, models or frameworks) are relevant to our digital research?
- methods are relevant to the research?
- is the context of the digital research?
- is the contextualised phenomenon that is relevant to the digital research?

What conceptualisations are relevant to our digital research?

As researchers we move from concrete observations of phenomena in the 'real' world to some conceptualisations based on those concrete observations (i.e., theory development), or we take previously developed conceptualisations and consider how well those conceptualisations explain sets of concrete observations (i.e., theory testing). In other words, we move between the concrete and the abstract in our research. The particular conceptualisations we use are the theories, models and frameworks relevant to our disciplines. Any particular research project either uses these conceptualisations to develop the research aims and/or objectives, or examines unexplained phenomena to develop new conceptualisations (McGrath and Brinberg, 1983). With digital research, we need to consider the relationship between these conceptualisations and the digital environment. Suler (2016), for example, looks at how psychological theories need to be reconceptualised for the digital age. However, using digital methods will not necessarily lead to a 'digital' conceptualisation of the phenomenon, as the digital method might only be used to access the concrete observations. For example, citizens' understanding of their employment rights when examined through questions posed on Q and A websites and forums is unlikely to result in a reconceptualisation of employment rights.

If we are considering phenomena in the digital environment, then we need to consider how our conceptualisations relate to the characteristics of the digital domain. We need to understand the extent to which our conceptualisation is derived from and embedded across the digital environment. For a conceptualisation developed in the digital environment, we need to consider how its conceptualisation is related to the macro-level questions considered earlier. If the conditions under which the conceptualisation previously occurred no longer exist, then we need to consider how those changes might impact on (if at all) our conceptualisation in this time and place. Specifically we need to ask what our current context shares with the context that the theory/model/framework was developed in. For example, research attempting to conceptualise the 'sharing' society needs to consider the movement away from open profiles to private profiles on Facebook as abuses of privacy, perceptions of control over content, etc., changed as the digital platform evolved.

When we want to understand how non-digital conceptualisations apply to problems in the digital environment, we also need to understand how the theory/model/framework was conceptualised. What are the characteristics of the conceptualisation (or the digital environment) that make it interesting to explore in the digital space? How much do we know of the conceptualisation in digital space? Indeed, why do we believe a non-digital theory is relevant in the digital environment? For example, a research study interested in fashion clothing purchasing behaviour and the influences involved may consist of taking non-digital theories of influence and applying them in a digital context, or the researchers involved may take the view that none of the established theories are relevant in the digital context.

What methods are relevant to the research?

Every time we conduct research, we need to consider how we will access information to help us address the research questions we are asking. Understanding how we access information is not unique to understanding digital research. While not the focus of this book, whether we are conducting digital research or not, we need to consider ontology (what we believe exists) and epistemology (how we can know what exists). More pragmatically, we also need to consider whether the methods we propose to use fit with the particular problems we are studying. Because research in the digital environment is less well established and continues to evolve rapidly, we need to consider carefully how our choice of research methods will impact on the data we can gather, how that data can be analysed and, in turn, how that data might shape our findings. For example, we might gather data about attitudes from tweets or personal blogs. Tweets are short, so any attitudinal data are likely to be summative – good/bad – not nuanced. In contrast, personal blogs can be extended, and attitudinal data here may not provide an overall summative statement but instead explore both positive and negative attitudes towards something. As such, the characteristics of the data from a particular data source can shape the research insights found, so when choosing digital methods, we need to ask ourselves questions about those methods in order to help us understand how they might shape our understanding of what we are researching. This will help us choose the methods most appropriate to our research.

Do we even need digital data?

As digital researchers, we need to consider whether we actually need to gather digital data to explore the phenomena that we are interested in. Here we might need to separate out whether we are interested in the entity (person, organisation or thing) or the digital manifestation of that entity (e.g., tweet, personal blog, navigation behaviour, network connections). The distinction between the entity and its digital manifestation (digital footprint or shadow) is important. If the digital footprint/shadow is of interest, then we need to consider how to appropriately access that footprint/shadow. Here we need to reflect on issues related to authorship and ownership of the data, as well as matters relating to privacy. These issues are explored in more detail in later chapters. In contrast, if our research question focuses on the entity (person, organisation or thing), then we may not need digital data at all as non-digital methods may be better suited to directly access that entity.

It might be that the data manifestations we require are digital (e.g., Twitter, Facebook, Instagram, WhatsApp and WeChat), but to access those manifestations for a particular entity requires non-digital data collection (i.e., recruiting an individual who will allow access to their phone, tablet and computer). When considering the relationship between an entity and their digital manifestations, we might also want to consider how close the digital manifestation is to the entity. Someone's personal blog is closer to the entity who wrote it than a tweet about that blog, an individual's Instagram account is closer to that individual than a selection of those photos compiled by someone else. This reflection on the relationship between entity and manifestations is concerned with the proximity of the data to the focus of the research, and would be included under primary or secondary data considerations when not in the digital space. However, data in the digital space might not be easily classified into primary/secondary and this is considered in more detail in Chapter 3. The proximity of the material to the individual may also have implications for the content of the data.

Some digital research methods are derived from more traditional research methods, others have developed as we have explored phenomena in the digital space. When we adopt non-digital methods (e.g., questionnaires, interviews, focus groups, experiments), we need to consider how the digital environment impacts on those methods. For example, we may need to consider: How does the participants' ability to look up information online impact on responses to questionnaires or in interviews? How might the loss of body language and facial expression between people impact on the interaction in interviews and focus groups? Or, how might the dynamic possibilities of online research impact on experiments? Overall, when using adaptations of established methods in the digital context we need to consider how the characteristics of the digital environment will impact on those methods.

When considering methods developed in the digital space, we have to explore how well understood those methods are in the digital context we are using them in. Are the methods known in our discipline, for example, or in related disciplines? Have the methods been used with a particular technology or platform? Using a digital method that is already established within a discipline will require less justification to convince others of the value of the findings we produce. If we are introducing a digital method to our discipline, then we will need to fully understand, and be able to explain, how that method relates to accepted methods. Some digital methods that have been used extensively and are now relatively well developed are netnography and geo-location based mapping (see Kozinets, 2010 and 2015). Other digital methods are still under development (e.g., STACKS, an open source research toolkit designed to collect, process and store data originating from various social networks) or require more extensive justification (visualising results rather than providing numbers).

We also need to consider how the development of a digital research methods tool might have impacted on the data it produces. The technical development of some methods (e.g., sentiment analysis) could be criticised for taking too simplistic a view of how sentiment is expressed through language. Similarly qualitative data coding software used in but not limited to digital research, such as NVivo, has been criticised for being overly reductive and attempting to overlay quantitative analytical approaches onto qualitative data, including social media text and image based data. What we need to ensure is that, overall, we consider the relationship between the research method chosen and the data we gain.

A further consideration is practical. We need to consider, when looking at digital methods, whether we have the skills and/or resources required to implement them (i.e., our expertise). Many of the technical skills required to implement digital research methods fall outside the social science disciplines, such as the ability to write computer code or manipulate complex data sets across different software systems to create an integrated data set. While technical skills can be learnt and/or bought in to a project, there are significant time and financial resource implications in doing this. Other skills may be needed that are found within the social sciences but outside your own subject area, for example, skills in setting up experiments, frequently found in researchers from psychology, some areas of economics and even education. If you are researching in a team then it is valuable to identify the existing skills your team may have in relation to digital research, and if you are in a position to recruit or access other researchers think about where the technical skills gaps lie that need to be filled in order to execute your project. Small scale digital research studies may be successfully conducted without the use of complex or costly technology. However, naïve execution of digital research methods leaves us vulnerable to criticism as we might not be able to determine whether the method genuinely allows us to access interesting and valuable data or whether it is a digital methods equivalent of a cat selfie (i.e., a fad) and only provides data of limited value in terms of representativeness and longevity.

What is the context of the digital research?

The context of the research is related to the event the phenomenon is concerned with (McGrath and Brinberg, 1983). When we undertake any research the context may be of central importance to the research question (e.g., when investigating how people communicate online, the online context is central to the research question), or the context might be peripheral to the research question (e.g., when examining how information about innovations are spread, no specific context is central to the research question). With digital research the methods might be embedded in the digital context, the phenomenon might be digital, or both might be bound by the digital context. As such, we need to understand how the digital context impacts on our research. For example, the video gaming context can be considered as spanning the boundary between digital and physical spheres, as those people engaged in online video gaming are sitting somewhere either by themselves or with others while they interact online and their physical as well as digital behaviours may be of interest to a researcher. Networks offer a further example: the context of a network may be a digital social network or a physical social network, which involves actual interaction between people. These networks might consist of individuals limited to either the digital or the physical network, or there may be multiple individuals that span the boundary between both types of network, thus blurring the distinction between the digital and physical networks.

Understanding the context of the research helps us to make choices concerning how we access data for our research problem or question. Considering the context of the research can also help us identify the particular types of event(s) we need to explore to answer our research questions – the context might reveal multiple types of events that are related to our research question, or reveal particularly important time-based elements related to the research question (e.g., gaming behaviour might include cooperative or competitive behaviour, and this could relate to length of association between individuals or groups, or other contextual factors). While the previous factors relate to how we access the most appropriate data for our research, the context also needs to be considered in relation to ethical questions.

Ethical questions that arise from the context include the potential to take data out of context. As digital researchers, we have the ability to isolate and atomise data in more ways than previously possible. For example, it is an easy task to perform hashtag searches for key words on many social media platforms but how were those keywords used in relation to the context they are describing? Once we lose Krippendorff's (2004) 'keyword in context' ideas about content analysis, then those words can be given very different meanings from their original intent. As such, it becomes relatively straightforward to remove data from their context and in doing so, open up the possibility of misinterpretation or selectively choosing 'soundbite' data to fit our purposes. The edit and retweet function on platforms such as Twitter can also assist in distorting an original context. Contemporary, tribal, sub-culture 'slang' and language usage in digital communication should be treated with care to avoid misrepresentation.

Another contextual issue that we need to consider carefully surrounds whether data are public or private (see also Chapter 6). This established division within research methods is linked to issues of consent, which are also explored in Chapter 7. Data produced online might be intended for public or for private distribution. An online newspaper article, a tweet, an open-access blog and searchable YouTube videos might all be considered as being produced with the expectation that they would be publicly consumed. In contrast, a Facebook post, an email, a Wikipedia correction and a text message are not produced with the expectation of public consumption. Consequently the specifics of the digital context of the data can lead to consideration of how we report that data. Reporting practices associated with non-digital data (e.g., interviews) such as quoting verbatim are not necessarily appropriate for online data (e.g., tweets) as the data can be traced back to individual research participants through straightforward internet searches. Even if the original data were created with the expectation of it being consumed publicly, digital research does not remove our responsibility as researchers to protect the anonymity of our participants.

We also need to consider who owns the data we are collecting. This is not a straightforward question in the digital environment as individuals who consume digital services (as well as researchers themselves) are not always aware of the terms of use associated with those services. This can make it difficult for the researcher to untangle who to seek consent from for their research – specifically, should they ask the digital service provider as the legal owner of the data, or should they seek permission (if at all possible) from the producer of the data? Data ownership is given further discussion in Chapter 6. This issue has implications for both the relevance of, and feasibility of gaining, informed consent.

Whether the data are produced actively or passively is also a contextual issue that we need to reflect upon and this is discussed in more detail in Chapter 6. Active digital data include the manifestations of deliberate actions by a 'participant.' These could include any comment or image posting made, as well as online purchases, and connection invitations accepted. These actions are known to the participant and might be equated to their active identity construction. Passive digital data occur naturally, for example, the navigation data produced when someone is searching for and purchasing a particular item or geo-spatial data created by an advertising app. While participants may be aware of this passive data collection, it is not something they generally pay attention to when they are going about their daily lives.

The context of the research can also alert us to ethics questions that we need to consider. For example, if we are interested in researching particular types of people, we might recognise that they represent a vulnerable group. This would require us to take measures to help ensure that the safety of vulnerable participants was not compromised by taking part in the research (Cresci, 2015). For example, research focusing on the integration of recent immigrant families, or the use of illegal pain medication by chronic disease sufferers. Interestingly, the anonymity of digital research can be more comfortable for some vulnerable groups than the personal exposure associated with non-digital data collection. The digital context can act as a buffer zone, which is perceived by the research participant as offering a safety mesh through which to voice their experiences in matters ranging from product complaints to articulating domestic abuse.

Finally, thought should be given to collecting data across multiple contexts. That is, a research study may be investigating a phenomenon across several contexts and each context needs to be considered individually and also together as a whole. Further to this, the layering of contexts could inadvertently reveal the identity of an individual or group. This issue is of particular relevance to the anonymisation of data and how much information needs to be removed to ensure that anonymity is maintained.

What is the contextualised phenomenon that is relevant to the research?

Contextualising the phenomenon in many ways reflects the macro-considerations of time, place and space discussed earlier, but at the micro-level, it is applied more specifically within the research design frame. Within this contextualisation, the phenomena being investigated in digital research may, or may not, be digital; it may be deductive (i.e., derived from theory) or inductive (i.e., observed in the digital space or non-digital place); it may, or may not, be confined to a particular digital or non-digital space/place. However the central phenomenon of interest is conceptualised; to fully develop an understanding of that phenomena we need to identify, define and even explore its boundaries. Questions to consider here include:

- How is the phenomenon of interest bound by time, place and space?
- How do time, place and space impact on the proposed research methods?
- What is the impact of the socio-cultural context on the research study?

Contextualising the phenomenon helps us to separate out the different influences related to that phenomenon. In the digital space, this requires us to think about the extent to which the phenomenon is digital and/or a digital manifestation of non-digital behaviour. That is, what 'space' does this phenomenon occupy? This is likely to require us to carefully consider interactions between the (digital) environment where the phenomenon is observed, and the need or desire the behaviour fulfils. For example, social network platforms fulfil a need to interact with others, the dark web fulfils a desire for privacy, and navigation data fulfil a desire to understand customer movements. Thinking of each phenomenon in terms of the need it fulfils can also help us to identify whether it is likely to be an enduring aspect of the digital environment (i.e., potentially a new trend), or whether it is likely to be more fleeting (i.e., a fad), or something in-between (i.e., a fashion). Contextualising the phenomenon includes us considering what it is about the digital environment that enables the phenomenon to either emerge on, or transfer to, the digital context. Depending on the amount that is known about the phenomenon we are interested in, contextualising the phenomenon might itself be integral to answering our research questions. If this is the case, we might not be able to address all of the above issues when developing the research. However, maintaining an awareness of these issues can help us to identify potential contributing literature that might not otherwise have been considered.

Contextualising the research will also involve thinking about the extent to which it can be understood in, or through, digital methods – how are the methods used impacted by time, place and space? In some instances, research might not be fully realised by drawing data from within the digital context – that is, the research question goes beyond the boundaries of the digital context. In others, the research question might be answered with only digital data. Whether or not the research can be fully addressed from within the digital environment may be related to whether the underlying focus of the research is the entity that acts in or on the digital space, or the manifestations of the entity's action (i.e., a person, versus that person's digital footprint). If the focus of the research is the entity outside the digital space, then the relationship with their digital manifestations needs to be explored to determine what can be understood through digital research methods and what needs to be explored through non-digital means (for more discussion see Chapter 5). This is akin to considering the problem of using behavioural intentions to infer actual behaviour, or of using self-report measures to assess individual characteristics. It is not that inferences cannot be made, just that we need to be aware of the disconnect that exists between how we are assessing the data and what we are making inferences about.

The socio-cultural context also needs to be considered in relation to the phenomenon of interest, and the methods of study. Specific consideration can be used to contextualise the phenomenon in time, including: the lifecycle stage, stability and potential longevity of the technologies/platforms that are associated with the phenomenon or methods; the rate and magnitude of change in the digital environment; whether the specific phenomenon is related to specific events; the prevailing disciplinary research norms and legal restrictions on research; whether there is a cyclical element to the phenomenon; and the planned duration of the research project. In addition, the socio-cultural context can be used to contextualise the sensitivity of the topic with specific groups, as well as the research methods proposed. Both direct and indirect influences are important as while research that considers digital manifestations might have little direct impact on the entity that produced those manifestations, indirect influence is still possible – perhaps, for example, research findings on how to improve website conversion rates lead to website design changes that impact positively on vulnerable consumers who might otherwise not have purchased particular goods.

Entities (e.g., individuals, organisations) that directly provide research data might also be impacted by research findings. When this occurs, there is a possibility that participation in the research directly impacts on the participants. This is sometimes straightforward to identify (e.g., action research in organisations), but can also be more subtle (e.g., knowing about the 'bystander effect' makes people less susceptible to it). As researchers, we need to contextualise what we wish to gain by investigating the phenomenon we are interested in within a framework that allows us to assess the potential benefits and harms that may result from our research. Just because we can research something does not mean that we should, and whether we should is dependent on our socio-cultural context. While this discussion has restricted itself to the direct or indirect participants of the research, wider stakeholder groups might also need to be considered, and these include all the potential research audiences identified earlier.

Overall, there are various elements we need to consider about the digital phenomenon we intend to research and/or the digital methods we intend to use. These include both macro-level factors related to our research choices, as well as more micro-level factors related to specific research projects.

Digital research design in the changing research landscape

The complexity of digital research whether due to phenomenon, method or both has design implications for us all as researchers. In common with non-digital researchers we have to ensure that the different elements of our research fit together (McGrath and Brinberg, 1983) in order to effectively address our research questions. However, this 'fit' in digital research occurs within a complex, diverse and rapidly changing research environment that is almost impossible for a single researcher to fully understand. As a result of the dynamic nature of the digital environment, successful digital researchers often draw on skills and expertise outside their own discipline, which may involve working in multi-disciplinary teams. The dynamic digital environment presents huge opportunities to provide new insights, but also leads to problems analysing and integrating the different data types/formats. The complexity in the digital environment also lends itself to more complex designs; see, for example, the variations of mixed methods designs identified by Creswell and Plano-Clark (2011). So even if other factors did not impact on the usefulness of qualitative/quantitative labels, the advent of mixed methods as a relatively common feature of digital research makes labelling many research studies as qualitative *or* quantitative problematic.

SUMMARY

In this chapter, we have outlined that some of the previously distinct aspects of research are becoming increasingly blurred in the digitalised research environment. We have clearly delineated both the macro- and micro-level reflections required of a digital researcher when considering research. Importantly we have foregrounded the central role of contextuality and its importance when making digital research decisions. These are all important when considering ethics, expectations and expertise in digital research.

The 3Es

With research in the dynamic digital environment, we, as researchers, have to identify and examine our expectations of research purpose and research practices. We have to consider explicitly how time, place and space impact on the purpose of research (macro-level questions) as well as how we practise research (micro-level). Examining macro-level considerations such as our expectations concerning the longevity of the research we are undertaking will help us unpick what binds our phenomenon to the specific socio-technological context in which it is undertaken. This reflexive practice will also help us to understand when changes in the socio-technological context make it necessary to re-examine the phenomenon of interest. Examining micro-level considerations, such as our expectations of the research methods used, will help us to identify the strengths and weaknesses of particular research designs – possibly prompting us to combine different methods such that one method's weaknesses are mitigated by another method's strengths.

The dynamic digital environment also places demands on us as researchers to identify not just what digital and methodological expertise we have, but also acknowledge where our expertise is lacking. We may, for instance, not fully understand the digital and non-digital ecosystem we are working within, or we may recognise that our ability to extract data from the digital environment is hampered by a lack of technological knowledge. Carefully examining what expertise is needed to achieve our research aims within the complex macro- and micro-level factors will help us to identify who we may need to collaborate with, or what knowledge we need to gain. Alternatively, identifying weaknesses in the research team's expertise might prompt a redesign that plays to the strengths of the research team, yet still achieves the research objectives. Careful consideration of the impact of macro- and micro-level factors, including the expertise needed to deal with those factors, is required to ensure any research insights gained are sound.

Ethics are themselves bound by the socio-cultural context in which the research takes place. What was ethically acceptable in the 1960s when Milgram undertook his obedience experiments where participants believed they were administering electric shocks, or in the 1970s when Zimbardo conducted the Stanford prison experiments, would not be considered acceptable today. Ethics, like language, evolve in a broader context. They are related to societal, institutional, disciplinary and individual norms and values. Examining the macro- and micro-level factors that impact on our research allows us to examine the underlying assumptions we are making. Micro-level factors might mean that established research practices used to protect participants, such as gaining consent, are not fit for purpose in the digital context. For example, if a technological platform protects individual participants' identities what is the purpose of gaining consent when that could reveal participants' identities and inadvertently expose them to 'harm' by uncovering their use of a particular technological platform (think of users of a chatroom that supports domestic abuse suffers)? At a macro-level, consideration of changes in socio-cultural norms – such as what 'privacy' means – might reveal changing standards that open up, or restrict, the use of different data sets. For example, comments on publicly accessible forums may be posted with no expectation of that comment being public (e.g., online communities that support people with specific health issues), these comments may be akin to private conversations over lunch – made in a public place, but not for public consumption. Consideration of the macro- and micro-level factors that influence your research should help to unpick which ethical issues are pertinent to the research project, and how they can best be achieved.

Overall, the content of this chapter challenges us, as digital researchers, to examine how the contemporary state of dynamic socio-technological context relates to, and impacts on, our particular research project. The questions posed, and issues discussed, help us reflect on the digital context, on our expectations of and for our research, on the expertise need to undertake that research, and on the ethical issues we might need to consider.

Questions

1. What macro-level considerations should you reflect on in relation to your digital research?
2. What micro-level considerations should you reflect on in relation to your digital research?
3. How might thinking about contextuality within digital research impact upon your own research design?

FURTHER READING

Charmaz, K. (2002). Qualitative interviewing and grounded theory analysis. In J.F. Gubrium and J.A. Holstein (eds), *Handbook of Interview Research: Context and Method* (2nd edn). Thousand Oaks, CA: Sage.

Iphofen, R. (2011). *Ethical Decision Making in Social Research*. New York: Palgrave.

Lewis, S.J. and Russell, A.J. (2011). Being embedded: A way forward for ethnographic research. *Ethnography, 12* (3), 398–416.

Williams, S., Clausen, M.G., Robertson, A., Peacock, S. and McPherson, K. (2012). Methodological reflections on the use of asynchronous online focus groups in health research. *International Journal of Qualitative Methods, 11* (4), 368–383.

REFERENCES

Cenni, I. and Goethals, P. (2017). Negative hotel reviews of TripAdvisor: Across-linguistic analysis. *Discourse, Context and Media, 16*, 22–30.

Cresci, E. (2015). #timetotalk: Is social media helping people talk about mental health? The *Guardian*, 5 February. Available from: www.theguardian.com/technology/2015/feb/05/time totalk-is-social-media-helping-people-talk-about-mental-health (accessed June 27 2016).

Creswell, J.W. and Plano-Clark, V. (2011). Collecting data in mixed methods research. In *Designing and Conducting Mixed Methods Research*. Thousand Oaks, CA: Sage, pp. 171–202.

Hughes, C.E., Moxham-Hall, V., Ritter, A., Weatherburn, D. and MacCoun, R. (2017). The deterrent effects of Australian street-level drug law enforcement on illicit drug offending at outdoor music festivals. *International Journal of Drug Policy*, *41*, 91–100.

Kozinets, R.V. (2010). *Netnography: Doing Ethnographic Research Online*. Thousand Oaks, CA: Sage.

Kozinets, R.V. (2015). *Netnography: Redefined* (2nd edn). Thousand Oaks, CA: Sage.

Krippendorff, K. (2004). *Content Analysis: An Introduction to its Methodology*. London: Sage.

McGrath, J.E. and Brinberg, D. (1983). External validity and the research process: A comment on the Calder/Lynch dialogue. *Journal of Consumer Research*, *10* (1), 115–124.

Newton, I. (1676). Letter from Sir Isaac Newton to Robert Hooke. Historical Society of Pennsylvania, Philadelphia, PA.

Suler, J.R. (2016). *Psychology of the Digital Age: Human Become Electric*. New York: Cambridge University Press.

Tuten, T.L. and Solomon, M.R. (2018). *Social Media Marketing* (3rd edn). London: Sage.

Wallace, M. and Wray, A. (2016). *Critical Reading and Writing for Postgraduates* (3rd edn). London: Sage.

PART 2
Assessing Digital Data

In this part, we examine what we need to think about when assessing information in the digital environment. Overall, we consider questions concerning the 'what', 'when', 'who' and 'how' of assessing digital data. First, we consider the characteristics of digital data – the 'what'. Some of the issues here are not qualitative changes in the type of data that is available – social science disciplines have established diverse traditions using most of the data formats that are available digitally. Rather it is a quantitative difference – that is, the accessibility and volume of data available means that digital researchers look outside their discipline's 'core' data formats. Understanding the range of data formats that are available in the digital context is a key element to understanding both the opportunities afforded digital researchers as well as the challenges faced by them. Data formats are considered in Chapter 3.

Second, a more contemporary characteristic of the digital environment is that it requires researchers to think about the temporality of their data – the 'when' of digital data. Time, in the 'real' world, leads to problems with assessing data from previous time periods. The loss of raw data from previous time periods is reflected in our language – what is 'past' is gone, it's historic. The 'past' is remembered and interpreted, not observed directly. The data storage capacity of the digital environment means, however, that raw data are available from previous time periods, and as digital researchers we need to consider the issues associated with changing the past from being remembered, to being an observed state. Temporality, however, is not restricted to the past, present and future, it is also related to how we 'chunk' time (e.g., whether an interaction is synchronous or asynchronous depends on how we interpret a time period), whether we perceive something as continuous or disjointed, and our ability to absorb information (e.g., the difference between sensory information that is registered by our sensory organs – awareness of sound generally – versus sensory information that is paid attention to consciously – listening to a specific conversation) in a particular time period. These temporal aspects of how we consider data are all impacted by the data processing capacity that is a characteristic of the digital environment. The temporal aspects of digital data are considered in Chapter 4.

The third aspect of assessing information in the digital environment is identifying our data source(s) – the 'who'. As social scientists we are, overall, interested in understanding humans in their environment(s). However, different social science disciplines focus at different levels – e.g., anthropologists look at groups, psychologists consider individuals, whereas communication scholars consider interactions. Consequently, one of the challenges of digital research is to unpick what our level of focus is, and how that is reflected in the digital context. We need to pay particular attention to this in the digital context as we could easily be overwhelmed by the volume of data that is available to us. We also need to consider whether our research question requires us to directly interact with the person(s) that produce the data, or whether our understanding of the phenomenon of interest can be achieved through looking at the digital artefact(s) that are left behind; that is, is our data source a person or a thing. This question is particularly pertinent as digital's data storage and processing capabilities mean that 'things' can be accessed directly, even if they are historic. It is also important because the digital context enables a separation between physical/real identity and digital identity. These data source issues will be discussed in Chapter 5.

The fourth and final aspect of accessing digital information that we consider is the process of accessing that information – the 'how' of digital data collection. Here we explore issues concerning the agency of both researchers and participants – how active or passive are they in digital data collection, how informed and empowered are they to make research choices. The sometimes contentious issue relating to the disclosure or non-disclosure of researchers within digital data collection environments is highlighted and reflection is made about the care needed when taking such decisions. Aspects such as sensitivity of topic, vulnerability of groups and individuals as well as norms of behaviour within context are raised. A central issue that we recognise here is the impact of automation on social science data collection. In our discussion automation includes the impact of algorithms on both data collection and analysis, and how this can impact on the rigour of research outputs. Within automation, big data are foregrounded as an increasingly used data source and an important area that digital researchers need to reflect on. These digital data collection process questions are considered in Chapter 6.

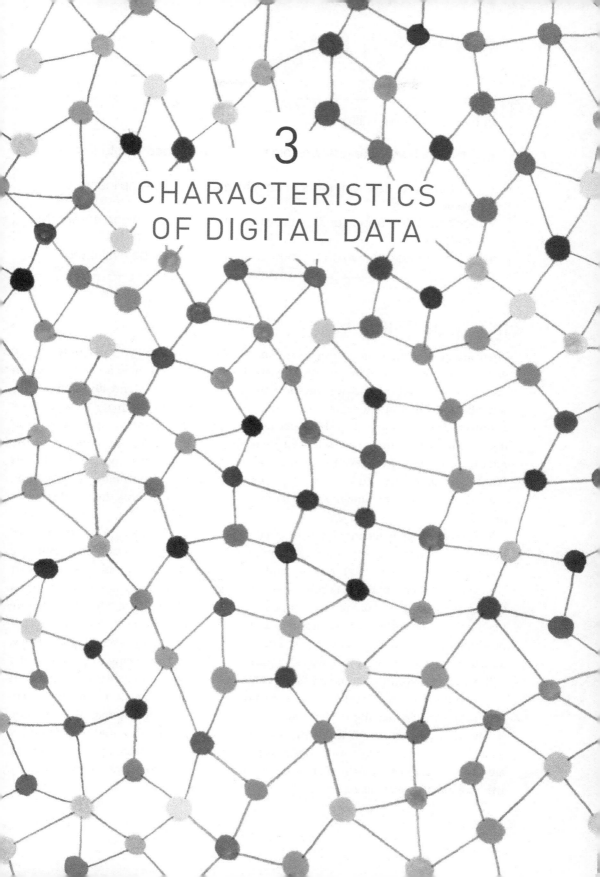

3

CHARACTERISTICS OF DIGITAL DATA

In this chapter we will:

- discuss how the digital domain requires us to reconceptualise data sources
- outline new developments in data formats and the implications for researchers
- consider the opportunities provided by co-produced and co-created data
- suggest ways in which the new data formats may be evaluated.

INTRODUCTION

There are now genuine opportunities for knowledge gaps to be filled through the use of digital research. As we alter the ways in which we think about how and why research may be conducted, and as we question the established norms and divisions within schools of research methods, we may create fresh insight through digital data and new approaches to analysing data. New perspectives and novel methods can create fresh insight but within the social sciences, there remains a lack of understanding of the relevance of the new types of data and the possibilities provided by the digital tools (Meyer and Schroeder, 2015). One of the aims of this text is to contribute by developing understanding and encouraging acceptance of digital research across the social sciences for researchers.

The use of digital technologies in social science research is creating a blurring of boundaries between our previously established notions of, for example, qualitative and quantitative (Chapter 2), primary and secondary classifications, and naturalistic or contrived research contexts. Furthermore, while non-digital research sometimes has a tendency to use attitudinal proxies for behavioural variables that are difficult to capture (e.g., behavioural intentions rather than actual behaviour), we need to be alert to the possibility that the digital environment's data storage capacity may reverse this tendency. So where the balance was once tipped towards attitudinal data, owing to the increasing ability of technology to capture and store behavioural data, the balance is now tipping in the opposite direction. The abundance of behavioural digital data may, if care is not taken, lead to researchers making conclusions that go beyond behavioural data: that is, using behaviour as a proxy for attitude. However, it is worth mentioning that much inferred data are used within industry and business focused reports. As researchers, we need to be alert to the danger of drawing conclusions from our research that are not supported by the type of data we are using.

In this chapter, we will outline the new types of data formats made possible through digitalisation. Our focus is on the variety of data, their ability to be combined and their possible uses in answering various research questions. The adoption of digital technologies and social media platforms has resulted in complex and multi-layered data, also referred to as deep data (Salmons, 2016). These new types of data reflect, in part, peoples' lives, which makes these data particularly attractive to social science researchers. The variety of data formats now available (e.g., static and moving images, sounds, texts, numbers, and combinations thereof), and the synergistic effects of being able to triangulate data, present the researcher with the opportunity to develop a greater depth of understanding. The variety of digital data formats available now necessitates a broader skill set to analyse them than is commonly used for more traditional research projects. These new data types and the size of data both challenge and call into question previously established orthodoxies of research (Borgman, 2015; Rogers, 2013).

This chapter explores the characteristics of different sources of digital data by first considering the questions about data we need to reflect on in relation to general research design – for example, do we intend to go out and collect data or search for data that already exist? This section considers how established ways of looking at data characteristics translate to the digital context. For example, it expands on non-digital characteristics concerning the nature of what is studied (i.e., are the data attitudinal or behavioural?) and the closeness of the research data to the original data (e.g., primary, secondary) by considering how these might need to be reconceptualised in the digital domain. Other issues, such as the impact of the digital characteristic of practically unlimited data storage, are also considered. This section then looks at the characteristics of digital data sets such as 'big' and open source data. The use of third party data such as open access data, big data or data collected by organisations such as Google are relatively new phenomena that researchers are now embracing. This chapter will provide guiding questions to help when considering the use of all these data in a research project including the research design.

Following this, the specific information characteristics of the data are considered. Information characteristics are considered both in terms of how the information is presented in digital format (text and numbers, static and moving images), and in relation to the different types of information we might want to extract from the data to answer our research questions. While each of the information formats is available in non-digital versions, in many cases it is the ease with which we can access, produce and upload these types of information, and the resulting volume of that format of information that is available digitally, which changes how we use it for research. The different types of information that we extract range from self-tracking data recorded, for example, via the use of fitness wearables, through to assumed to be accurate factual information such as profile information or Wikipedia contributions, to our opinions based on our experiences (e.g., product reviews) and/or values (e.g., comments in response to news stories). Both the variety, and the abundance, of these data present opportunities for, and challenges to, digital researchers.

This chapter then changes tack to consider digital data from an ethical standpoint. Here it considers what constitutes 'ethical' in digital research and how that relates to what we consider 'good practice' in the established research traditions. Ethics questions relating to accessing information in the digital environment are also provided in order to help shape and develop a research proposal. This chapter closes by looking at some of the 'bigger picture' issues associated with digital data – for instance, how research is designed to take advantage of different data formats and the impact of changes in data on how we analyse and interpret digital data.

DIMENSIONS OF DIGITAL DATA

Forcing ourselves as researchers to review and potentially revise the way we think of digital data and how we understand the characteristics of different types of data may appear unnecessary but, by delving into how we conceptualise data sources we may gain additional clues and insight into 'what' we actually require from the data to address our research question(s). That is, where the core value of the data might lie. Considering these questions seriously may provide us with alternative data sources, identify alternative perspectives on the problem to be explored, and/or expose weaknesses in the conceptualisation of our research problem. By thinking carefully about the dimension of the digital data required to address the research question given our resources, as well as possible alternatives, we will also be able to develop sound justifications for our research design choices. This process may also help us to overcome potential roadblocks to our choices by showing that clear consideration of the issues surrounding different aspects of data have been thought through. In this section we suggest different dimensions by which different data points and data sets can be evaluated.

Individual data points

When looking at individual data points, digital researchers need to ask themselves questions that explore how the data point(s) identified impact on the quality, and/or ethicality, of their research design. Broadly, these questions are:

What type of data do I need to answer my research question? How does the data type impact on how I address my research question?

How close is the data to the desired source? What is the impact of distance from the data source on the research quality?

Are there naturally occurring sources of the data I can use or do I need to actively 'produce' the data to address my research question?

How visible was the original data intended to be? Do I need permission to use the data? If so, whose permission is appropriate?

Data type: Attitudinal or behavioural

An established way of thinking about the type of data that we are using is whether it represents internal attitudes or observable behaviour. As social science researchers, we can classify data about humans/societies according to whether the data collected are focused on an internal characteristic (e.g., state or trait, attitude, opinion, cultural characteristic) or an external behaviour or manifestation of that behaviour (e.g., shopping or exercise regime, diet, sales figures, disease outbreaks, voting behaviours). (We recognise, as authors, that some ontological/epistemological perspectives maintain that it is not possible to research internal characteristics of individuals. Unfortunately, it is beyond the scope of this text to explore the implications of digital research from multiple or different ontologies/epistemologies. Rather our intention is to highlight the methodological questions that the digital domain 'throws up', which apply broadly across ontological/epistemological perspectives.) Attitudinal data can be concerned with relatively surface characteristics (e.g., attitudes towards a brand, opinions about smoking) and easily voiced through the explicit use of language or images. Attitudinal/internal data might also be concerned with the underlying drivers and/or socio-cultural assumptions that make up the individual's ideology (e.g., values and beliefs). These deeper internal characteristics may be harder for the researcher to access as the researchers' own internal characteristics may interfere with the interpretation of the data. The preceding statement is of course true for all research not just for digital research but it is worth pointing out nonetheless. Alternatively, it may even be that the participant themselves is unable to identify their latent beliefs and values as they are just 'natural'.

Attitudes can be expressed digitally through texts, videos and images. As such, they can be found virtually everywhere on the web, including on social networking platforms, discussion boards, blogs and photo-sharing websites. Digitalisation has also resulted in a profusion of behavioural data that are relevant for the social sciences (e.g., navigation data, purchase basket contents), including personal tracking data (e.g., health data such as step counts, location data). Behavioural data are created in many ways, commonly through Internet Protocol (IP) tracking and the use of cookies to piece together individuals' search and online behaviour histories through the devices they have used. Behavioural data can be observed and collected through directly observing activities (e.g., number of comments on a politics blog, CRM system failure, timing of customer complaints on social media), or through considering the artefacts of the behaviour (e.g., navigation archives, system downtime records, responses to complainant). Furthermore, if needed, direct questions can be asked about behaviour that has occurred.

Both attitudinal and behavioural digital data can be captured and recorded through the digital traces we now all leave in our wake. However, as researchers we need to be cognisant that while the existence of these data is known and visible, that does not necessarily mean that we can easily access these data for research purposes. Just because we can access a single data point, it does not follow that we can access the data set (e.g., access to individual tweets is open, whereas accessing Twitter's database is not). The characteristics of a data set, however, across the different dimensions of individual data points, are discussed in the next section.

The existence of digital behavioural data – both of non-digital activities captured digitally (e.g., people's singing recorded at a music festival) and digital behaviour captured digitally (e.g., online shopping behaviour) – may soon outstrip attitudinal data. The presence of so much behavioural data does counter a general criticism of non-digital research that was concerned with researchers using attitudinal data as a proxy for behavioural data (e.g., using behavioural intentions rather than actual behaviour when investigating the usefulness of the Theory of Reasoned Action – Fishbein and Ajzen, 1975). To expand, much previous research in the social sciences has researched and reported attitudinal research as being a base for informing policy, making predictions about people's behaviour and/or commercial decision-making. Yet what people say (attitudinal research) and what people do (behavioural research) are not the same – see, for example, research regarding attitude and behaviour towards household energy usage (Frederiks et al., 2015) or choice making in sustainable tourism (Juvan and Dolnicar, 2014). The emergent quantity of 'doing' data (behavioural data) has helped in overcoming the previously held criticism but only to a certain point. A further critique has developed which suggests that this digital behavioural data should not be mistaken for behaviours more generally and that some behaviours and interactions are now over researched (such as follows, likes and posts on social media or even specific platforms such as Twitter and Facebook) and over reported and could thus skew information about how life is lived in the twenty-first century. Furthermore, questions may arise for researchers in future years concerning whether the increased volume of behavioural data 'blinds' researchers to certain types of research questions that address areas such as motivation. In addition, reflection may be necessary as to whether inferences made from behavioural data can be used to understand patient/citizen/consumers' attitudes, and if so at what level (i.e., surface or deep); that is, can behavioural data be used as a proxy for attitudes, as attitudes were once used as a proxy for behaviour?

Distance from the data source: Primary or secondary

We classify our data to allow us to assess the degree to which they are produced by the person or thing that represents the phenomenon of interest. In other words, we classify data according to whether the data point is derived from the focus of our research, or whether it has been 'filtered' in some way. For instance, if we are interested in consumers' experiences of a hotel, then we might interview a selection of those consumers via Skype. These primary data are the raw data from the original source(s); they are as close as we can get to that original source. However, if we used reviews posted on TripAdvisor of that hotel or bloggers' reports of other people's experiences of a hotel, then our digital data source is one step removed from the original source of the desired data. These secondary sources have been filtered in some way – as well as the content being influenced by the raw data, it is also influenced by the interpretation put on that data by the author(s) of the blogs or the reviews. When accessing primary data sources, we are accessing that data in order to address a particular research question. In contrast, secondary sources did not collect the raw data with our research purpose in mind. Consequently, the specific aspects of the data they paid attention to, the amount of data they collected and when they collected the data, as well as how they collected and interpreted the data, will all need to be assessed before we can be confident that the source of data is suitable for our research purpose (see Figure 3.1).

Secondary data's main advantage over primary data to non-digital researchers was that fewer resources were required to use the data (if the data were considered suitable for the research question). However, this advantage is greatly diminished in the digital environment. In the digital environment, assessing the quality of non-primary data sources can encounter two serious information shortfalls. One of these is that it may be difficult to determine the distance of the source from the primary data. Part of this difficulty stems from a lack of explicit attribution (source of information and/or authorship of original information on a webpage for example) that can occur with digital data. This makes it difficult to trace ideas back to their origin, and as such difficult to determine how far the non-primary source is from the starting point/original source of the data. For example, Wikipedia entries are an amalgam of multiple different (potentially anonymous) authors. The difficulty of determining closeness to, or level of distance from, the data source makes assessing the quality of the secondary data source more resource intensive. Another issue is concerned with identifying when a digital data source was created or modified. Unless, for example, the website owner supplies this information as part of the content (e.g., dated news stories) or page properties, it can be quite resource intensive to determine the currency of a digital data source. Again, if the currency of the digital data is important, this adds to the resources (e.g., time, expertise) required to assess the quality of the secondary data.

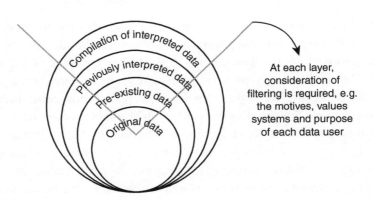

Figure 3.1 Proximity of research data to data source

In contrast, the plethora of digital data now available and the feasibility of using previously generated digital data for our specific research question impacts on the resources required to access primary data. The characteristics of the digital environment, particularly its data storage and processing capacity, and its dissolution of geographic boundaries, have had a considerable impact on reducing the resources needed to collect primary data. Digital's data storage and processing capabilities mean that, if the researcher has the technical resources, it is much easier to find and extract some, if not all, of the raw data from the person or thing that is the focus of the research.

For example, data mining/scraping can be used to extract specific information from multiple websites or social media platforms. One consequence of the dissolution of geographic boundaries is that the economic resources required to, for example, talk directly with someone in the next town via Skype are the same as those needed to talk to someone in a neighbouring country, and talking to someone in a distant country is now hampered more by time differences than cost. So, on the one hand, the digital environment makes assessing the quality of secondary sources more difficult while on the other hand, it makes the collection of primary data easier. As such, in the digital environment where resource demands differ from the non-digital research context, using secondary data sources may be much more difficult to justify.

Digital researchers should not automatically discard thoughts of using secondary data, however, but factors other than the ease of accessing the secondary data should be considered. These factors are concerned with how the data set is compiled and are discussed in the next section.

Data generation: Synthetically manufactured or naturally occurring

Until recently in the social sciences, there has been greater emphasis on collecting data based on researcher interventions in a contrived setting where the researcher asked specific questions via a 'created' research context such as interviews, focus groups or questionnaires. These data are effectively manufactured for the research study. Exceptions to this generalisation do exist; for example, the anthropological discipline has routinely observed community interactions in their natural context, and particular approaches in some disciplines, such as the discursive tradition in psychology, favour naturally generated data. We are not using 'contrived' or 'manufactured' as pejorative terms, rather that the research setting is not naturalistic, and the data would not be happening if the researcher was not present to intervene in the environment. Synthetically manufactured research data allow the researcher to retain some control over the data that are generated. This type of data also ensures that there is sufficient data available for the non-digital researcher to address their research question(s). Unlike non-digital researchers, digital researchers can be confident that there will be a sufficient volume of accessible, naturally occurring data for them to address their research questions. The volume of digital data generated naturally, alongside the digital tools that allow digital researchers to identify natural data that are relevant to a particular research question, have enabled the collection, storage and subsequent analysis of naturally occurring data from almost the entire spectrum of human life and interactions. This naturally occurring data should help us to better understand 'life as lived' (with certain caveats outlined elsewhere in this text).

Naturally occurring data are data that would exist without the presence of the researcher. Naturally occurring digital data may take the form of online community discussions, images and posting to social media platforms such as Facebook, or videos of activity in public places such as filming of sports fans at a football match. There are several benefits of naturally occurring data for researchers. Naturally occurring data are not limited in the way that data collected by a researcher with a specific narrow focus may be. Naturally occurring digital data can also be useful to sensitise us as researchers to the context that we might be researching before we further define and narrow our focus. For example, from observing online community interactions of the 'skater' community we may be better able to formulate questions using the terminology that the members of the skater community use in their exchanges to describe their skateboards, activities and lifestyle. Observational and interactional natural digital data may present ethical and practical challenges, which are discussed throughout the book. Naturally occurring digital data may well provide insight in ways that could not be foreseen in a staged research setting. Furthermore, naturally occurring digital data may be provided from harder to reach research participants and those who may be suspicious or anxious about a formalised research setting, such as refugees or people with criminal records. Nevertheless, research questions that have more causal objectives might not be possible without some intervention. As such, it may be possible and even preferable to combine both contrived and natural data in a research study, depending on the research question.

Data visibility: Public or private

While it is not the intention of this text to re-enter the continuing contentious debate of what type of digital data may be considered public or private data, it is worth explicating how decisions about this divide may impact digital research. Three areas are considered in relation to the visibility of the data: the implicit or explicit intent of the data originator; the socio-cultural context and norms of the digital community; and the terms and conditions of the digital platform.

A helpful heuristic for researchers, to determine whether the large amount of data that can now be accessed should be accessed, is to consider what the *original intention* might have been for those who originally posted/wrote and/or shared the data, alongside the norms of online behaviour within the communities and groups you may be researching. For example, much data are created to be shared as that increases the influence of the creator, such as videoblogging material. Based on this original intent, an argument can be created and defended that the data are, and have always been, in the public domain, and that the originator always intended the data to be widely disseminated. That is, there was no expectation of privacy when the data were created and posted. In contrast, while an online parenting support group might be public and require no registration or password to access, those posting to the site cannot be assumed to want to actively disseminate their data. They are unlikely to regard sharing their interactions (whether anonymised or not) as desirable. These types of digital data are akin to a private conversation that takes place in a public place – such as a chat between friends while walking in a park – it is possible to overhear what is being said, but those conversing are not actively encouraging others to listen into, or take part in, their conversation.

As 'sharing' has become increasingly common across many, but not all, cultures and generations, the socio-cultural norms and expectations of privacy are changing. Much is made in the UK and European media about generation Z, the generational cohort who were born after 1995 and come after the Millennials, and their supposed lack of concern about privacy. The concept of 'oversharing' and the impact of the disinhibition effect that is present in the digital context have also been studied (Suler, 2016). However, some of this generation have moved away from Facebook, and other popular digital platforms, as they wish to prevent their digital activity from being watched and/or commercialised. For example, some people are turning towards TOR (a free software system that enables total anonymity in searching and communication, via multiple encryption layers), not necessarily for nefarious purposes but merely to avoid being monitored by the platform providers. Thus, while there may well be a disinhibition effect online, assumptions made about generational differences in attitudes towards the sharing of data may not be valid. In a similar vein what is shared across social media differs across cultures, and despite the 'globalisation' of the internet, social media and mobile phone adoption, careful consideration should be given as to cultural nuances and norms of how data are perceived by different cultural groups to avoid alienating potential research participants or creators/sharers of the digital data, or, indeed causing 'harm' to research participants because of violations of offline socio-cultural norms.

Moderators of online forums and communities play an important role as gatekeepers in allowing or blocking access for researchers to their respective communities. While these moderators may be nominated, or even self-nominated, they act as intermediaries for approving or not approving research activity. As members of the online communities they are embedded in the socio-cultural context of that community, and as such, are more sensitive to the level of visibility that is acceptable to their community members. How these moderators view their members' content should be carefully considered by digital researchers who wish to access these groups.

Pursuant to privacy concerns is the need for digital researchers to be mindful of privacy agreements that are often buried within the lengthy terms and conditions of social media platforms and commercial or company owned websites. For example, strictly and legally speaking Facebook owns all Facebook posts, but this source and others continues to be used without disclosure in research at all levels including published articles. TripAdvisor, at the time of writing, also contained a clause within its terms and conditions about not using TripAdvisor data for research purposes. While we, as authors, do not wish to actively encourage any researcher to contravene any legally binding conditions, we do believe that these terms and conditions are highly unrealistic and that, in practice, they are unenforceable. The probable original intent was to avoid the data being used for commercial market research, not individuals' academic research. If in doubt, the terms and conditions can be consulted and advice could be sought, ideally from an experienced digital researcher, before a final decision regarding the suitability of the data is made. An additional precaution may be to anonymise the specific source of the data before writing up the research for publication. Further discussion and guidance on privacy and good research practice can be found in Chapter 7 as well as from recognised bodies, such as the Association of Internet Researchers (AoIR).

Determining the boundary between public and private data can leave researchers, supervisors and some examiners feeling insecure when using informed judgement as suggested in this matter. The emergent types of digital data and the dynamic nature of data in the digital environment requires reflection of the research purpose alongside the data context in order to justify the use of public/private data. The digital domain is a young context for research and, as such, the 'rules' are still being negotiated in the digital context itself, in the academic context and within specific disciplines. Many highly experienced researchers, as well as some institutional ethics bodies, may lack expertise in digital research. Their approach may be framed by a lack of contextual knowledge and in firmly rooted notions of data. This lack of expertise may manifest itself in a defensive or even negative viewpoint. A researcher wishing to pursue digital research may need to provide very detailed explanations over the data choices made in order to reassure and educate institutional colleagues. Citing other published work, even beyond the specific subject area, which has taken similar positions over data choices may help to persuade sceptics.

Characteristics of digital data sets

As well as understanding the dimensions of the desired digital data, it is also useful to consider the way in which the data set is organised.

Big data

Although the term 'big data' originated from computer science to define immensely large data sets with diverse data, which involved complexity in their management and processing, big data has now become a fashionable term to describe any very large amount of data that may come from one or more sources. Big data are complex and very large data sets where identifying correlation rather than causation is the aim. Defining what 'a very large amount' is, however, proving somewhat elusive. The elusiveness is captured in Boyd and Crawford's 2012 definition focusing on the mythology of big data. They define big data as a tripartite phenomenon based on the interaction between technology (digital's data storage and processing capacities), analysis (identifying patterns in data), and mythology (the belief that more data are more truthful, objective and accurate). Despite the difficulties of defining the boundaries of big data, social science researchers do use big data (for examples, see Deardorff, 2016). Researchers using big data might draw data from different raw data sources, so they will need to master the mechanisms for matching cases across databases, and the techniques for cleaning the resulting data set. Big data that are frequently used by social science researchers for digital research are often social media content data, which until fairly recently, has been easy to access. We say 'until fairly recently' because in 2011 Twitter altered its API (Application Programming Interface) structure, which limited the data available, and Facebook also made significant API changes in 2015. The potential commercial value of some social media data, means it is likely that there will be further restrictions on the access to these types of big data.

Given the resources required to access and analyse big data sets, it is difficult for lone researchers to use big data beyond limited social media scraping, and there are now certain institutions specialising in using big data to understand societal topics. These institutions are found throughout the world, and have multiple, ongoing, large scale research projects not only examining the data but also designing new computing code to better mine the data assembled (see, for example, the Oxford Internet Institute in the UK, Monash University's Centre for Data Science in Australia, and Berkeley's Institute for Data Science in the USA).

So what might a big data social science project entail? As an example, business research-ers' have worked on data accessed through relationships formed with companies. These researchers, given access to the huge volumes of company data, sometimes combined with publicly available data, have investigated various business issues, such as the link between data use and performance, and improving airline estimated arrival times (e.g., McAfee and Brynjolfsson, 2012). Overall, big data sources can be distilled into four broad areas (Borgman, 2015), each of which presents different opportunities and challenges. First, there are data collected and stored by commercial firms. These data may have commer-cial value to other organisations (e.g., credit card details and usage patterns, landline and mobile phone call history), or may contain competitively sensitive information. As such, these data can be difficult to access. Second, there are data held by public bodies and government agencies. These might include our education profile, registrations for voting, criminal convictions and public health data. This information may be sensitive to the indi-vidual. Some of these data are searchable online, however, accessing the database holding the raw form of the data would require identifying the data 'owner' and gaining permis-sion for the data's use. Third, there are the data created by digital footprints of individuals. These data are held and sometimes shared by internet providers, such as text message his-tory, geo-location data, web search activity. Fourth, there are user generated data provided by individuals such as uploading of photos to Facebook or Weibo or blog or vlog posting.

Big data can comprise not just of one large data set but of multiple sources of overlaid data and these offer enormous opportunities for digital researchers but there are significant challenges in the integration of the data sets, cleansing the data and repurposing it for purposes other than for which it was originally collected (Borgman, 2015). The completeness and representativeness of big data may be questioned and there are research ethics questions heightened by these types of data. For example, what are the unintended consequences of combining different data sets on the anonymity of the people described? These issues are beyond the scope of this text but as researchers, we should be aware of them (for further information see, for example, Zwitter, 2014).

Open data

Open data have emerged out of a rise in demand for transparency and accountability in many countries including the UK, USA and parts of Africa. As a consequence, it is now possible to access various types of government data (local and national), and data collected as part of government sponsored research projects (e.g., ESRC research projects). In addition to the mutually beneficial data/research arrangements in the commercial environments mentioned in the section above, and open data associated with governments, there are also data philanthropy initiatives that aim to provide data that can lead to social rather than commercial benefit. These enable social science researchers and others to access big data sets, such as the United Nations Global Pulse project, or the UK Data Archive (www.data-archive.ac.uk). While open access data sets provide access to a great deal of information, as digital researchers we need to be alert to the possible boundaries around the open data sets, despite having stated that digital data generally may now be border and boundary-less. These boundaries may be related to the age of the data, changes in data collection procedures, or institutional policies concerning how the privacy of data providers is maintained. Consequently, while there may be open access to a great deal of information, what is provided may be a relatively small proportion of the whole data set. Nevertheless, open access initiatives do promote data as a public good, which should be shared rather than concealed. Open data, even if not central to the research question pursued, may still provide a useful resource whether as a starting point for understanding a digital phenomenon or as a means to confirm other findings.

Information characteristics of digital data

The research implications arising from information characteristics include the form in which the data are recorded or uploaded, the level of aggregation of the data as recorded, and the purpose to which the data are put. Particular information characteristics, while sometimes associated with particular platforms, are not tied to those platforms. So while the platforms for sharing these particular data formats will appear and disappear (for example, WhatsApp may not exist in ten years' time and may be supplanted by another new platform entrant), the sharing of data through increasingly sophisticated digital technology, as well as the variety of content types, is expected to increase.

Encoding format

Each of the information characteristics of digital data places boundaries on the digital data. As digital researchers, we need to consider how the information format of digital data impacts on the collection, collation, integration and analysis of our data. When thinking about the format of digital data there are three areas to consider: (1) whether the data are based on text/numbers, or whether they are based on images (though we acknowledge that some data will have both); (2) whether the data are static, or dynamic; and (3) whether the data are derived from an individual, or considered at the group level. The first two areas for consideration interact, as text/numbers can be static (e.g., reviews) or dynamic (e.g., podcasts), and images can also be still (e.g., photographs) or dynamic (e.g., vlogs). Consequently the following section on text/numbers-based digital data includes both still and static formats, as does the image-based digital data section. While we can attempt to separate digital data by the way they are encoded, it is important to remember that, in the digital context, we often encounter data that transcend boundaries. For instance, text captions might supplement the meaning of visual data on an Instagram post, or the use of emoticons might steer the interpretation of text.

Text and numbers

Social science researchers are used to dealing with text and numbers, though not necessarily at the same time, and the digital environment provides a vast repository for both text-based and numbers-based data. Text might be in different languages, but it is nonetheless the written word, or the spoken word transcribed into the written word. Static digital text can range from posts and comments on social networking sites, through website content and reviews, to personal blogs. There may be text comments underneath YouTube postings that are of interest, consumer generated reviews of products written on company websites, or Facebook interactions between people. Dynamic text can take the form of podcasts and radio transmissions, or be found in a live Twitter feed. The temporal element to text-based data may be minimised via the way the data are prepared for analysis (e.g., transcribing a podcast reduces the transparency of its temporal element as something that was dynamic is now static and 'placed' on a page of text), however, the original format of the digital data remains dynamic. (Chapter 4 discusses the temporality of digital data in more detail, and as such, this aspect of the data format will not be considered further here.) Text-based data, whether digitally static or dynamic, can be diverse in terms of style, tone and quantity. Determining whether comments are ironic, rhetorical or humorous can be challenging, especially with static text-based digital text, and care needs to be taken when using any content analysis software over the nuances of language use. Furthermore, users have adopted emoticons that give 'clues' concerning the tone of written text although these too can have a disingenuous meaning and are often sub-culture specific. Whether emoticons (discussed under image-based data) count as text- or image-based digital data may be debated, with the final decision likely to be closely linked to the research question and its specific context. Some automated methods of extracting text-based data are unable to reliably identify these nuances within text-based digital data. (Chapter 6 considers how automation impacts on research in the digital domain; as such, this aspect of the digital data format is not explored in detail here.) So we, as digital researchers, need to be aware of multiple issues when using text-based digital data.

Numbers are also regularly used by social scientists and can range from economic and behavioural data, to the more error prone measurement of internal characteristics using attitudinal and/or psychometric scales. Static numbers-based digital data can include the output from fitness wearables, bounce rates and other website statistics, as well as the results from online questionnaires collecting data on attitudes and individuals' psychometric attributes. While these numbers may initially appear straightforward, as digital researchers we need to be aware of how the numbers are produced – for instance, being aware that watching a downloaded video does not necessarily count as 'activity' on a website will enable the researcher to better interpret time-out statistics when comparing different webpages. Dynamic numbers-based data can be used in digital research to illustrate change as it occurs, this might, for example, include how social network connections change over the course of an event (e.g., an election campaign) or over different time periods such as music downloads or film streaming by an individual recorded in a single week. Researchers working with both static and dynamic numbers-based digital data need to be fully aware of what the numbers represent to be able to accurately interpret their meaning.

Text- and numbers-based digital data have also given rise to novel social science phenomena. The interactive and connected context of the digital environment, for instance, has led to text-based phenomena such as collaborative authoring (e.g., wikis, open source software). Whether something like a wiki is considered as a static or dynamic example of text-based digital data, however, depends on the research focus. Some numbers-based digital phenomena, like citizen science projects such as the Royal Society for the Protection of Birds' (UK) 'Big Garden Birdwatch' (in which citizens are asked to count and identify the birds that appear in their gardens over a set time period and then upload that information via the internet to input into a national bird count), can also be attributed to the interactive and connective nature of the digital environment.

Images

In line with numbers- and text-based data, we, as social science researchers, have had the ability to use static image-based data, such as photographs, diagrams, storyboards, animations and infographics, for a considerable time. These images can be both non-digital, specifically old photographs produced in the pre-digital era, but increasingly these materials are either converted into digital images or created as a digital image in the first place. These images could be used as prompts to elicit responses from participants, through using techniques such as photo-elicitation, or researchers might themselves have directly interpreted images provided by participants. The digital context has, however, changed how we, as people, use images. Digital devices have reduced the resources we need to produce images – for example, we can now take multiple photographs of the same thing on a smartphone and then instantly evaluate them before deleting those that we do not want. Digital devices such as smartphones also provide us with the data storage capacity to carry around thousands of static and dynamic images in the form of photographs and videos. Digital devices also have the processing capacity to manipulate these images, as well as allowing us to manipulate other data into a different visual format (e.g., infographics, cartoons). Alongside the digital capacity to store and manipulate images, increases in the speed with which data can be transferred make it easier to share the images we produce as well as to consume the images produced by others.

Novel social science phenomena have emerged within the digital context. The ability to create and share static-digital images has produced new ways for people to interact with their environment and others. An example of how meaning is created through user generated static images is food consumption. Digital photographs of food served in restaurants taken on mobile phones are instantaneously uploaded and shared around the world. This has become a social phenomenon to the extent that many restaurants have tried to ban the taking of photographs of plates of food, and 'food envy' has become a much used phrase as a result of the prevalence of sharing food-based images (Kozinets et al., 2016). New phenomena emerging from the digital context are not confined to static image-based data. Digital technologies have reduced the technical knowledge necessary to manipulate dynamic image-based material. This enables us as digital users to, for example, fabricate images. Interesting 'news' videos, such as birds of prey swooping down on small dogs and flying off with them, once broken down into still by still images, reveal that different sources have been spliced together to produce a meaning that is different from that conveyed by either of the original sources. While the fabrication of data was not unknown in the non-digital context, the easy accessibility of digital technologies that allow us all to create professional fabrications is a social phenomenon unique to the digital environment.

The meaning of text-based digital communications can also be modified by image-based data. While understanding the impact of emoticons, smileys and other symbols on meaning within digital text research is still in its infancy, social media and other digital data offer a rich landscape in which to collect this type of informal data. The use of emoticons and other images of this type can be bounded within particular socio-cultural contexts, or self-bound interest groups (e.g., Line in Asia and South America). In places, these types of images can form a complete 'language', entirely replacing text-based communication. Consequently, the understanding of the meaning of these communications can be challenging for digital researchers who sit 'outside' these groups.

While creating meaning through the inclusion of an image, or image manipulation (whether using static or dynamic images), may be a phenomenon worthy of study by social scientists, the ability of users to use images in these ways necessitates that we, as digital researchers, exercise caution when interpreting image-based data. Just as we need to check the veracity of text- and numbers-based data, we also need to ensure that we understand how participants are interpreting image-based data and, as much as possible, that image-based data are genuine. Happily, as well as providing the means to fabricate material, the digital environment also provides many of the resources necessary to check the veracity of our data. For example, First Draft News (https://firstdraftnews.com) is a verification source used by journalists to determine the origin and potential credibility of possible news stories. We as digital researchers need to adopt a critical approach to our data – especially when those data purport to provide evidence of actual, physical events. If we do not scrutinise the sources of our data, we may damage the credibility of our research outputs through the inadvertent use of non-authentic material.

Digital users also express what is important in their everyday lives through image-sharing platforms, and these digital platforms can be used to investigate non-digital phenomena. Instagram and Flickr are popular social media sharing platforms that host predominantly visual content created by the account holders. Pinterest as a visual platform functions differently. In this case, images already available on the internet can be 'pinned' to a board to create a page dedicated to a specific interest, such as weddings or classic cars. These images may be professionally taken, computer generated, or created by an ordinary citizen. YouTube, and non-Western platforms such as Weibo, are increasingly popular as repositories of video data. While much video material is not live streamed, platforms such as Periscope offer the opportunity to live stream video material of current events such as festivals. Live streamed video data are also used to overcome geographic boundaries. In medical teaching and research, for instance, open-heart surgery has been live streamed (with the consent of the patient) from Texas, USA to surgical teams around the world as a way of disseminating medical knowledge.

The immediacy, visual content of the data and ease of use are the predominant influencers in the use of image sharing (Van Dijck, 2013). Images can be powerful and the ability to convey a meaning or an event without typing text into a message screen has facilitated the number of images shared. There is some evidence to suggest that image-based data may surpass text-based data in the near future, as the number of images posted, video streaming and infographic sharing continues to rise dramatically, it may make up 74% of internet activity by the end of 2017 (Meeker, 2017). For researchers the broad array of images, from pets to mountains, now available for research purposes creates opportunity but also challenges. As most of us live within text-bound cultures, analysis of images can be more alien than the analysis of words and text. Analysis of images involves interpretation; it is worth remembering that defending how we have interpreted images and gained meaning from visual data is not straightforward. Helpful insight into visual analysis is provided by both Rose's (2013) and Spencer's (2011) seminal works on visual methodologies, much of which is transferable across to the digital context.

Individual, group or organisational data

Considering who provides the data is worthy of reflection as this provides clues concerning how the data are likely to be organised, and who the information should be attributed to. Individual digital data can take the form of one person's comments or perceptions, or expressed attitudes towards an event. In marketing and business research this might be viewed as consumer generated content, more generally it is termed user generated content. These types of data are perceived to be of value as it generally comes directly from individuals' experience of their life as lived. Social science researchers might be interested in these types of data as comparator data, for instance comparing different experiences of education, or local government services. Data can also be generated by groups, such as shared interest groups, and capture the overall experience of those communities. Homophilic groups are common across social media and digital online communities. These groups may share a common characteristic (e.g., a medical condition, children at the same school) and/or purpose (e.g., the 'Black lives matter' movement, or the recent Nepal earthquake disaster relief), so can provide insights into behaviours that may be of interest to a range of social scientists.

Having identified the shared interest or purpose that is the focus of the research, the locating of these groups can be completed via search engine searches. Localised groups such as choirs, or patient and carer groups, can be found via these searches while more dispersed professional body groups such as chartered engineers can be found as LinkedIn groups. Highly focused data relevant to specific research projects can be collected from or through these groups. Data might also be formatted at an organisational or business level. Organisational and/or business generated digital data can be of interest to those investigating a specific industry, for example, website data concerning human resource training resources within the school teaching sector or hotel responses to poor online reviews. For example, video data may be generated by organisations for official purposes, such as product demonstrations, or by individual citizens who wish to film friends and family activities, or vloggers who use video as a main source of communication and interaction for a community of interest, such as beauty and lifestyle.

Separating data into singular or collective categories in the digital environment may create a false distinction. Digital data are complex and it may be that we need to consider how data are both singular and collective, rather than whether they are one or the other. Digital data are often interactional in nature, owing in part to the nature of the digital exchange mechanisms. Thus limiting analysis to the group level may result in important insights at the individual level being missed, and limiting data collected to, for instance, an individual's contribution may limit the ability to produce a holistic view by only utilising one side of an interaction. An individual's view or perceptions may also not be representative of the sample you are interested in. Pursuant to this is the criticism afforded to social media, and online communities in particular, that these groups are narrowly constituted and reflect only the more vocal members of the shared interest community. That is, those who have access to, and expertise in, communicating via digital technologies. As a counter to such criticism some social science researchers such as Simões and Campos (2017) have identified that 'peripheral' groups have been given a voice through social media and online communities. In Simões and Campos' paper, subculture groups of protest rappers and graffiti artists in Portugal found digital media to be a facilitating voice. Further examples of groups important to researchers yet on the fringes of society, including survivors of domestic abuse, refugee seekers and those involved in the sex industry, have all had their voices heard through research projects where anonymised sharing of experiences as data has proved valuable to all involved.

USE OF INFORMATION

Digital data can be used to disseminate information for or about a variety of purposes. The main purposes to which digital information can be put are discussed below.

Review-based data

Review-based data have the primary function of sharing actual experiences and information regarding an undertaken activity. For example, the experience of having stayed in a particular hotel, bought a specific TV, visited a doctor's surgery, or attended a named university may be reviewed and shared digitally. These reviews frequently have a ratings system of stars or points. They may be held under an aggregator of reviews such as TripAdvisor, or by a specific retailer or service provider. Review-based data may comprise stars, a mark system, images of the product or service, or service environment, as well as written comments concerning the activity undertaken or product purchased. Review-based data posted on digital platforms, or passed on through other forms of sharing such as emails, may be of interest to social science researchers interested in, for instance, key influencing factors for consumers, how individuals understand particular experiences, and/or how people's communication styles differ across contexts. However, researchers should be aware of the potential for spurious reviews and paid-for reviews, which might impact on their research findings. An interesting article by Chen (2017) on the website www.digiday.com explains how Amazon reviewing works and the challenges faced by incentivised reviewers.

Commercial interaction data

Commercial interaction data can include online purchase related data. This is likely to be of interest to business and management, or psychology researchers, as well as computing software researchers. Data that could be collected might include observational data of how customers navigate e-commerce sites, analytics data concerning page dwell time, interactions with customer help functions such as live chat, as well as data capture surrounding the purchase/payment. A challenge faced by researchers wishing to understand, or make connections between aspects of, e-commerce is the access to the data compiled on commercially owned websites through analytical tools such as Google analytics. In order to collect aspects of commercial data, access has to be permitted by the e-commerce organisation and/or its partners. Consequently, an inability to access these types of data will impact on the researcher's ability to study commercial interaction data. Postgraduate students are often disappointed to find that commercial interaction data will not be shared by consumer brands and marketing firms or that certain firms have contractual relationships to only share their data with core business partners. They perceive that the commercial value of the data outweighs the potential value of any results derived from sharing that data with academics, or feel that sharing their data may expose them competitively.

Lifestyle data

The ability of digital technologies to facilitate the sharing of different facets of people's lives, in both public and private settings, could be considered a source of useful data for certain research topics. Blogs of people's interests can highlight trending topics and brands. The focus of the information may move from niche to mainstream as the blogs gain followers, interactions and shares. Blogs and micro-blogs such as Twitter, as well as WhatsApp, can illustrate a variety of interactions across different groups. The content of, and interactions associated with, these platforms can act as mirrors reflecting contemporary life as lived by specific groups. For example the use of Skype, enabled through iPads, by elderly people to contact and stay in touch with family in other countries can provide an insight into how families are now communicating as well as how technology can enable socialisation for potentially isolated older people.

Gaming data

Digital data concerned with gaming include scores, interactions between gamers, in-game micro-payment for advantageous tools, as well as data focusing on the subcultures involved in gaming. These data might prove useful for anthropologists and other social scientists that benefit from studying defined groups, as well as providing more practical insights for game developers and designers. The instantaneous and dynamic nature of gaming interactions can contribute a rich stream of data for a wide range of research projects. Commercial organisations are employing gamification within some of their engagement and promotional activities in order to grab consumers' attention, for example, financial services providers in the UK as well as energy providers in the United States (Palmer et al., 2012).

Virtual world data

Virtual world immersion environments, such as the immensely popular Second Life virtual world, have and continue to be used as a source of data by commercial firms as well as individual researchers. People take on characters and avatars in these 'virtual' landscapes and while not a game as such the escapism offered by virtual world environments is of interest to a wide variety of social science researchers. Although the manufactured characters are unlikely to reflect their real world creators' actual real world habits, researchers still find valuable data in areas such as the speed of learning to operate in technology bound imaginations, the role of escapism in stress management, perceptions of self-identity and technology enabled relationship formation, as well as the level of engagement with brands embedded within a virtual world environment.

Virtual reality data

The advent of further digital technology advances has enabled immersive virtual reality environments. These environments use headsets to create a three-dimensional environment within which the participant can engage. Companies such as Occulus Rift have been swift to enter the marketplace and while accessing headset data is likely to be beyond the bounds of most researchers, interesting research questions and data could be obtained from those who have participated in virtual reality. Simple virtual reality headsets are being developed by Google for school use to enable, for example, geography field trips to take place while pupils remain inside the classroom. Data of value to researchers might include; pre- and post-experience data, headset suitability data, physiological data readings, and educational outcomes. Thus, virtual reality environments present rich possibilities for social science researchers.

Self-reported data

Digital data also include data reported by individuals who choose to upload, comment or share data about themselves. This is sometimes called self-reported data. In the pre-digital age, self-reported data were criticised for being inaccurate as individuals over or under assessed their own activity. However, with the adoption of digital technologies by people, data can now be far more accurately recorded and uploaded in real or near real time for analysis. For example, full body photographs of before, during and after exercise and diet regimes are now commonly posted to lifestyle Instagram accounts as documentary evidence of an individual's changing body shape. These self-reported data are often met with supportive and encouraging commentary by the followers of those accounts.

A fascinating area of self-reported data is the popularity of quantifying one's physical activities and sharing these digitally. For example, fitness wearables, containing the ability to record and transmit personal physical activity data, will tell us how many flights of stairs we have climbed and enable us to share these data with others. Likewise, websites and online communities such as Strava provide routes and times for runners and cyclists based on self-reported data, and early stage research has indicated that chronic conditions such as diabetes may be better managed through the use of self-reported digital data (Comstock, 2015). Self-monitoring of sleep patterns, heart and/or breathing rate, as well as calorie consumption, are among the personal data that can be tracked. This tracking is often done with an aim to increase the individual's wellbeing through helping them take control of their own actions. Further insight into the quantified self through digital tools can be found in the work of sociologists such as Deborah Lupton (2016).

The ability to digitally record and share one's self image and to make public chosen expressions of ourselves is a consequence of having the digital technology that facilitates such behaviour. For researchers these types of data have created a treasure trove of digital data to examine, if they can access the data. The global social phenomenon of 'selfies', for example, is one form of such self-monitoring behaviour. If a researcher is interested in concepts around self-branding, or even narcissism, then these data images may provide a naturally occurring type of data to investigate.

ETHICS CHALLENGES

The existing ethics questions asked of and by researchers and the institutions in which we work and study become increasingly complex when we enter the domain of undertaking digital research. In fact, not only do the established ethical questions get more complicated but the advent and adoption of new data formats also raises new ethics questions altogether. The new types of data that are now easily collected, such as video material downloading or covert scrapping of social media data, have created new and different ethics questions that require more explicitly contextual justifications than were previously required. Maintaining the 'do no harm' principle of research ethics requires careful appraisal in relation to the collection and use of digital data. New data types will continue to emerge as digital technologies and platforms morph and advance. So, there are understandable difficulties in trying to 'fix' a set of ethics codes and 'rules'. Rather, there is a need to recognise the necessity for a contextually based, flexible approach to ethics decisions for digital researchers. This is not to suggest that anything should be acceptable, but rather that acknowledging how the changes in the socio-technological context impact not only on the conceptualisation of harm, but also on the possibility of doing harm. Helpful general insight has been provided in Chapter 7, which references recognised external sources of research ethics guidance relevant to social scientists. In addition, the research ethics officer within your own university or institution should be able to articulate institutional good practice advice, although in the nascent area of digital research it is often more helpful in the first instance to speak to someone who has or is researching digital phenomena and/or is using digital data in their own work. At the time of writing this text there is a dearth of expertise in how to approach the more complex ethics questions raised by the new data formats. The suggestion that the questions remain the same as with non-digital data is necessarily naïve but the suggestion fails to acknowledge the complexity and specifics of the digital environment.

Based on our own experience of undertaking research and supervising those who research using digital methods, and those who undertake research looking at digital phenomena, we suggest asking yourself the key questions below to help you unpick some of the tricky ethics dilemmas over the use of the new types of data formats available digitally. While these questions are presented here, some refer to other chapters in this section, and we have indicated this at the end of the questions.

How vulnerable are my chosen participants?

The level of participant vulnerability, while strictly not related to digital data *per se*, is one of the areas digital researchers need to consider when unpicking the ethical challenges related to the digital data they wish to collect. Vulnerability also relates to the sensitivity of the research topic and aspects of participant vulnerability are discussed in Chapter 5. For example, online transgender communities would be considered as a potentially more vulnerable group than a LinkedIn group of wine industry professionals. Vulnerability may also be fluid in terms of the people within that group at the time of research but who may not remain within that group, for example, Fergie, Hunt and Hilton's 2016 research on young adults' production and consumption of social media in relation to mental health (Fergie et al., 2016). Vulnerability, and the potential to cause harm, may be related to the type of data that are being collected. For example, if 'big data' are being explored where multiple data sets are combined, individuals across those data sets might be exposed (de Zúñiga and Diehl, 2017) because of the composite of information compiled from different sources (see discussion in Chapter 6). In contrast, if the data collected consisted of analysing digital interactions on a discussion board where participants' retained their anonymity, then, as researchers, we could be more confident of not exposing potentially vulnerable participants to harm.

How sensitive is my research?

Some social science researchers will be involved in social research that is easily identified as sensitive – for example, the use of legal highs by adults in the UK, or subjects such as identity conflict in transgender communities. Alternatively, research may focus on understanding activism within extreme political parties in Greece, or research that requires data about illegal activity, such as communication patterns and content between organised gang members. Other topics may only be sensitive in particular individual or cultural contexts. In all cases, we need to consider both who and where a topic might be sensitive, and how likely our data are to intersect with individuals or societies where sensitivity levels may result in the data collected 'doing harm'. For example, research into how people connect with 'romantic' partners digitally may not be sensitive to single urbanites in Western cultures; it may be highly sensitive if the research participants are married, from small communities or from socio-cultural backgrounds with more traditional views on romantic relationships. Chapter 5 also discusses issues related to the focus of the research, which may help unpick issues related to the sensitivity of the research.

To what extent is the use of digital data in my research critical?

Although apparently counterintuitive to the premise of this book, we suggest you ask yourself if it would be appropriate and possible to use non-digital data sources to answer your research question. This allows you to consider the relationship between your research problem and the data you intend to collect, as well as providing you with a justification for the necessity of digital data (if non-digital sources are not feasible). Can non-digital material be collected and if so how? Indeed, it may be desirable to collect both digital and non-digital data, especially if your research questions are linked to knowledge bases that have developed outside the digital context. It is likely, however, that if your research concerns a digital phenomenon, for example, analysing a social media network's influence in the take up of alternative treatments by cancer sufferers, then it is probably desirable to access digital data in order to fully answer your research question.

How can I manage third party data capture?

As digital researchers, we are much more likely to involve, and either deliberately or randomly collect, third party data. By third party data, we mean participants who might join in an online community conversation without being aware that the data are being collected, or individuals who share information with contacts without knowing that their contact is participating in research. Third party data do not arise with more established research techniques, such as interviews or focus groups, where the number of participants is finite, pre-determined and screened, and the data collection takes place in a secure environment. However, the interactive and connected nature of the digital context, where sharing of material is common, exposes a multitude of third party data to the researcher. For example, a Facebook feed will contain images uploaded by individuals other than your participants; it is common to forward emails to others interested in a particular issue; and reposting tweets is a positive action (though not necessarily an endorsement) in relation to that microblog. All of these common digital behaviours expose the researcher to third party data. In some cases, these third party data might be important for your research. For example, if you are a researcher investigating the use of images to denote self-identity or consumption practices then you might wish to include such third party data. Consequently, as digital researchers, we need to explicitly consider the ethical implications of using third party data, even though it is unrealistic to suggest, and would probably be dismissed as unnecessary by the originators, that we attempt to contact the third party data providers even if we had their contact details. This might include us considering how 'public' the third party data were intended to be, looking at the issues concerning who 'owns' the third party data (Chapter 5), or the means by which the third party data were captured (Chapter 6). Overall, our aim is to unpack the issues surrounding third party data, bearing in mind the underlying principle of doing no harm to known (or, indeed, unidentified) research participants.

Data formats and active management of anonymity

While the ubiquity and versatility of digital data present great opportunities for social science researchers, they also present complexities in the levels of anonymity required. Two aspects of anonymity need to be considered: (1) protecting participants' non-digital identities, and (2) protecting participants' digital identities. While the characteristics of the digital environment mean there is not necessarily a correspondence between the digital and the physical identity, combining different digital data sources or using digital data located in physical things may allow a connection between physical and digital identities to occur. For example, the use of geo-location data, with the identification of precise streets or exact neighbourhoods, may cause issues for those inhabitants. Studies such as those looking at crime or school performance need to carefully consider how accurately they may wish to 'pinpoint' the location of particular findings, particularly when presenting results using visualisation tools and maps. Neuhaus and Webmoor (2012) have an interesting early paper on this matter while more recent commercial realisation and developments can be read in Cui (2017). Some published research (e.g., Kemshall and Maguire, 2011; Li and Goodchild, 2013) suggests broadening the location so that specific locations cannot be identified, thus preserving the anonymity of those residents and communities.

Protecting participants' digital identities is made more difficult by us all being able to search digital platforms, either through the functionality of the platform itself, or via the use of internet search engines. For example, it is not sufficient to remove a Twitter handle and the unique referencing number of the Twitter interface API from a tweet to protect the Twitter user's digital identity. This would not prevent someone from searching for the original tweet via its contents being put into a search engine and consequently being able to uncover the digital identity of the source. This creates a potential issue for the researcher. A question to ask yourself here is how important is it to report or quote verbatim your digital source material? If content analysis is not your aim, and thus exact content is not the core focus of your data, then the substitution of words without changing the central meaning will significantly improve the anonymity of the data. For example, certain published sociology work takes this approach (Sugiura et al., 2016).

BIG PICTURE DIGITAL DATA ISSUES

This chapter has so far focused on digital data characteristics. However, we must recognise that as social scientists we are not interested in digital data *per se*, we are interested in what digital data reveal to us about lives as lived. This section considers broader issues we need to be aware of when attempting to understand how we might use digital data. Three issues are considered:

1. non-human generation of digital data
2. implications of digital data on research design
3. how we analyse digital data.

An assumption that has been implicit throughout this chapter, and in later chapters, is that the digital data we are concerned with are created by humans. However, this does not necessarily hold in the digital environment. Intelligent 'Bots' are now able to write product reviews, respond to questions in online communities, pose questions as 'interviewers' and even provide branded content messages in non-commercial digital spaces. As researchers, we should be aware of the increasing volume of non-human digital data generation, and consider whether we wish to (attempt to) exclude this type of data from our research. Non-human data may be useful for our research, for example, an interesting study could be made comparing 'Bot' and human responses to Q and A on citizens' advice websites. Chapter 6 considers the impact of automation on digital research in further detail.

Data format challenges

The problems we investigate as social scientists are not tied to particular data formats, rather we select one or more data format that we believe will help us to gain insight into the research problem we are concerned with. However, digital data are rarely isolated to just text, numbers or images, for instance, text can contain emoticons and images as well as captions. This leads to two main challenges: (1) how do we develop the skills to appropriately evaluate the potential of different data formats? And (2) how do we integrate our findings across data formats? The former challenge requires us to be open-minded to different research traditions, and consider how guidelines and frameworks across the social sciences (and possibly beyond) can be applied within our particular discipline(s). While there is no one solution to this problem, a common approach is likely to include working in cross-disciplinary teams who consider a particular research phenomenon from different perspectives. Integrating findings from different data formats, the latter challenge, may also be problematic. We might want to start by considering whether the insights we have gained are complementary, can co-exist, or appear to contradict each other. Another approach might be to look towards the mixed methods literature (see for examples the *Journal of Mixed Methods Research*) to see how this challenge has been addressed.

While integrating findings from different types of digital data is one challenge, actually analysing digital data can also present challenges. There are multiple ways of categorising and coding digital data formats. This creates opportunities for reflection on how we might approach the analysis of such data and whether existing data analysis tools remain relevant.

Analytical software such as NVivo may be used to assist researchers in managing and making sense of large quantities of digital text- and image-based digital data. The ability to categorise and sort digital data such as social media dialogue, images or video using these tools can help the researcher to identify patterns, commonalities and key findings. However, the existence of set parameters designed by the software developers may, to some extent, place restrictions on how the data are coded with the knock-on effect of limiting what is seen by the researcher in terms of the emerging patterns. Pre-determined codes and the subsequent grouping into categories have their limitations: if images comprise both people and landscape, can they be categorised as both? If video material consists of music, commentary on the music, and is in a different language, how should it be coded? The analysis of numbers-based data faces similar issues. Much early analysis of digital data and social media content focused around frequency, or crudely put, the 'counting of stuff'. More recently, mapping and visualisations have become popular as analytical tools become available that portray overall patterns. However, these tools rely on frequency of occurrence to draw the density of influencers with social media groups via software such as NodeXL, assuming that frequency equates to influence. The sheer quantity of digital data now available for research projects necessitates, to some extent, a movement away from manual analysis of the data and towards the use of either open or closed source software tools to help unlock the data. However, we need to understand the impact of using such tools on what we can find, and it is our responsibility to remember that how data are analysed shapes the type of insights we are able to produce (Belk et al., 2013).

SUMMARY

In Chapter 1, we proposed that the digital environment requires a more reflexive approach to research. There we acknowledged a need to be iterative when considering how to address our research problems, moving between our research questions, the digital data that might help us understand those questions, and the internal and external constraints placed on us as researchers. In reality, even this iterative approach to digital research may appear rather simplistic, as one of the barriers to undertaking digital research is the 'unknown unknowns' that this novel environment contains. Ultimately, as researchers working in the digital domain, we have to be pragmatic. Having an interesting research question about which you cannot gather sufficient data will not be productive. Neither, however, will researching social media owing to its availability and volume necessarily lead to interesting and valuable insights. In relation to digital data, it is important to acknowledge that different types of digital data will result in different types of information being gathered, and the type of information we have will shape our insights. For example, the insights gained from Facebook data will be different from those gathered from online community data, which in turn will differ from Flickr generated insights. Pragmatically, we may need to be open to the complementary possibilities of using non-digital data sources to understand digitally derived insights, for example, online community interactions combined with face-to-face interviews of citizens' experiences of local government service provision may better address a research question than the digital data alone.

The 3Es

Detailed discussion has been provided in this chapter on important ethical considerations in relation to data and the authors will not repeat themselves here. However, it is worthwhile recognising that data sources require careful reflection in relation to the ethics issues surrounding the access of digital data, the ownership of the digital data collected and used in research and also the blurred boundaries of the perceptions of whether data might be public or private. Expectations of the researcher should be considered in terms of what the data can actually provide rather than what the researcher would like the data to provide. Further to this, there are often unrealistic expectations over the available access to digital data sets and the completeness of that data. The expectations of the participant and/or the provider of the data should also be contemplated to avoid ethical blundering in the use of the data and also to uphold the rights of the participant above the needs of the researcher. Expertise or lack of expertise by the researcher in accessing, managing and making sense of both big data and open data should be identified prior to the commencement of the research project. Honesty in the ability of the researcher to assess the quality of any pre-created data sets of whatever volume is important too as this will impact the credibility of the research project.

Questions

1. To what extent have you evaluated the level of vulnerability of any of your proposed sample/participants?
2. What will be the source or sources for your data? Will you include both digitally sourced and non-digitally sourced data, and if so how will you access these?
3. Are there aspects of your data that can be co-produced, and if so how might you approach this?

FURTHER READING

Cresswell, J.W. and Plano-Clark, V.L. (2011). *Designing and Conducting Mixed Methods Research*. London: Sage.

Rose, G. (2013). *Visual Methodologies*. London: Sage.

Spencer, S. (2011). *Visual Research Methods in the Social Sciences*. London: Routledge.

REFERENCES

Belk, R., Fischer, E. and Kozinets, R. (2013). *Qualitative Consumer and Marketing Research*. London: Sage.

Borgman, C.L. (2015). *Big Data, Little Data, No Data: Scholarship in the Networked World*. Cambridge, MA: MIT Press.

boyd, D. and Crawford, K. (2012). Critical questions for big data: Provocations for a cultural, technological, and scholarly phenomenon. *Information, Communication & Society*, *15* (5), 662–679.

Chen, Y. (2017). Confessions of a paid Amazon review writer. Digiday UK, 20 March. Available from: https://digiday.com/marketing/vendors-ask-go-around-policy-confessions-top-ranked-amazon-review-writer/ (accessed 15 September 2017).

Comstock, J. (2015). Survey: Diabetes patients who use digital tools self-report better health. Available from: http://mobihealthnews.com/40600/survey-diabetes-patients-who-use-digital-tools-self-report-better-health (accessed 27 June 2016).

Cui, W. (2017). Project PrivTree: Blurring your 'where' for location privacy. Available from Microsoft Research blog: www.microsoft.com/en-us/research/blog/project-privtree-blurring-location-privacy/ (accessed 15 September 2017).

Deardorff, J. (2016). Big data to transform social science research. Northwestern University, News, 23 May 2016. www.northwestern.edu/newscenter/archives/special/data-science/day-3.html (accessed 14 January 2017). See also Northwestern's take on big data/data science: www.northwestern.edu/newscenter/archives/special/data-science/index.html (accessed 15 September 2017).

de Zúñiga, H.G. and Diehl, T. (2017). Citizenship, social media, and big data: Current and future research in the social sciences. *Social Science Computer Review*, *35* (1), 3.

Fergie, G., Hunt, K. and Hilton, S. (2016). Social media as a space for support: Young adults' perspectives on producing and consuming user-generated content about diabetes and mental health. *Social Science & Medicine*, *170*, 46.

Fishbein, M. and Ajzen, I. (1975). *Belief, Attitude, Intention, and Behaviour: An Introduction to Theory and Research*. Reading, MA: Addison-Wesley.

Frederiks, E.R., Stenner, K. and Hobman, E.V. (2015). Household energy use: Applying behavioural economics to understand consumer decision-making and behaviour. *Renewable and Sustainable Energy Reviews*, *41*, 1385–1394.

Juvan, E. and Dolnicar, S. (2014). The attitude–behaviour gap in sustainable tourism. *Annals of Tourism Research*, *48*, 76–95.

Kemshall, H. and Maguire, M. (2011). Sex offenders, risk penality and the problem of disclosure to the community. In Matravers, A. (eds), *Sex Offenders in the Community: Managing and Reducing the Risks*. Abingdon: Routledge, pp. 102–124.

Kozinets, R., Patterson, A. and Ashman, R. (2016). Networks of desire: How technology increases our passion to consume. *Journal of Consumer Research*, *43* (5), 659–682.

Li, L. and Goodchild, M.F. (2013). Is privacy still an issue in the era of big data? Location disclosure in spatial footprints. In *Geoinformatics, 2013: 21st International Conference on Geoinformatics*. IEEE, pp. 281–284.

Lupton, D. (2016). *The Quantified Self*. Cambridge: Polity Press.

McAfee, A. and Brynjolfsson, E. (2012). Big data: The management revolution, *Harvard Business Review*, October, 60–68.

Meeker, M. (2017). *Internet Trends 2017 – Code Conference*. Available from: www.kpcb.com/internet-trends (accessed 15 September 2017).

Meyer, E.T. and Schroeder, R. (2015). *Knowledge Machines: Digital Transformations of the Sciences and Humanities*. Cambridge, MA: MIT Press.

Neuhaus, F. and Webmoor, T. (2012). Agile ethics for massified research and visualization. *Information, Communication & Society*, *15* (1), 43–65.

Palmer, D., Luceford, S. and Patton, A.J. (2012). The engagement economy: How gamification is reshaping business. Deloitte University Press. Available from: https://dupress.deloitte.com/dup-us-en/deloitte-review/issue-11/the-engagement-economy-how-gamification-is-reshaping-businesses.html (accessed 15 September 2017).

Rogers, R. (2013). *Digital Methods*. Cambridge, MA: MIT Press.

Rose, G. (2013). *Visual Methodologies*. London: Sage.

Salmons, J. (2016). *Doing Qualitative Research Online*. Thousand Oaks, CA: Sage.

Simões, J.A. and Campos, R. (2017). Digital media, subcultural activity and youth participation: The cases of protest rap and graffiti in Portugal. *Journal of Youth Studies*, *20* (1), 16–31.

Spencer, S. (2011). *Visual Research Methods in the Social Sciences*. London: Routledge.

Sugiura, L., Wiles, R. and Pope, C. (2016). Ethical challenges in online research: Public/private perceptions. *Research Ethics*. DOI: 10.1177/1747016116650720

Suler, J.R. (2016). *Psychology of the Digital Age: Human Become Electric*. New York: Cambridge University Press.

Van Dijck, J. (2013). *The Culture of Connectivity: A Critical History of Social Media*. Oxford: Oxford University Press.

Zwitter, A. (2014). Big data ethics. *Big Data & Society*, July–Dec, 1–6. DOI: 10.1177/2053951714559253

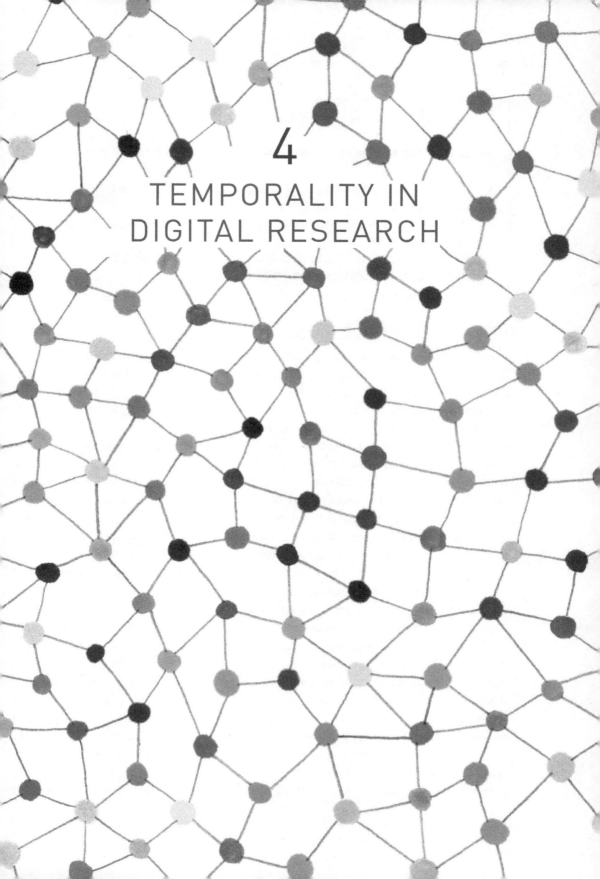

4

TEMPORALITY IN
DIGITAL RESEARCH

In this chapter we will:

- outline the nature of temporality and its implications for digital researchers
- propose the dynamic nature of digital research and its new opportunities for researchers
- discuss the dynamic nature of digital research and its challenges for researchers
- offer suggestions to optimise the dynamism and mitigate the challenges through the design of research projects.

INTRODUCTION

The digitalised environment has led to us, as researchers, needing to rethink our conceptualisation of time and temporality. In the context of our digitally enabled lives, we hear and use terms such as 'always on', '24/7', and 'real-time' as well as experiencing a 'culture of immediacy' where even a second feels too long to wait for a website to download. As digital researchers, we need to reflect on how this change in time/temporality impacts on the digital phenomena themselves, as well as consider how time and temporality affect the use of digital methods as our instrument of research. The consideration of the temporal aspects of the digital context includes exploring how established norms based on temporal assumptions might change lived experiences (e.g., comments on live performances are now shared before performances are completed; this could change both how the performance is experienced and the nature of how the creator designs the performance to unfold; for examples see Blast Theory's artistic work (www.blasttheory.co.uk/)).

In addition, consideration might expose temporal assumptions underlying established theories/concepts (e.g., temporal restraints to product comparisons have been removed in many product categories by comparison websites; this potentially affects how the concept of product involvement impacts on search behaviours). Furthermore, temporality could add complexity to social phenomena and to digital as an instrument of research (e.g., the impact of 'immediacy' on when digital data collection occurs and on how long the research findings remain 'current'). How we define time, as in past, present and future, objectively and/or subjectively, and what this means in terms of the phenomenon we investigate, data collection, data reporting, the interpretation of research currency and the value of digital research as a result, is a main theme of this chapter. The technology-driven, interactive, connected environment creates dynamic activity, which is reflected in digital research data. Not only do the dynamic nature of data, their availability, and in some cases their chameleon-like qualities, have implications for research, but research in the social sciences is now able to utilise and benefit from accessing new types of data (as described in Chapter 3) from which to develop knowledge and scholarship. This dynamism creates both opportunities and challenges for researchers.

Understanding the impact of temporality on digital research benefits from a quick review of how established research designs implicitly accounted for time. Established research designs have generally taken data from a particular point in time or from multiple points in time. Established research taking data from a particular point in time often implicitly made the assumption that points in time were equivalent; only when the research was related to a temporal event (e.g., an individual's transitional event such as a marriage, or external environmental events such as a terrorist attack) would explicit acknowledgement of the temporal element be made (generally in relation to the event concerned). This approach to gathering research data gave the researcher a snapshot of the citizen or consumer (i.e., cross-sectional research) and included methods such as surveys and focus groups. Research across multiple points in time (i.e., longitudinal research) acknowledged temporality as an important factor when addressing the research problem.

The addition of a time-based element to the research design makes the collection of data more complex as data might be required from multiple time periods and other research design elements, such as whether the same research participants were needed over time and how earlier participation might influence responses in later time periods, need to be considered explicitly. One of the decisions that all longitudinal researchers needed to make was when each time-bound set of data should be collected. In shorter studies, such as pre- and post-test experimental designs, time might be needed to allow either the influence of the pre-test questions to dissipate prior to an intervention, or for the intervention to 'take hold' before post-test measurement occurred.

In longer studies (e.g., understanding childhood development), decisions concerned with when each 'snapshot' was taken would need to be examined. For instance, an *event-based* study on child development might collect data related to particular milestones (e.g., first birthday, pre-school, primary education, secondary education, puberty) or might collect data according to a *fixed-time interval* (e.g., every three years until adulthood). These longitudinal studies (of both short and long duration) resulted in a series of static pictures that appeared to show movement (similar to that of a cartoon flick book); so, for example, changes in voting intentions in successive national elections would be apparent through a comparison of the results from one time period with an earlier time period, and trends over time might be shown using graphs.

With the acceptance and adoption of digital technologies, a more dynamic view of the citizen, consumer or patient can emerge. In the digital context, we can use technology to access continuous data as they are recorded. Once accessible, these real-time data can be viewed at any point in time. For example, real-time data streamed from health apps and fitness wearables could be used to show how research participants were behaving at any particular point in time. This could allow health researchers to examine natural variations in health/fitness activity, look at the impact of external events on behaviour (e.g., how is exercise impacted by adverse weather conditions), or, as part of an intervention study, looking at who responds 'best' to different interventions over time. When taken along-side the data storage characteristic of the digital environment that allows huge volumes of continuous data to be stored, access to 'real-time' data can be retained after they have been produced. This combination of data storage and continuous data allows researchers to make research design decisions after the real-time data are collected. For example, one of the author's colleagues was pondering the research questions that could be investi-gated with a complete continuous data set consisting of more than 10 million geo-located tweets (from a defined geographic area) collected (using an algorithm) over a two-year time frame. Their eventual research design choices might be based on looking at patterns in the data set found through data mining, or they may examine external events (e.g., elections, natural disasters) relevant to the geographic location and examine how those are reflected in the data set, or they may start from a theoretical perspective (e.g., theories of information dissemination) in order to guide their research design choices. Their access to this time (and geographically) bound, but completed, set of continuous data allows them to take an emergent approach to research design that would not have been possible in a non-digital research environment.

The accessibility of continuously available data to us as digital researchers is an example of where digital as a research instrument needs to be examined as a digital phenomenon in its own right. Looking at the dynamic nature of digital data as a phenomenon can lead us to consider parallels in financial market research where stock market data can be 'diced and sliced' into different time frames (e.g., considering share price movements ranging from seconds to years). Financial researchers have considered how these different time frames influence the patterns found in the data, and the subsequent impact this has on the theories considered (e.g., market volatility). They have devised ways of deciding rel-evant time frames in terms of identifying appropriate fixed time intervals for particular research questions, and have developed techniques to understand event-based influences on the market. Digital researchers may need to consider how the tools and techniques that have been developed in some areas of social science like finance might be applied to other social science problems where the temporality of the digital domain changes the nature of the data that researchers can access. Understanding the impact of temporality on digital research methods will help us justify our research design choices and unpick how the data we collect represent the phenomenon (whether digital or not) that we are investigating.

The digital environment also facilitates the analysis of data in real-time. Algorithms, which are discussed in more detail in Chapter 6, are, for example, used on commercial websites to automatically analyse search terms and display relevant advertising, as well as offering consumers aid when navigation behaviours indicate they are not progressing with a purchasing decision. While technology also allows researchers to analyse data sets whenever new data are added, this facility does not necessarily 'fit' the way in which academic work is reported and used. However, the real-time analysis of data could provide insights related to research methods phenomena, such as whether early and late responders differ in their responses (e.g., with survey responses), or how temporal factors impact on data quality (e.g., is there any evidence that time of day/day of week impacts on consistency of responses). This 'live-streaming' of data creates both opportunities and challenges for the researcher.

This chapter begins by discussing temporality and how time can be thought about in relation to digital research. Different aspects of temporality are then considered including the nature of longevity in the digital context; how spaces/places such as work and leisure are blurred as temporal boundaries between them are eroded; how temporal factors impact on communication; and the temporality of digital data. Next, some of the opportunities presented by, then the challenges of, digital temporality are discussed, before the chapter concludes by briefly considering how temporality impacts on the 3Es – ethics, expectations and expertise.

WHAT IS TEMPORALITY?

Temporality has been stated as being foundational in social science research and is important in understanding casual relationships, as relationships develop over a period of time (Maggetti et al., 2013). Temporality denotes that a relationship or entity exists within a time frame, whether the time frame considered is objective and able to be measured by external means (e.g., a stopwatch), or subjective and related to how we perceive time passing (e.g., a child's perception of the length of a school day). This is an important distinction in the digital context. Objectively, the digital environment reduces the time it takes to undertake some activities, for instance, communication between distant individuals is much faster now than it was previously, both qualitative and quantitative data analysis can be undertaken faster than in the pre-digital era, and finding the answers to many questions can now be achieved almost instantaneously.

Our subjective experience of time has also been altered by the digital context. Online 'flow' experiences can accelerate our perception of time to such an extent that time almost disappears (Voiskounsky, 2008 as cited in Suler, 2016: 43), while the ability of the digital environment to store our personal records can enable our identity to transcend time boundaries creating the potential for psychological conflict as our identities continue to change over time (Burkell, 2016). How temporality is experienced in the digital environment can also be ephemeral; applications such as Snapchat, for example, deliberately offer fleeting, time-limited, interactions. Lastly, while experiences such as flow can skew our perception of time passing, ultimately, we are physical beings with physical needs and these can force us to return to the physical world. As such, digital temporality cannot be considered as totally isolated from the physical world; digital time intersects with the physical time we experience in our everyday lives (Suler, 2016). Understanding the temporal aspects of digital phenomena requires us to reflect on multiple facets including the digital platforms we are considering, how people interact with those platforms over time, and how those platforms intersect with our physical world. Getting pulled into some temporal aspects of the digital world might lead us to neglect our physical safety, as is demonstrated by road safety campaigns that encourage us not to engage with the immediacy associated with text messaging (and other apps) while driving.

Many of these temporal aspects of the digital context have created phenomena that are worthy of our consideration as social science researchers. An illustration of this can be seen in business and management research, where the 'always on' phenomenon is of interest and value to those seeking insight into how the constant connectivity to work communications may be impacting the wellbeing of employees. In psychology, researchers might be interested in investigating how the real-time digital recording of early childhood events affects the construction of identity in later adult life. Those involved in politics research may find value in examining the spread of instantaneous communication in the formation of networks of influence in political decision-making and/or behaviour tracking of political candidates following social media content surges.

The notion and use of 'time' in research can be categorised in three ways. The first is the notion of time as a verb. Here time is used as a period of measurement indicating how long something took to do, for example, the time taken to complete a PhD or an experiment. This notion of time can be objective (seconds, hours, months) or subjective (long, short, average). Second, time can be used as an adjective, such as when a supervisor says 'this is a timely piece of research' or when time passes quickly or slowly. Third, time can be used as a noun denoting an event; for example, 'the time my interview respondent said …'. How we think of, and use, the word 'time' and how we conceptualise the temporal aspects of the digital context is important within the context of digital research. For example, the digitalisation of our environment has led to the perception by some of increasing time pressure. One of the characteristics of digitalisation, that of immediacy, includes the ability to immediately connect with others and thus an expectation that an immediate response can be gained. This creates an implied pressure to enact a certain set of behaviours for both us as researchers and for our respondents. This might mean that research participants do not take time for reflection when taking part in digital research. In addition, the lack of temporal cues in many digital environments can result in us, as researchers, forgetting the physical time in which we and others are operating, leading to the phenomenon of an 'always on' expectation in digital communication, which is unlikely to be conducive to attracting and retaining research participants. A further reflection on temporality within the digital context is the option of asynchronous interaction despite the immediacy offered by social media. We can connect and respond instantaneously to each other via social media but can also choose to interact asynchronously by responding to a text message, for example, at a later point in time; this is not possible with offline face-to-face interactions.

Digital technology affords us the opportunity not just to reflect on temporality, our research and the lived experience of those we wish to engage with in our research, but also offers us the tools with which to implement our research in novel ways. Prior even to the early adoption of digital methods, organisational researchers were calling for a more considered approach to temporality in social science research. 'We need to embrace more nuanced and dynamic notions of temporality as a means of grounding our research in human experience' (Cunliffe et al., 2004: 262). Digital technologies allow us to ground our research in the 'life as lived' of human experiences in a way that has never before been available. To what extent have we as researchers adapted our research practices as a result of reconsidering temporality in the digitalised environment? What have the expectations of immediacy brought to both the participants of research and researchers themselves? Has the 'when' as well as the 'what' of research altered owing to digitalisation, as suggested by Marres and Weltevrede (2013)? These questions are worth considering at an individual research project level by individual researchers but also at a broader research methods level.

LONGEVITY IN THE DIGITAL CONTEXT

A pertinent aspect of temporality is in relation to currency issues associated with research within a dynamic environment. The longevity of research on or through the digital context may be fleeting and ephemeral or enduring and timeless. Whether a particular research project is ephemeral or enduring depends on how the digital context evolves. Consequently, as digital researchers we need to be alert to the impact of digital environmental changes on:

- the phenomena we study
- the methods we use
- the relevance of the specific digital context (e.g., social media platform) we select.

First, we need to be aware that our research phenomenon might have a short 'shelf life' or be perceived as owing its value to its topical nature. The impact of the socio-cultural context on theories and concepts is a long standing idea in the social sciences – aspects of Freud's (1856 –1939) work in Vienna, for instance, were recognised as being, to some extent, 'of their time and place', by psychologists such as Karen Horney (1885–1952).

In the digital context, the fast-paced changes in the environment impact on the socio-cultural context, that is, the digital environment has an impact on established human behaviours (e.g., meeting a suitable life partner) and enables new behaviours to emerge (e.g., online dating or the use of dating apps). Consequently, the dynamic digital environment may lead to research whose insights into the human condition are 'in the moment' in a way that researchers have not previously experienced.

Second, and beyond the temporality of the digital phenomenon studied, there may also be a currency aspect to the research tools used to investigate the phenomenon. Digital research tools can also be subject to the relatively fast changes associated with technology itself. Upgrades of software can and do result in research tools morphing with little or no notice, and this too has implications for researchers. For example, the functionality of digital recording devices may change, or the NVivo software tool may change its version and require patches or updates to allow you to continue working. In some cases 'upgrades' may change the format of data previously stored and/or partially coded or analysed, or changes to improve the interface may require effort to identify previously familiar analysis functions. All of these occurrences can be frustrating and waste resources; however, they are now a normal aspect of research and should be acknowledged as potential challenges when planning research.

Third, the specific digital context selected as a platform for study might also be ephemeral. For example, a research project involving analysis of short video material produced by Vine, an app owned by Twitter, would be problematic as that app ceased to exist in 2016 and the videos produced by Vine are now not searchable or retrievable (Perez, 2016). Although researchers cannot guarantee the continuation of their selected research vehicles, it may be worth either using more than one platform (e.g., research using both Vine and YouTube) or planning a contingency, alternative platform in case of merger/acquisition or shutdown. Here the ephemeral aspects of temporality play out in a different way from that of Snapchat. Researchers have not previously needed to account for such fast-paced change in the socio-technological context of their research projects. Consequently, as researchers we need to ask ourselves whether our research topic will still be of interest to readers and examiners once it is completed, and/or look for insights that will endure beyond the specific socio-technological context we examine. With a masters' level project that may take one year these questions will be less relevant than for a doctoral study that may take up to three or four years to conduct and write up. For academics who want to create insights and build on those insights to establish and develop their research careers, the stakes are much higher.

The impact on research of accelerated changes in the socio-cultural and technological context, through the medium of data capture, the speed of resulting data flows, and the immediacy of interactions between people through digital technologies, should not be underestimated. Acceleration can be exemplified via the ephemeral nature of time and data when someone chooses to interact through Snapchat, giving a very short time window to view an image and message, and possibly capture that data for research. This ephemerality of digital platforms through their design (i.e., Snapchat) has been used effectively by groups wishing to keep content restricted and as a way of limiting their content on a publicly accessible digital archive. Teenagers may use this format for instantaneous fun and to avoid display to potentially disapproving parental figures, disreputable groups may also use it to communicate messages or images of illegal activity. However, the ephemeral nature of these platforms makes it difficult to capture data from them. The rate at which data accumulate online creates its own ephemerality as what is not seen when it is posted needs to be consciously sought out. The sheer volume of new postings on platforms like YouTube, or social media sites like Twitter, also creates a pressure to be 'always on'. As social science researchers, this 'always on' social phenomenon creates opportunities for researching digital phenomena and needs to be considered in relation to digital research methods. These issues are discussed in the next section.

Whether digital research is fleeting or enduring should also be considered in relation to the lifespan of data. As researchers, we acknowledge that data continue to be generated after we have stopped collecting them for research purposes. For example, comments on YouTube do not cease just because we have ended our data collection period, people's online behaviours will continue and additional data accumulate. The data we have captured, however, become frozen data. The technical ability to store digital data has and continues to grow such that we can store, indefinitely, far greater volumes of digital data every year. These frozen data are enduring, as our ability to store data is not now limited technologically, and they are timeless, as the data are not subject to decay (Burkell, 2016). The digital imprint, the archive and the footprint of digital content remain firmly in existence. What is, will always be, at least in relation to data content. Nevertheless, while data may be timeless and enduring, the usefulness of the data and how they might contribute to understanding the human condition may be fleeting and ephemeral.

The accelerated perishability in the value of digital research is directly related to the dynamic nature of the digitalised society. As changes in the socio-cultural and technological environment impact on how we behave and the attitudes we have, the frozen data quickly become out-of-date as a representation of the human condition. This leads us to consider the extent to which digital data and data produced about digital phenomena might be perishable. While the lifespan of research outputs on digital phenomena were considered earlier, we also need to reflect on the 'lifespan' of digital data, and data about digital phenomena. The acceleration of society could be argued to be shortening the lifespan of digital (indeed all) research about human (including digital) phenomena. To illustrate, research about a digital phenomenon may have a shorter life for research contribution as that phenomenon may significantly alter based on changes in technology use and adoption. Early published research on the characteristics or influencing factors for online purchasing is now being superseded as more consumers are using their mobile devices to make purchases, as opposed to laptops and PCs.

TEMPORAL BLURRING OF SPACE AND PLACE BOUNDARIES

The experience of temporality in the twenty-first century and the speed of data flows influence the researcher, those researched and even the phenomenon researched. For the researcher immediacy, and the immediately available data, can have implications for the management of the resulting data. For those who are participants or co-producers in research the speed at which data accumulate and the immediacy of the data can lead to expectations about research results being available and disseminated more quickly than previously. Research topics can also be influenced by this accelerated access to data making it possible to conduct 'live' research, for example, trending topics on social media such as hashtag #blacklivesmatter or #MeToo, or video footage of political unrest in specific countries. Thus, the speed of data flow can be both an advantage and a challenge. On one hand, the speed of data can ensure currency and up-to-dateness. On the other hand, the management of the data flow may be difficult. Analogous to the decision to sell shares on the stock market, the best point concerning when to 'cut off' the live data stream and commence analysis is a difficult exercise.

The ubiquitousness of digital tools in our lives has led us, as individuals, to blur the boundaries between different aspects of our lives. This merging of previously distinct times for different activities impacts on our lives as digitalised individuals and on our activities as researchers. This phenomenon resulting from the pervasive nature of technology is most prevalent in the blurring of the boundary between work and non-work life. For many this boundary has become hazy as emails, calendar updates, etc. are all sent to and accessed through our smartphones. French legislation, which came into effect from 1 January 2017, reflects the pervasive nature of these blurred boundaries. For workers in companies with more than 50 employees, there is now legislation to support their freedom to ignore emails or phone messages outside of normal office hours known as the 'right to disconnect'. While for some having the flexibility to answer work related emails wherever and whenever is helpful in the management of their lives, for others it is seen as an implicit expectation and encroachment on non-work life (Wajcman, 2015). Even within our social lives, time to disconnect from others is less available. Social media platforms such as Facebook and Twitter bring others into our homes and on our holidays, they even allow those to whom we are connected to accompany us to work and intimate social events (e.g., dates). While it is still possible to physically separate ourselves from others, digital separation is more difficult and can be accelerated by a 'fear of missing out' (i.e., FOMO). Connection to, and yet distance from, others when we choose is widely seen as desirable and the resulting blurring of boundaries between different aspects of our lives is an important social phenomenon. As digital researchers we need to acknowledge and respond to this merging of different spaces/places, and the simultaneous desire for control of connections with others.

In digital research, the blurring of space/place boundaries across work and non-work can be seen by looking at the time stamps of online questionnaire responses, even taking into consideration global time zone differences. A recent online study of European small and medium enterprises' (SMEs) attitudes towards digital technologies conducted by one of the authors of this text collected responses recorded well outside 'normal' working hours, for example 11.30 p.m., and 6.20 a.m. A hypercritical argument could be created concerning the impact of completion of online questionnaires late at night and the likelihood of respondent errors and therefore less valid data. This argument could be countered with reference to how those participating SMEs decided when they wished to complete the questionnaire; they controlled the connection to the research instrument and fitted in the completion to suit their lives. Alternatively, the question of whether responses were impacted by when the data were collected could also be answered methodologically by analysing the responses themselves. For example, were there more missing responses on 'out-of-hours' questionnaires, were measures noticeably less reliable? Digital researchers cognisant of the potential impact of the blurring of space/place boundaries on how participants interact with research projects can investigate the digital research methods they use as a digital phenomenon in its own right, alongside the other phenomena their research focuses on.

TEMPORAL FACTORS OF COMMUNICATION

Communication in the digital environment occurs along a spectrum from instantaneous and interactive, to delayed and non-reciprocal; from synchronous to asynchronous. Communication by and through digital means presents huge potential for researching the meaning making of a digital phenomenon. Synchronicity underlies areas of digital research such as telepresence and interactivity. Synchronicity may impact on digital phenomena, such as how social norms are formed on different digital platforms and how meaning is negotiated through digital communications. Digital identity construction, particularly social identity, is likely to be influenced by the temporal element of synchronicity as asynchronous platforms allow more time for reflection than synchronous ones. The perception of synchronicity, while not restricted to the digital context, is an important phenomenon itself where insights may be gained through digital research. Communication is pervasive in human behaviours. Consequently, the ability to observe and potentially manipulate synchronicity, a key characteristic of communication, which is afforded by the digital environment presents broad possibilities for social science researchers.

Synchronicity also needs to be thought about when considering digital research methods. While much is made in the media of the immediacy of computer mediated technology, be it the internet or social media, in reality when we as social science researchers use digital research methods to conduct research and collect data, an important temporal element we need to consider is whether that method is (or is perceived by participants as being) asynchronous or synchronous.

When we collect synchronous data, we are collecting data as they are being created. For example, we can measure when pupils access their virtual learning spaces, observe when people stream videos to their mobile phones, scan when researchers use Skype to record online interviews with research participants, or record participants' responses to website stimuli when interactive experiments are conducted. This information is synchronous as it is captured while it is happening. Prior to the advent of digital technologies access to synchronous data did not exist. Researchers would analyse notes from interviews or observations, or analyse experimental results when participants had completed the study. Now, as researchers we need to think if our research question requires the collection of synchronous data. While synchronous data can be valuable to academic researchers, they are particularly important to commercial organisations. Real-time observation of website navigation behaviour might, for example, prompt pop-up chat windows to appear or customised advertising to be displayed. Real-time adaptations on websites or e-commerce sites are made and the reactions of populations are monitored to maximise organisational objectives. Real-time website usability experiments can help ensure that organisations quickly maximise the potential of their website design, minimising disruption to their customer base and optimising the conditions for achieving revenue goals. As academic researchers, however, unless we are conducting action or some experimental research, our research objectives are unlikely to require us to collect synchronous digital data. Most academic research in the digital environment does not require truly synchronous data collection. Exceptions might include experimental research with dependent variables such as response time, and research questions that use digital tools to capture ongoing experiences (e.g., tourism with Go-Pro cameras and participant commentary).

Asynchronous data are more commonly used in social science post-graduate and doctoral research, as well as in individual academic research studies. Here, data have been created and we are collecting them after the event of creation, at one or more different time intervals. Asynchronous data occur both as primary data, for example, a research question posted to a community forum on the experience of voting online in an election, and as secondary data such as the scraping of tweets regarding the Euro 2016 football tournament. Although social media is commonly thought of as immediate, it is frequently an asynchronous exchange as a comment is posted and a reply is made later when someone checks their social media feeds. Near synchronous data (Salmons, 2016) are a midway point between synchronous and asynchronous data. Some short exchange types of data may also be near synchronous, such as 'liking' an image on Instagram, which takes very little time to complete. Near synchronous data collection may include sending an email containing a link to a questionnaire about healthy eating where someone may open the email, have a cup of coffee, click on the link and complete the questionnaire that is then uploaded to the online questionnaire provider, such as Qualtrics, later on the same day that the original email was sent.

Synchronicity might also impact on the dissemination of research results. Interactive digital displays through visualisations of both 'live' data and asynchronous data are now possible thanks to advances in computer sciences. Human geographers can synchronously observe real-time mass movement of people through public transport systems in Mexico City, London or Tokyo via geo-location devices and touch-in touch-out smart cards. Yet they may also produce asynchronous visual displays of earthquakes and tremors along the San Andreas Fault in California over the past 50 years. The subsequent display of 'moving' data is appealing as a communication strategy for research results as it gains and holds the attention of an audience, as we are drawn to moving images (Rosling, 2006). The cost of producing interactive and/or moving visualisations of research data is falling but as of 2017 it still remains outside the scope of most individual social science (academic) researchers. Less complicated visualisations of digital data, for example, non-moving, static images, can be created at low cost via widely available software or through using specific programing languages such as R. The University of Washington Interactive Data Lab in America has a valuable resource centre for data visualisation tools (http://idl.cs.washington.edu/).

DIGITAL TIME AND SELF-AWARENESS

Temporal incongruities exist in the intersection between the digital and physical worlds. These incongruities exist because time is perceived differently in the two environments. Issues related to intersectionality may manifest in phenomena concerning how we perceive time to be passing, in the way in which processes unfold in the digital environment, how we manage our lives, as well as in the expectations we have concerning how long things will take.

A temporal phenomenon in the digital context is when we perceived time as disappearing when in the digital environment ourselves. A further attribute of digitalisation that can be related to temporality is the immersive nature of certain online and social media behaviours, where we dissociate from our physical selves. Deep involvement with online gaming through handheld devices, or virtual reality headsets, the scrolling through and engagement with social media feeds about celebrity gossip, searching and tracking down the 'perfect' gift through multiple e-commerce sites or identifying original sources of specific information through visiting multiple hypertext links on a library database can all create 'online flow experiences'. Being 'in the flow' results in a sense of loss of time, hours can be spent performing these online, highly immersive activities and this can have positive and negative consequences for people's productivity and time management, both as citizens and researchers.

The digital environment can also immerse us 'in the moment'. This multi-faceted phenomenon raises questions concerning both digital as a social science phenomenon and digital as an instrument. For instance, does 'in the moment' refer to being physically present during a phenomenon, or can it refer to being remotely present through technology? Does researching 'in the moment' refer to the collection of only synchronous data or can it also and should it include asynchronous data too? Does researching 'in the moment' and 'life as lived' lead us to need a more complex understanding of people's relationship with time, one that is less fixed and more fluid? Does the embedded nature of technology in everyday lives require us to reconsider our understanding of time?

An illustration of the complexities surrounding considering the phenomenon of being 'in the moment' can be made through a project aiming to understand the influence of digital technologies on millennials' purchasing decisions. A typical participant's behaviour might include engaging in both individual and social activities, absorbing both real-time and asynchronous data, while switching between multiple technological platforms to simultaneously perform different but related tasks, all with constant but partial attention. For example, she might be:

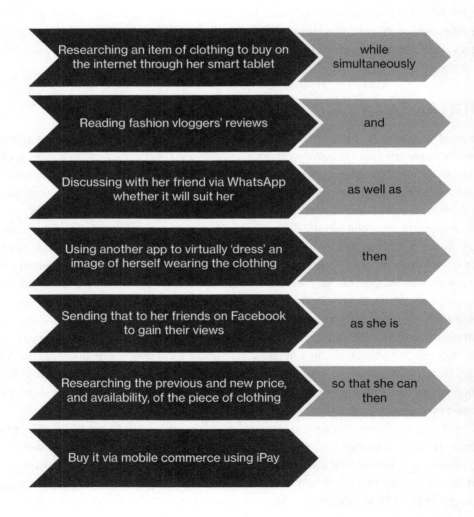

While there is constant attention on the matter in hand (i.e., clothing purchase) by the research participant, there is partial attention given to each platform and network of communication. The goal of whether or not to purchase the clothing remains consistent with technology-free purchasing decisions. However, the purchasing process itself, which moves at a rapid pace between information gathering and evaluation, through individual and social influences, and across different modes of interaction, means that the digital decision-making appears to bear little resemblance to its non-digital counterpart. The layered data necessary to understand the digital purchasing process as a phenomenon cannot be captured through a single digital platform, and while each element is essential to the research phenomenon, it is not necessarily appropriate to disentangle them to create a linear process resembling our established understanding of purchase decision-making as much of the activity is simultaneous. Market research firms, however, and their clients, may argue that it is of commercial value to learn which platform or interaction was most influential in the purchase decision-making.

The pervasive nature of technology in our lives impacts on how we manage our time and activities. Self-management through apps (those specialised software applications designed to perform a narrow function on your mobile phone or computer, for example, a weather app or a currency converter app) designed to assist our lives and help us not to forget events or actively remind us to do something is now almost inescapable. Whether the app we use is as general as an electronic calendar, or whether we use different apps to monitor specific activities (e.g., steps, heart rate, productivity), technology has changed how we manage our time. Many of these apps are believed to help us change our behaviour, to remind us to walk more so we improve our health, to breathe more deeply to alleviate stress, or to help us focus on the task in hand. However, whether this is achieved, or whether personal analytics do not in fact empower us but rather overwhelm us, is a question that has not yet been fully answered. These now routine accessories to everyday life can act as useful data capture tools for researchers, as well as cross-reference points in terms of checking reported behaviour against actual behaviour of research participants.

The digital environment impacts on how long we expect things to take. For instance, while physically present in a service environment such as a bank, we might be willing to wait several minutes for service, whereas if we are experiencing the service digitally seconds is too long to wait for the service (often a website) to be available to us. The expectation of the instant gratification of our information and entertainment needs is a phenomenon of the digital environment, and impacts on digital research methods. Consequently, managing our own, and others, expectations of digital research is an important aspect of managing research in the digital age, and involves managing expectations across digital and non-digital contexts. This intersectional temporality creates temporal incongruities in research projects when online and offline research designs are implemented. Different time frames of data collection can be commonplace in social science research, such as interviews conducted over a period of six months or two sets of interviews conducted as a 'before and after' scenario. How these disparate time frames are integrated in the analysis and writing up of the research results will depend on the original research objectives. When research methods involve both digital and non-digital data collection methods, thought is needed concerning when each element should be collected. The speed with which digital data can be collected alongside the rapid changes that can occur in the digital environment mean that planning is needed to minimise the impact of temporal intersectionality.

Temporal intersectionality might also need to be considered at the level of the research project. Portrayed temporality refers to how any time-framing or time-shaping might be illustrated in research reports. Pre-digital research was often conducted, written up and communicated as linear, with a defined starting point and an end point. Digital research can take on a different guise with multiple start-stop points, multiple interactions and could be described as messier, non-linear, deviating and disruptive, with less clear time lines. Whether or not this can be used as a criticism against digital research will depend on your ontological position and your own perspective on the nature of research. Another temporal incongruity between digital and non-digital contexts occurs when we consider how research is reported. Digital information contexts thrive on content; content is turned over quickly as new content is always available. Academic research reporting, however, requires reflection and careful consideration, which is incongruous with the quick news environment of the digital contexts. This can be frustrating for academic researchers who are used to the norms of digital information acquisition and dissemination. Digital research disseminated through established academic means such as conferences may feel outdated by the time it is shared, and dissemination through media whose fundamental processes were designed in a non-digital age (i.e., academic journal articles) may lead to the latest academic findings being 'behind the times' when they are eventually published.

TEMPORALITY OF DIGITAL DATA

The digital environment's rapidly increasing storage capacity means that a vast volume of usable data exists, and this leads to the need to consider the temporal aspects of digital data. The temporality of digital data is related to its currency (broadly discussed when looking at the ephemerality/timelessness of digital data), and the time frames of the digital data being used.

The first aspect of the temporality of the data source considers the separation, if any, between when the data were produced and when they are used for research. In the non-digital environment, data that are not collected specifically for research are automatically considered to be secondary data. As a consequence of the data being secondary, we would assess whether the data were appropriate for our research project across multiple different dimensions including the data collection unit, the data content, and the currency of the data, the dependability of the data source and multiple other criteria (specific criteria can be found in general research methods texts). However, unlike non-digital data, pre-existing digital data can be the raw data we would be interested in collecting for our specific research purposes. For example, if we were interested in how parents' make restaurant choices for family celebrations we might look at discussion forums on parenting sites like Mumsnet. These pre-existing data were not produced for our research purposes, and as such would fall under the established definition of 'secondary data'. However, this digital data may still be accessible in their raw form, so only the currency criterion related to the evaluation of secondary data needs to be considered. As such, while 'historic' digital data are not, *per se*, primary data (i.e., they were not collected in order to answer a specific research question), neither is it appropriate to assess their usefulness using the criteria applied to non-digital secondary data.

To differentiate between pre-existing digital data and digital data that are generated or collected to answer a specific research question, a temporality dimension is useful. In this instance, we consider whether the data have been generated and/or collected contemporaneously, or whether they are gathered from historic records (however closely in the past that historical record was produced). Two factors can, as such, be used to classify the relationship between digital data and their source – temporality and closeness (from Chapter 3). It is important here to remember that whether a source is primary or secondary is dependent on the research question. A travel blog, for example, would be a primary source of information concerning a holiday location if the blogger has visited the area and was reporting on their attitudes and experiences. However, the blog would be a secondary source if the blogger was passing on others' attitudes and experiences, and would be a tertiary source if the blogger was reporting on a newspaper report of consumer attitudes and experiences in the area concerned.

Table 4.1 Temporality and closeness to data

		Time when data was produced	
		Historic	Contemporaneous
Closeness to the data source	Primary		
	Secondary		

Understanding the relationship between digital data and the data source helps us to consider a number of questions concerning the potential for the digital data we are using to represent the phenomenon we are interested in. The previous chapter discussed the general relationship between the closeness to the data source and data quality, and is not repeated here. Instead, we consider why it is relevant when the data were produced. Essentially, knowing when the data were produced enables us to assess the currency of the data. Given the dynamic nature of the digital environment, and the impact of technological changes on human behaviour, we need to be able to evaluate the data in relation to any socio-technological changes that have occurred. Questions we might consider would include: Has a new platform/app been launched, or an old platform/app closed, that is relevant to the research question we are interested in? Are there any new devices that have changed how people interact with the platform we are accessing? Has the platform/app that the data are from updated its interface in a way that will impact on the phenomenon we are interested in?

The second aspect of temporality that needs to be considered in relation to digital data is related to determining whether the research requires a shorter or longer data collection period. For example, it is relatively straightforward to collect one week's worth of Twitter content without complex scrapping software, and it is possible to set up your computer to collect tweets at regular intervals. However, it is far more resource intensive to collect Twitter data for an extended period of time. This is partly owing to the huge volume of tweets produced: the total amount of tweets is known as the Twitter firehose. The Twitter firehose is the complete stream of public messages on Twitter. Access to this complete stream is highly limited to a few organisations, largely based on ability to pay very high charges and the ability to process such high volumes of data. Consequently, as researchers we need to consider how much data we require, and whether it is useful to have a temporal dimension to our data. Questions that need to be asked here include considering how long it will take to collect a sufficient volume of data to address our research question, whether the time period we are using is typical of the phenomenon that is being researched (i.e., what environmental factors might have impacted on the data), whether seasonality might impact on content, etc. A further consideration might be between whether we need one period of data collection or multiple periods. While continuous data might be available, using continuous data might not be the best way to produce robust insights into the research phenomenon we are investigating.

OPPORTUNITIES CREATED BY DIGITAL TEMPORALITY

Dynamic rather than static data have created multiple opportunities for social science knowledge development. In the commercial environment, real-time data from EPOS (electronic point of sale) systems and e-commerce platforms have provided far greater responsivity by retailers to customers. The live testing of online advertising options for brands, as used by Zara among others, can help the efficacy of their implemented advertising, inform manufacturing decisions, and enable tailored offerings to local markets. The instantaneous feedback afforded by dynamic digital data means that marginal adjustments can be made in almost real-time to enhance commercial activity. In the education sphere live monitoring of learning platforms can tell us much about the most accessed revision topics for children sitting exams, or contribute to understanding how young adults share information via social media to make decisions.

The established research process of designing, piloting, then refining data collection followed by implementing the main data collection and analysing the data, before designing any follow-up investigations is still valid. All the stages are still present, however, the time delay between stages has been significantly shortened and the research turnaround time can be much shorter. The shorter research process cycle can limit time for reflection, and may also mean that it is useful for the researcher to consider how their research design choices might limit the longevity of their research (Figure 4.1). For example, we no longer need to wait for the postal return of completed questionnaires to input data, as data can be automatically uploaded from online questionnaires to a cloud-based storage facility, which may also include software to enable faster analysis. The sharing of research project data between research partners, or between research student and supervisor, has been greatly expedited through computer mediated technologies.

Dynamic data also afford effective plotting of certain types of behaviours of individuals or groups such as networks of relationships in LinkedIn business groups, or movement of people through the London underground tracked by Oyster card usage. These data can be accessed and integrated into online data feeds to produce 'living' insight of behaviour, for example, the reporting of internet broadband speed across different country regions. Geo-spatial dynamic data are used by water management companies, logistics firms and public health bodies to better manage resource availability, and to even out supply and demand where possible. Police organisations in the UK use geo-spatial, dynamic data to monitor known crime hotspots, and plan relevant activity and human resource deployment based on these data. In America dynamic crime data are publicly accessible and downloadable, helping citizens to be better informed about their neighbourhoods. As individual researchers we can also make use of dynamic data in a scaled down version, our data can be mapped and presented via visualisation software, some of which is very low cost or free. As new approaches to research are opened up through the continual development of new digital technologies, new avenues may also be created and new perspectives found in digital data.

Other opportunities are presented by the dynamic nature of digital research including that of research topic identification. Digital data highlight emerging topics, and researchers might previously have been unaware of the extent of interest in that topic. Trending topics on social media identify what issues large numbers of people are commenting on at that moment in time, some of which (e.g., global warming, or the potential repeal of the Affordable Care Act in the USA #save ACA) may prove fruitful ground on which to develop research projects that have contemporary relevance. The alternative view, though contentious, is that if a potential research project wished to focus on a named organisation, or specified activity, and there was no digital conversation or social media content about that entity, then the silence may indicate that the subject is of limited interest to a wider audience.

A further opportunity provided through digital research and its dynamic nature is the ability to reach and involve previously hard to access groups and to engage with those groups of people. Some of these groups are at a transitional stage in their lives (e.g., recent migrants), whereas others may be more stable, but seeking to change their circumstances (e.g., domestic abuse suffers). Reaching these groups offline may be difficult due to the transitory nature of their experience, or because identifying particular individuals might make them vulnerable as research participants. Thus temporality can be manifested through the stages in life a person or group of people are experiencing and this time-based stage can be a coalescing point through which researchers may be able to engage with those potential participants.

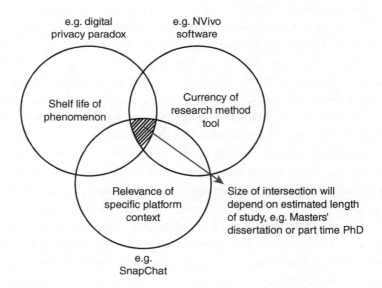

Figure 4.1 The factors impacting longevity of digital research

CHALLENGES OF DIGITAL TEMPORALITY

Knowing when how much data are enough data is a question faced by all researchers both digital and non-digital. In the dynamic digital environment one challenge we face is when should we stop collecting data? The volume of digital data now generated and archived is far greater than ever before. While this presents exciting opportunities, the sheer amount of data, and the fluidity of these data, creates a significant challenge for digital researchers, particularly when using social media data or 'big data' sets. Part of the challenge associated with digital data is that they are not only large, but also changeable. When the data are dynamic and liable to change then how can we gather 'representative' data? How do we avoid the pitfalls of atypical data collection? Time is important to this problem in two ways. First, we need to consider how long is long enough to collect sufficient data; second, we need to consider at what time, in a socio-cultural sense, we collect the data.

Thinking first about how long we collect data for, we need to consider the volume of data we need to address our research question. Just because we can access more data does not mean we should. However, if we can access data across a number of different time periods (e.g., days of week, hours of day), then we might consider sampling data from different time frames rather than collecting a continuous stream of data. Whether this is suitable or not will, of course, depend on our research objective.

The second aspect of the problem is when, in the socio-cultural sense, we collect the data. Think, for example, of the impact of the Boston marathon bombings on the hashtags that trended on Twitter, such as #BostonMarathon, #Bostonbombing, #BostonStrong and #prayforBoston, and how that unexpected event would have impacted on someone studying the content of tweets. Less dramatically, consider the difference between the Twitter interactions in the UK over a two-month period in the run up to the EU referendum (#euref, #eureferendum), and how they would compare to those found in Australia at the same time, or in the two months after the EU referendum in the UK – which would you consider more 'typical'? To unpick the impact of expected or unexpected socio-cultural events on how well our data might represent the phenomenon we are interested in, we need to be aware of the events that are happening in the environment which are relevant to our research participants, and we need to consider the relationship between those events, our participants and our research question. For example, a linguist looking at how tweets are structured might not be overly concerned about whether those tweets were collected at a politically sensitive time, however, it is unlikely that a political science researcher could ignore the signification of the EU referendum. If the research question focused on trending topics, responses to news updates and the temporality of the data are a plus rather than an issue. However, temporality is unlikely to be a core concern for researchers studying the impact of website colour on the navigation behaviour of users.

The rapid changes in the digital environment may make it more difficult to replicate research findings across different time periods. This fluidity may draw criticism from the sceptics of digital research that a lack of replication infers a lack of rigour and thus the value of the research contribution is diminished. The challenge for digital researchers, then, is to separate out those research insights that are related to the digital context as it is/was when the research was conducted, from those insights that are less dependent on the specific context. Returning to the example earlier of Freud, the feminist criticisms of his work came about because Freud failed to separate out the desire to be in a powerful position, from the desire to be male – the group in power in the socio-cultural context he operated in. As we increasingly investigate the digital phenomenon as well as using digital research methods, we will become better at unpicking the insights that transcend the socio-technological context from those that do not. Though, as digital researchers, we need to guard against digital research being viewed as the 'new toy' for social science researchers. Inappropriate use of digital methods, questionable ethics decisions and over-researching specific phenomena just because we are now able to access certain content, behaviours or groups of people will not improve the case for digital research. Nevertheless, greater exposure to digital research for those who are sceptical of its value will help to open their eyes to the possibilities that digital research presents, and allow them to draw more informed conclusions. Digital research, as it becomes increasingly mainstream over time, and those involved in research within the digital domain, will facilitate the development of criteria for rigour. We hope that this text will enable and encourage this to occur.

Other time-related challenges faced by digital researchers relate to the choices that need to be made over when to 'stop the clock' on data collection, and the 'gap' between each snapshot (or the duration of the 'reporting' cycle) that is appropriate in an online research project. While 'always on' data generation and analysis is now possible, at some point the digital researcher must make the decision to stop the flow of data so that analysis, interpretation and reporting can take place. Making this decision should be part of the research design process and should relate to the research objectives. As a general rule, data sufficiency should provide a guide here: once no new pertinent data are being collected, then the data collection process should stop (Fusch and Ness, 2015; O'Reilly and Parker, 2013). The decision concerning the duration of the 'reporting' cycle is related to the interaction between the environment and the research question. Stable environmental conditions are likely to be reflected in stable results and consequently result in relatively long gaps in data collection. In contrast, changing environment conditions are likely to lead to more volatile results and require shorter 'reporting' intervals. This presents the problem of whether the data are used to identify changing environmental conditions, or whether the researcher needs to be alert to changes in the environment so that volatile results can be examined to capture and unpick the impact of those changes. A challenge for digital researchers is how to manage these dynamic reporting cycles with the resources available to them, and what mechanisms are needed to ensure changing conditions are noticed.

An important challenge to acknowledge within digital research is the reliance on technology. Technology underlies the data that are generated and how they can be collected. It is generally used to analyse the data, and influences how results are portrayed. Digital researchers need to have a sound grasp of the underlying processes related to the technologies they use, and consider the potential effects and limitations of these on their research (boyd and Crawford, 2012; Snee et al., 2016). Further discussion of the impact of automation on digital research can be found in Chapter 6. However, it is worth noting that the technologies that researchers depend on themselves have a limited shelf life. It is also worth noting that compatibility of technologies and platforms used in digital research may create a practical challenge for researchers. For example, at the time of writing, there are differences between the formatting structures for Twitter and Instagram data as uploaded to NodeXL, which creates complexities when trying to compare semantic networks of social media hashtag content.

SUMMARY

This chapter considered the multiple ways in which the digital environment forces us to think about time and temporality. After unpicking what temporality is, in both objective (i.e., measured time) and subjective (i.e., felt time) forms, we considered some socio-cultural impacts of digital temporality such as the 'always on' phenomenon. Temporality has an aspect associated with the rate at which change occurs, and this was also discussed. For instance, how the rate of change in the digital context influences the longevity of our research findings and the currency of our research methods were both examined. This discussion included considering how change in the digital environment impacts on the usefulness of our research findings over time. Temporal aspects of the digital environment also blur space and place boundaries. The speed (a temporal dimension) at which information can be transmitted digitally, for instance, removes geographic boundaries making distant parts of the world closer, and remote individuals accessible. Blurred boundaries also impact individuals in their day-to-day lives as the separation between work and leisure is less clear cut. The blurring of these boundaries was discussed, and its implications for digital research considered.

Not surprisingly, temporality also impacts on communication. We discussed how communication can be synchronous or asynchronous, and how we need to consider this dimension of digital communications when looking at what our research methods can (and cannot) achieve. This chapter also explored the intersection between the digital and physical spaces, where transitioning between the two can make time seem to have disappeared or dragged depending on the activities being undertaken. The intersection between digital and non-digital time was also considered, including how we now manage our time, and some possible implications of changes in time management on the lives we now live. Crossing over with Chapter 3, this chapter also explored temporality in relation to digital data. Questions such as how long is the gap between data production and data consumption by the researcher, and how long we should collect data for, were considered here.

The last two sections considered some of the opportunities and challenges of digital temporality, including, for instance, discussion of how temporal dimensions impact on the research process, and concerns about what constitutes 'enough' data to ensure that neither the digital environmental nor socio-cultural phenomena produce (overwhelming) anomalies that might influence research insights. Overall, this chapter provided a discussion of the different temporal dimensions of the digital context that can and do impact on digital research, as well as providing some guidance on how to unpick these dimensions.

The 3Es

Ethics, expectations and expertise are all impacted by the temporality of the digital environment. When we examine how temporality impacts on the ethics of digital research we have to consider the interactions between the researcher, the research participant and the research user. The researcher is trusted by both the research participant and the research user to provide a fair representation of the digital phenomenon they are examining. This responsibility is particularly pertinent when we consider the relevance of research. The question of the longevity of research findings and research data is significant here as we, as digital researchers, need to reflect on the longevity of our research findings. Our expectations as researchers in the digital environment can be challenged by the complexity of that environment. Expectations are challenged by the blurring of boundaries that result from the removal of temporal constraints on activities – for example, the ability to respond at any time to work emails blurs the boundary between work and leisure, or research participants engaging in multiple activities simultaneously. These blurred boundaries challenge us as researchers when we attempt to unpick the complexities of digitally intricate behaviours in order to report our results. Capturing the temporal complexities of the digital environment, while making those complexities accessible to our research audience, is a challenge that is likely to remain. As researchers we may have expectations regarding the desired immediacy of obtaining our research results if the collection instrument was digital but as has been discussed participants may respond synchronously but are more likely to respond asynchronously. Do researchers working in digital research expect the results to be enduring or to have a 'shelf life' as digital technology continues to evolve? Will the practical implications of the research results remain relevant to those using the research in different disciplines or will the usefulness and value of the research diminish with time?

Maintaining expertise in relation to temporality and digital research is challenging. The speed of change and evolution of digital research tools, currency in the prevailing attitudes and remaining up to date with ethics knowledge requires much from a researcher. Lastly, when we consider how temporality is related to digital research expertise, one area for focus is the need to develop criteria for making temporally related research design decisions. There remains a need for published guidelines concerning appropriate 'reporting' cycles, for example.

Questions

1. When looking at your own research project, what aspects of temporality will you need to explain or defend?
2. What is your justification for collecting your data at a particular point in time? Are there any environmental events that you need to account for? Are there any changes in the digital context that you need to consider?
3. How do you justify your methodological decisions related to time (e.g., time intervals between data collection points)?
4. How will you show that your research insights remain current? What are the insights you have derived from your data that might be bound within a particular socio-technological time period? What are the insights that are relatively robust to changes in the environment over time?
5. What challenges have you faced through using dynamic data, and how have you overcome these?

FURTHER READING

Wajcman, J. (2015). *Pressed for Time: The Acceleration of Life in Digital Capitalism*. Chicago, IL: The University of Chicago Press.

REFERENCES

Boyd, D. and Crawford, K. (2012). Critical questions for big data: Provocations for a cultural, technological, and scholarly phenomenon. *Information, Communication & Society*, 15 (5), 662–679.

Burkell, J.A. (2016). Remembering me: Big data, individual identity, and the psychological necessity of forgetting, *Ethics in Information Technology*, 18, 17–23.

Cunliffe, A.L., Luhman, J.T. and Boje, D.M. (2004). Narrative temporality: Implications for organizational research. *Organization Studies, 25* (2), 261–286.

Fusch, P.I. and Ness, L.R. (2015). Are we there yet? Data saturation in qualitative research. *The Qualitative Report, 20* (9), 1408.

Maggetti, M., Gilardi, F. and Radaelli, C.M. (2013). *Temporality in Designing Research in Social Science*. London: Sage.

Marres, N. and Weltevrede, E. (2013). Scraping the social? Issues in live social research. *Journal of Cultural Economy, 6* (3), 313–335.

O'Reilly, M. and Parker, N. (2013). Unsatisfactory saturation: A critical exploration of the notion of saturated sample sizes in qualitative research. *Qualitative Research, 13* (2), 190–197.

Perez, S. (2016). Twitter is shutting down Vine. Available from: https://techcrunch.com/2016/10/27/twitter-is-shutting-down-vine/ (accessed 31 October 2016).

Rosling, H. (2006). The best stats you've ever seen. TED2006 Available from: www.ted.com/talks/hans_rosling_shows_the_best_stats_you_ve_ever_seen (accessed 23 January 2017).

Salmons, J. (2016). *Doing Qualitative Research Online*. Thousand Oaks, CA: Sage.

Snee, H., Hine, C., Morey, Y., Roberts, S. and Watson, H. (2016). *Digital Methods for Social Science*. Basingstoke: Palgrave Macmillan.

Suler, J.R. (2016). *Psychology of the Digital Age: Human Become Electric*. New York: Cambridge University Press.

Wajcman, J. (2015). *Pressed for Time: The Acceleration of Life in Digital Capitalism*. Chicago, IL: The University of Chicago Press.

5
DATA SOURCES FOR
DIGITAL RESEARCH

In this chapter we will:

- provide different ways to consider data sources when conducting digital research
- outline who and what can be accessed through digital research
- highlight population and sampling concepts as they relate to digital research
- propose different possible foci for sampling considerations
- contribute key reflective questions to ask when making sampling decisions.

INTRODUCTION

As researchers conducting primary research, whether digital or not, whether positivist or interpretivist, we need to access data either from people (who), or events or things (what) (i.e., entities) to examine the phenomena that are of interest to us. This research entity needs to be defined and identified if we are to be able to gather information from or about it in order to answer our research objectives. The research question asked should drive the sample selected and this research question will require reflection on whether or not broad generalisation is a goal of the research.

It is important to think carefully about the relationship between the phenomena we are interested in and the entity – whether human, event or thing – and how this provides us with access to information about those phenomena. In most research, once we have defined/identified the 'who' or 'what' of our research, we do not draw from all possible examples but rather from a limited selection. The characteristics of the digital environment, including the volume of information available, the anonymity afforded to individuals and the dynamic structures of groups, impact on how we can identify and access information from these research entities (the who and the what). Consequently, we need to understand the impact of the digital environment on how we select the entities to investigate.

The terminology surrounding how we, as social science researchers, manage and divide the entities we wish to research is part of a larger debate concerning to what extent, if at all, the established norms of research methods language should be used in relation to the new world of digital research (Carrigan, 2014). In the same way that critics of quantitative methods of measurement suggest that marketers are using old ways of measuring to evaluate new digital interactions so digital researchers can question the use of terminology such as 'sampling unit' as this denotes an entity which is known, stable and fixed, and comes from the established view of research vocabulary (Nichols, 2013; Salim, 2017).

The groups of interest to a digital researcher may not be clearly known, nor fixed nor particularly stable. While this text does not intend to answer the question of whether researchers are inappropriately transferring the meaning of 'old' language to the new realities of the digital research environment, it is important to acknowledge that such critical reflection exists. The established way of thinking about research and the language tools available to us to describe the people/things we research may now require reapprais-ing, given the characteristics of digitalisation.

While we acknowledge that certain research terms can be value laden, to enable us to focus on understanding the digital research opportunities and issues rather than the debates between different research traditions, we refer to the pool of all possible instances of the entity from which information about the phenomenon of information will be gath-ered as the 'population', the source used to access that population as the 'sampling frame', with the limited selection that we select for the research as the 'sample'. The process of selecting the sample from the population is 'sampling'. For example, a research project wishing to investigate the impact of multi-modal online gaming (MMOG) on identity in the UK has identity construction in a particular group as the phenomenon of interest, so information needs to be gathered from online gamers in the UK (population of interest). The type of information gathered may be accessed directly through interacting with the gamers, in which case the research entity or sample would be the gamers themselves. Alternatively, it might be through looking at posts/threads on relevant online discussion boards, in which case the sample would be either the posts/threads themselves, or the discussion board (though this might pose problems with identifying specific UK gamers).

IMPORTANCE OF SAMPLING IN DIGITAL RESEARCH

Considering sampling in the digital environment is important for several reasons. Over the past decade far greater usage has been made of internet users as populations of interest and digital technologies as conduits for accessing those populations of interest. These groups have been considered relatively easy to access when compared to offline groups, as they are homogenous and focused and thus a resource efficient way in which to gather relevant data. However, when researchers do not understand the interplay between their population of interest and the characteristics of the digital environment, they cannot unpick how this interplay impacts on their research findings. For example, early published research on internet users (pre-dating the advent of digital and social media) was often based on largely educated, often white, American samples and as such under-represented certain groups within society. Critics have also highlighted respond-ent authenticity and instability of the respondent base as sampling limitations within the digital research environment (Xun and Reynolds, 2010). Whether this is important to a particular research project, however, is dependent on how that project defines its population of interest.

Many of the historic disadvantages of digital research samples such as particular groups' restricted access to technology are diminishing due to factors such as the decreasing costs of technology and web access as well as better coverage for the increasing population of smartphone users across the world. Consequently, researchers are able to reach more diverse populations through digital means. The digital context has opened up possibilities for research that were previously unfeasible due to participant reticence, excessive costs or perception of risks. For instance, a valuable aspect of digital media, specifically social media, is accessibility and allows engagement with 'new' groups. Some, often vulnerable groups, actively participate in social media because it is perceived as being 'neutral', 'private', 'hidden', thus digital media research can be inclusive in its parameters rather than restrictive. An illustration of this is the use of social media by refugee groups or the creation of informal social media groups supporting fellow domestic abuse sufferers. Thus, with care and sensitivity, these types of groups (the sampling frame) may now be included in research projects and their views, perceptions and experiences may be heard and published. This is an important and societally valuable aspect of inclusivity that is now possible in social science research.

With the wide adoption of smartphones, the opportunity to interact and research using mobile-based research instruments has never been greater. In regions of the world that were previously difficult to access for researchers, such as Africa, the smartphone penetration level has facilitated opportunities for digital research, for example, projects involving the tracking of micro-finance systems for Sub-Saharan farmers via their smartphone use or the sharing of relative wealth via mobile banking using M-Pesa in Kenya and Tanzania. These geographically dispersed individuals and groups can now be accessed as digitalisation has provided opportunities for both increased scope and broader diversity in sampling. However, the continued possible existence of a digital divide disrupting access to particular groups should not be underestimated (e.g., Davies et al., 2017). Nevertheless, a population becoming more accessible does not automatically lead to unproblematic data collection. For example, in parts of Asia the huge volume of online questionnaires disseminated through social media platforms such as Baidu has created issues for those platforms. Overall, the criticisms of digital research samples centre around the predominance of Anglo-American contexts with English language-based research instruments (e.g., Jankowski and van Selm, 2005), the over-use of student samples for online questionnaire completion within certain subjects in published social science (e.g., Hewson et al., 2016), and the over-representation of certain populations (e.g., Farrell and Petersen, 2010), now have a methodological basis rather than originating from the characteristics of the digital context.

Just as the digital context has broadened the populations that are accessible to researchers, it also requires us to re-evaluate the impact of how we access our sample. While using digital research tools to access participants and/or collect data necessitates that those participants (the sample) are present in one or more digital space, other factors also impact on how we assess the usefulness of digital research methods. The potential for anonymity afforded by the digital context can present us with clear challenges related to positively identifying our sample. Consequently, for any given research study, we need to be aware of which aspects of the sampling unit we need to be confident of, and which aspects are not important to the research project. Returning to the online gamers' example above, we would need to be confident that our participants were online gamers, however, would we need to know their age, gender, or personality, or any other individual characteristics to be confident of our findings?

While the anonymity of the digital context leads to clear issues related to the confident identification of the sample, issues occur when we consider the relationship between how we select our sample for inclusion in a study and the veracity of our findings. These sampling process issues are clearest with quantitative research where there is a relationship between the characteristics of the sampling process (i.e., probability versus non-probability) and the appropriateness of the analysis. The sampling process issues also relate back to how we define our population of interest, as a phenomenon of interest to social science researchers might be associated with individuals, groups (both formal and informal), and/or systems or interactions. Digital research methods can start with the group (e.g., online community), or interactions between individuals and/or groups, and drill down to individual behaviours within that community, which may then lead to translating that understanding to other groups.

Digital research is an emerging research discipline and thus currently, when compared to both established methodologies and also the social science phenomena researched, there is a limited published body of work. However, as the discipline grows and as the body of work increases, a justified critique may emerge questioning the early outputs in terms of the approach to sampling used. Early research conducted and published in the noughties contains very restricted justification of sampling or the issues surrounding the sample used. For example, the lack of completeness of social media samples is not mentioned, nor are the limits of representativeness with the use of Facebook samples (Tufekci, 2014). This period resembled the Gold Rush frontier mentality of early prospectors. The rush to find nuggets of golden insight from the exciting and new 'internet mediated' environment overshadowed consideration of rigour in the early exploratory digital research work. During this period of rapid exploration both Facebook and Twitter were over-used as sampling frames. As we can now just begin to look backwards and revisit this early body of work we can venture an opinion as to what extent there might be limits on the longer-term value of the work owing to some of the ad hoc early sampling undertaken.

The dynamism of the digital environment is no friend to those who crave stable, predictable sampling frames. Indeed this dynamism undercuts stable sampling as memberships of communities is fluid, friends and followers change, influencers' importance may wane overnight and achieving a classically desirable representative sample becomes more challenging. The established notions of using basic demographics to categorise and describe people's behaviours now play a lesser role in creating a sample, as these are frequently not the bases of interest to social science researchers pursuing digital research.

Researchers need to consider the advantages and disadvantages of using digital research methods in the context of the population they intend to research. Consequently, this chapter unpicks the issues that arise when considering who/what is, and how to access, the population of interest in or through digital research methods.

WHO/WHAT CAN BE ACCESSED ONLINE?

The distinction between digital as a phenomenon of research and as a method of research is particularly important when considering who (or what) to use as a basis for answering a research question or exploring the phenomenon we are interested in. When the digital domain is the phenomenon of interest, the population of interest and the sample will necessarily be available digitally (though it does not necessarily follow that the collection of data will be restricted to the digital environment). Here, the population, sample and sampling method can be defined and executed within the digital environment. In contrast, when the digital domain is used as a means to access information (i.e., digital as the research method), then the relevant population may be accessible both offline and digitally. Here it is important to consider additional issues such as sampling bias that might occur due to the sampling process if only a digital sample is selected. For example, a study of how mothers' exchange information as a way of enhancing their parenting skills would need to include multiple methods of information exchange and sampling would need to include mothers who chat face-to-face, mothers who chat on their mobile phones, and mothers who exchange information over community forums such as Mumsnet. Investigating this non-digital phenomenon using only the online sample might not provide a complete understanding of information exchange among mothers. That is, using only online community forums as the basis for the sample of interactions would be unlikely to be representative of all the behaviours engaged in by mothers' when exchanging information.

When looking at digital sampling, we need to consider the digital characteristics of the sample. Some characteristics of digital groups lead us towards drawing a sample from restricted sources while others require a broader based sampling strategy. Geographically dispersed (non-digital) populations would lead the researcher to use mail or telephone surveys, whereas a digitally dispersed population might be reached through advertising in/

on appropriate websites rather than a general call for participants on a social networking site. Both geographical and digital dispersion refer to the concentration of the populations at a particular (geographic or virtual) site. High concentrations at a small number of sites are easier to reach than dispersed populations. However, this does not mean that dispersed populations cannot be reached, only that more investment is required to reach the sample. In addition, unlike much non-digital research, which is generally geographically restricted, digital research needs to carefully consider the impact of time zones. This is particularly important when using synchronous data collection methods.

Potential populations of interest to digital researchers

The characteristics of the digital environment, including the dissolution of geographic boundaries and the potential for participants to either 'hide in plain sight' (through adopting different profiles) or remain anonymous, present both opportunities for access to previously difficult to reach populations as well as potential issues with how populations of interest are defined. People have always had a 'tendency to create homogenous groups and to affiliate with individuals who are similar in certain attributes, such as beliefs, education, social status and the like, (Granovetter, 1973 as cited in Colleoni, 2013: 126). These homophilic tendencies are apparent in physical space and have resulted in tools such as PRIZM and ACORN that geographically co-locate the habitats of people with shared characteristics. Interestingly, ACORN was predicated on the basis that neighbourhoods held people with shared identifiable common backgrounds, such as ethnicity-based areas within major cities, however, increasingly this is not the case as urban areas are increasingly multi-ethnic, multi-aged, etc. In physical space, homophilic tendencies tend to be restricted geographically by how far the potential members are willing to travel to take part in activities, or economically by whether individuals can afford to co-locate to share their interests. In the digital environment, where geographic boundaries have less meaning, there is a 'long tail' effect that impacts on the formation of homophilic groups (Anderson, 2008). These groups no longer have to physically be in the same space nor, beyond the ability to connect digitally, do economic barriers remain to accessing others with shared interests. So whether you are an 'ice-chewer' or a Christian 'furry' (both of which terms are deliberately obscure unless you are a member of these groups) you can connect with others who share your interests (Wolinsky, 2007). Consequently, the digital environment has opened up access to researchers to populations of interest that would not previously have been feasible.

The dissolution of geographic boundaries, however, does not mean that there are now no boundaries related to accessing specific populations of interest. While the digital environment is 24/7, that does not mean that anyone, anywhere can be accessed at any time by any method. Cultural barriers can still exist with accessing certain populations as there are differing norms related to whom one may be in contact with. More pragmatically, language barriers mean that while the technology may allow contact across the globe, that contact might not translate to being able to communicate with others (though images can sometimes be used to overcome this). Consequently, dispersed populations of interest demand that the researcher thoughtfully considers how their population of interest should be accessed to ensure that their sample fairly represents the population that is being researched.

The ability of individuals using the internet to maintain a separation between their physical and digital identities can present opportunities to, but also be problematic for, digital researchers in terms of sampling. Opportunities are presented as some vulnerable groups may feel safer communicating online. This safety may be both physical and psychological, for example, domestic abuse or forced marriage victims fear identification by those in power in those coercive relationships. Further examples include groups online who chose to engage or voice non-popular opinions, such as far right political views, which may make them vulnerable to attack through identification. However, even when the individual's identity is not fully hidden, the volume of information available digitally means that community participants feel safe hiding in plain sight, see, for example, Veer's (2013) research on 'pro-ana' (pro-anorexia nervosa) websites through which participants sharing their experiences in online communities gain both personal and community validation, leading to a feeling of acceptance.

Not being able to independently verify the identity of research participants or control who contributes raw data to a research project are examples of issues resulting from individuals being able to have multiple and often unverifiable identities in the digital environment. The former includes the ethical challenges associated with protecting vulnerable participants. (It should be noted that vulnerability takes many forms and vulnerabilities may not be known until research probes a particular phenomenon, see, for example, Iphofen (2011).) The labelling of a research participant as vulnerable as opposed to them self-identifying as such may have consequences for the participant and should be reflected on by both digital and non-digital researchers as a potential ethical issue. How, for instance, can digital researchers be certain that they are not including participants who are vulnerable if they cannot identify exactly who participants are? The lack of boundaries associated with verifying online identities may also impact on the assessment of whether a research participant is part of the population of interest in the research, especially if the digital environment is being used as a research tool and the population of interest is defined in non-digital terms. How, if participants are anonymous, can researchers assess whether they have a representative sample (in quantitative research) or a suitable range of participants (in qualitative research), if the only information they have about their participants is what they choose to say about themselves and what they do?

The potential to separate physical and digital identities can be potentially problematic for digital researchers. Whether this separation should be considered problematic, however, depends on the research objective and how the population of interest is defined. When the digital environment is used as a research tool to investigate a non-digital research question, then the researcher needs to ensure that the proportion of their total population which they can reach through digital means is, in substance, able to be representative of the whole population of interest. For instance, if the research question was concerned with how individuals transition from school to university in developed countries (a non-digital research question), then it is probably safe to assume that the vast majority of the population of interest had access to digital means of communication. However, if the research question was concerned with how low wage manual workers transition to retirement, then the researcher might find that not all of their population of interest had access to, or were comfortable using, digital communications; this would lead to potential bias if those with access were different in some important (to the research question) way from those without access.

When the research question is related to a digital phenomenon, then the whole population of interest is, almost by definition, engaging with that digital phenomenon. The question then becomes whether the research question focuses on the digital phenomenon itself – for example, do frequent and infrequent Twitter users tweet different content? – or on the producer of the digital content – for example, do the motivations of frequent and infrequent tweeters differ? With the former research question, the ability of the Twitter user to separate their physical and digital identities is unproblematic; with the latter research question, being able to explore non-digital aspects of tweeters might make it necessary to 'match up' a digital identity with the person it originated from.

The characteristics of the digital environment consequently require us to ask several questions when defining our population of interest; one of those questions is concerned with understanding the person, group, thing or interaction (research entity) that our research question leads us to focus on. How our research entity might manifest in the digital context is explored next.

WHAT IS THE FOCUS OF THE SAMPLING ENTITY?

When considering the digital research entity (the 'who' or the 'what') used to access information to answer a research question, the different broad research types – exploratory, explanatory, descriptive and causal – will lead to different approaches being used in relation to those research entities. With some types of research, generally descriptive and causal, the research design involves pre-specifying a particular research entity ('who' or 'what') prior to the data collection and there is little scope for flexibility. With other research types, generally exploratory or explanatory, the research design might specify one or more research entities as a starting point, but the focus remains fluid. So the research study may explore multiple perspectives (e.g., attitudinal/behavioural), or entities (e.g., individual/ group), in order to fully unpack the research question of concern. Nevertheless, when researching in a digital environment it is useful to consider what entity we intend to focus on, though at the beginning or our research, we might not necessarily know who or what will prove most helpful when addressing our research question. One of the things we ought to consider is that a characteristic of the digital environment means our expressed attitudes and our recorded behaviours are often more visible than we ourselves are. Owing to the increased accessibility of our digital traces, as researchers, we might find it easier to define our research entity in terms of those traces such as posts, tweets, navigation history, rather than in terms of the active producer(s) who left those traces.

Table 5.1 summarises the different ways we might think about the focus of our sampling. Thinking carefully about whether we are interested in the person (e.g., what are the characteristics of 'super-tweeters'?) or the traces a person leaves digitally (e.g., do 'super-tweeters' tweet differently than non-super-tweeters?), can help us determine where we can access information that will help us develop our research. Generally, research may focus on something, such as complaint behaviour or crowdsourcing, or someone, such as super-tweeters or activist groups. We might focus on singular instances and/or a number of those instances, for example, how individuals behave, or what is the outcome of a particular set of events. We can focus on collectives of our entity such as organisations, informal groups, or a series of events, and/or interactions between entities such as networks of people or organisations, or how multiple processes form systems and networks. Depending on our research approach, we might have to identify the research entity prior to collecting our data, or we might collect data from multiple different sources to gain different perspectives on our research question. Whether done at the research design stage, or as we access information about the question, we need to be open-minded about how we access data and consider particularly what and who will help us to understand the research question we are interested in. The discussion below considers the level of sampling more closely.

Table 5.1 Type and level of sampling entity

		Type/Form	
		Person/Who	**Things/What**
Level	Single	Individuals (e.g., blogger, consumer, patient)	Events (e.g., post, comment, hit)
	Collective	Groups (e.g., community, virtual organisation)	Systems (e.g., shopping visit, search behaviour)
	Interactions	Networks/relationships (e.g., social connections, communications)	Connections (e.g., memes, retweets)

Focusing on a single entity, individual or event

The separation of the single entity (the 'who' or the 'what') from the digital context can be problematic, especially when naturally occurring data are used in a study as in the case of archived chatroom data, as the action of focusing on a single entity rests on the assumption that the entity can be meaningfully separated from the collective in which it is embedded. The extent to which the separation of a single entity from its embedded collective context is problematic is largely dependent on the researcher's ontological and epistemological approach to research. For some research methods that have been translated into the digital environment, such as online questionnaires or digital interviews, the separation is less problematic than for others such as netnography. With other methods, such as online experiments, a single entity (in this case generally an individual) is considered an independent representative of the sample population. The digital design can minimise the need to identify individual participants through specific design elements, including randomly assigning and directing website visitors to different versions of a website.

Nevertheless, even with research methods where it is philosophically less problematic to decontextualise and isolate the single entity from its broader digital environment, there might still be practical problems to contend with when attempting to identify suitable events to study or individuals to use as participants. For example, exploring similarities and differences between the structure and content of blogs and vlogs using material from authors who have created both, we can isolate the structure and content of the material from its vehicles (the format and the platforms). In some cases it is easier to identify groups in the form of communities, organisations and discussions rather than relevant individuals/events that are part of those groups, such as the moderator, employee, or individual comments. So, in these cases to study single entities in the digital environment, the 'singular entity' may need to be picked out of the context in which it occurs. Take, for example, an individual who comments on videoblogs: the vlog needs to be identified prior to identifying the individual who posted comments related to that vlog. Alternatively, you might identify the individuals directly and then investigate their behaviour related to vlog comments.

Taking the perspective of descriptive researchers who might focus on describing individual behaviour, digital groups are akin to the sampling frame that is used to identify all possible members of the population of interest. However, while these digital groups may be where the researcher's population of interest can be found their fluid nature, prevailing usage norms, and governance structures, along with the ability of the individual to separate their physical and digital identity, often mean that the researcher cannot determine how many individuals are part of any given group (what is the total population?), or whether one (physical) individual appears across several groups (where/when does duplication in the sample occur?). This lack of what has been previously regarded by research methods authors as 'sample stability' may create challenges. These challenges include assessing the extent of generalisability and/or representativeness of the research findings if that is relevant to your research. As such, when we identify 'individuals' as our population of interest, we need to clearly define what we mean by an 'individual'. We should also be prepared to explain and make transparent our sampling decisions to enhance perceptions of credibility and rigour in the digital research and this may include far more detailed sampling process documentation.

While individuals can be examined through their digital presence, they do not actually exist wholly digitally. Rather what does exist digitally is a manifestation of the 'real' or 'staged' individual. Nevertheless, creating a dualism between the real/physical and the digital aspects of individuals would be a mistake, as the digital manifestations of the individual represent that individual's conscious or unconscious choices (Molesworth and Denegri-Knott, 2013). Consequently, their digital manifestations reflect different aspects of the individual:

- their geodemographic characteristics including personal and physical information such as physical image, location
- their attitudes, beliefs, opinions and values as reflected in the things they say, the valency of their comments and how they act digitally
- their external behaviours including search patterns, reading and viewing habits.

In terms of sampling, the digital environment contains the paradox that it can be much harder to connect any single digital event with a specific identifiable individual, while the co-mingling of data from multiple different events associated with a digital identity can make identifying a specific real/physical individual possible. Once that individual has been identified, the digital environment makes it much more straightforward to find out quite detailed and personal information about that individual. For example, attempts at large scale linkages of layers of digital data are underway in the UK and globally to produce Semantic Linked Data with the aim of producing a single distributed database that can produce what Google calls a Knowledge Graph – that is, a compilation of everything that is known about a person from these linked data. Similarly, commercial organisations such as large retailers are interested in producing a profile known as SCV – a 'Single Customer View' – which will provide a complete overview of one person as a customer. While these attempts to overlay data of an individual's digital behaviour are in the early stage of development and may appear peripheral to us as researchers, their existence suggests ethical concerns for digital researchers. First, it may be possible through the overlaying of an individual's anonymised data to identify that individual inadvertently. Second, this collage of data may contain several small inaccuracies, which could, when compiled together, result in the creation of an incorrect profile thus adversely impacting upon the 'truthfulness' of the sample, although what 'truth' is differs across research paradigms.

Putting aside the ethical issues for a moment, when sampling individuals we need to consider how the notion of the individual relates to our phenomenon of interest and research question. Specifically, we need to consider how we separate the individual them-selves from the manifestation of that individual (i.e., me as a person who uses a particular platform as distinct from my activities on that platform) to determine which is required for our purposes. That is, are we interested in the individual as an entity that is inde-pendent of, but present in, the digital environment or are we interested in individuals' manifestations in the digital environment?

Distinguishing exactly what our research questions are is necessary because, in the digi-tal environment, an individual may be present across multiple events or have multiple digital identities (multiple different accounts on a single social media site all with different 'personas' or several different email addresses). It is also possible that an individual digital identity is used by multiple individuals (multiple users of a single social media handle). Indeed, one individual can have multiple digital identities, some of which might be shared by others. Our ability to use pseudo-identities to create accounts (logins) in the digital envi-ronment can mean both that one account is used by multiple people (e.g., brand-based accounts) and that one individual can have multiple accounts on a single platform (e.g., a professional and a personal account). This, in and of itself, is not problematic. However, if we are not clear how our phenomenon of interest and how our research questions relate to our population of interest, and we have not clearly identified the 'individual' entity that makes up our sampling unit, then these complexities of the digital environment can cause problems later when we try to justify our sample and explain our results.

In the digital environment, it is necessary to decide whether our phenomenon requires us to understand the individual, or whether it is sufficient to understand individuals' manifestations in whatever form that constitutes. Table 5.2 clarifies the possibilities con-cerning whether the population of interest is the account or the individual(s) contributing to that account. So, as well as the issues surrounding our ability to associate a particular person with a particular account, thought needs to be undertaken regarding what/who exactly we consider our population to be.

Table 5.2 The potential overlap of users and accounts on a single digital platform

		Number of users per account/username	
		Single	**Multiple**
Number of accounts/ usernames per user	Single	'Physical/real' individual manifesting as a single 'digital identity'	'Physical/real' individuals subsumed within a group-based 'digital identity'
	Multiple	'Physical/real' individual manifesting as multiple 'digital identities'	'Physical/real' individuals subsumed within group-based 'digital identities'

If our research requires us to consider the 'real/physical' individual, then we will need to take steps to match-up that individual's digital manifestations. How we do this will depend on whether we are accessing information about the individual through non-digital research methods, digital research methods, or a combination of both. For example, Patterson (2013) investigated a digital phenomenon – the form, function and meaning of text messaging – by asking participants to keep a qualitative diary (not necessarily digital) related to their behaviours and thoughts concerning both incoming and outgoing texts. Here, the prevalence of the digital phenomenon (the text messaging) is so high in the general population that it is easy to identify suitable participants indirectly (not through the recruiting of participants via text messaging itself). Other researchers, however, might be interested in populations that are less common such as value derived by followers of world food blogs. While these researchers may well be interested in the individual behind the digital manifestation (the blog), they may have to start with the blog to identify their research participants. Once identified, the digital phenomenon may be investigated through digital or non-digital means, so in the example above, once the individuals have been identified, those followers could be researched through Skype interviews, or face-to-face interviews, and/or digital reflective diaries, and/or focus groups etc.

Some digital phenomena might require the researcher to access information from multiple digital data sources. For example, research questions that look at consumer search behaviours would need to account for consumers using multiple devices and accessing multiple websites, while research considering the impact of social media on mental health would be likely to include both social networking sites (Facebook, Twitter, LinkedIn, Instagram) as well as online communities focused on mental health. If digital phenomena that span multiple digital platforms are being investigated, then the researchers need some way of matching the physical individual across the platforms. This may be achieved through non-digital research methods such as the diaries used to explore texting (Patterson, 2013), non-digital methods translated into the digital environment (e.g., an online questionnaire), digital manifestations (e.g., tracing online navigation behaviour through tracking software looking at the online posts originating from logins using a common IP (Internet Protocol) address), or through a combination of them all. In research where online data collection is used, digital traces can be used to provide support for some participant details such as geographic location (e.g., looking at the IP address), and these digital traces can also provide the researcher with some basic indications concerning the quality of the data. For example, the length of time participants spent engaged in completing tasks associated with the research, either as discrete time periods (10 minutes to complete 20 questions of a longer questionnaire) or as the overall engagement (30 minutes to complete the online questionnaire, which was completed in three stages over two days). Nevertheless, it is important for the researcher to be aware of the technicalities of these digital traces. For example, using a virtual private network

(VPN) can change the geographic location of an IP address; if multiple individuals share devices then they will also share the IP address. (A VPN is a private network that allows individuals or groups to interact as though they were on a public network, but one that permits tighter security and management control; these are commonly used by organisations.) Furthermore, if a participant is multi-tasking then time spent completing an online study may not be a good indicator of the attention paid to it.

While researchers considering single entities might focus on an individual, they can also focus on an event or an instance of something. For example, research looking at website navigation behaviours might focus on website visitors (individuals), or it might focus on the website visit itself (event). Digital researchers focusing on the singular *thing* as the research entity (e.g., website visit, post, comment) often define the parameters of their data as they appear digitally. Consequently, defining the singular entity as a thing rather than an individual has the advantage of identifying the desired sampling unit as it is formed in the digital environment, that is, by what is visible digitally, rather than through reference to the physical. If the research problem being investigated can be investigated by referencing the digital manifestation as the sampling unit rather than through examining the producer of the digital manifestation (i.e., an individual), then it is likely to be easier for the researcher to connect their digital data with their research unit. Classifying the research entity in terms of a digital thing means that the researcher does not have to consider issues such as the potential separation between people's physical and digital identities, and ethical issues are likely to be more straightforward as the person behind the thing can remain anonymous. Research of this type might include, for example, looking at patterns in the spread of hashtags of social unrest in the Middle East or examining the characteristics of viral memes like the ice-bucket challenge.

Considering collectives: Groups and processes/systems

Mirroring research from traditions such as sociology, anthropology, organisational behaviour and others, digital researchers may be interested in investigating questions that focus on a collective rather than a single entity. When considering whether the collective rather than an individual is the focus of research, the researcher needs to think about when the phenomenon of interest can be confined within the individual entity. For example, both medical researchers and epidemiologists are interested in how diseases unfold. However, the medical researcher is primarily focused on how the disease develops within each infected individual and mitigating the consequences of the disease at an individual level, such as preventing HIV or managing diabetes. In contrast, the epidemiologist is interested in how a disease spreads through populations and managing the characteristics of the environment that impact on that diseases' dispersion, such as managing mosquitoes' habitats to slow the Zika virus, or restricting/monitoring air travel to prevent the spread of SARS. So, while both medical researchers and epidemiologists collect data from individuals, the medical researcher's focus is on the individual whereas the epidemiologist's focus is on the collective. Their explanations of the disease phenomenon will be at different levels, and their solutions for preventing/managing the disease may conflict with each other. For example, a medical response might flood an infected area with medical personnel to treat those infected, an epidemiological response might isolate an infected population to prevent new infections.

Digital researchers interested in a collective phenomenon need to understand how that collective is related to the digital sphere. Collectives of people (groups) might be confined to the digital environment, defined independently of the digital context, and/or span both digital and non-digital spheres. If a collective is confined to, and defined through, the digital space, then it may be impossible to explore that collective in a non-digital environment (see Geser, 2007). A collective that is defined independently of the digital context (patients of a particular disease) can be researched through digital methods. However, just as when single non-digital entities are researched using digital methods, we need to be conscious of any bias that might be introduced in our understanding of these non-digital collectives if we use digital methods to investigate them. For example, if a researcher only used digital methods to understand the efficacy of patient support groups, then the research findings could be biased as they would both ignore or under-represent those patients who had no, or restricted, access to the digital support groups; and overlook those support activities that do not occur online (house visits or other physical support), or occur differently online and offline (dissemination of up-to-date patient information). Some groups also span the digital and non-digital environments. Professional groups, for example, exist on social networking sites such as LinkedIn, and can have a digital presence through activities such as webinars, as well as having face-to-face networking events and other 'physical' activities. Consequently, the definition of the membership of a professional group may span both digital and non-digital contexts.

We refer to collectives of events as systems/processes. Events might not have a defined purpose, whereas systems and processes generally lead to an outcome (decision-making process), or are concerned with how different aspects of a whole fit together (e.g., economic system). While events and processes are related as a process is often a series of events, processes and systems are also related as systems are often made up of a number of different processes. So while events are relatively straightforward, for example, a website visit is clearly bounded within a particular digital space (the website) and time frame (i.e., the single visit), processes are more complex, for example, an information search, even one that is confined to digital sources, can span multiple digital formats (e.g., websites, mobile phone texts), and may take place over an extended time frame. Systems, as a group of processes, are even more complex, thus, a purchasing process is part of a larger consumption system that also includes the production process and the disposal process. While processes tend to be closed as they have an end-point, systems are more open. As such, when considering sampling entities we will focus on processes rather than systems.

The different events that make up processes can be digital or non-digital. The pervasive nature of digital tools in our daily existence means that, when looking at how multiple events fit into a process that produces an outcome relevant to the social sciences (i.e., relevant to the human condition), it is likely that both digital and non-digital elements will exist. For example, while travel booking systems are widespread and commonly used, you cannot actually arrive at a specific destination without interacting in the physical world. In the same way, many commercial websites have systems that facilitate all the stages of the buying process, but the (eventual) product purchased requires interaction with a physical entity or presence in a physical space (though notable exceptions do occur such as music, film and software downloads, and e-books, all of which can be purchased, delivered and 'consumed' digitally). As researchers investigating groups of events, we need to unpick which of the events in the system are digital, which are non-digital and which might be both. Doing this will enable us to ensure that we are uncovering the data relevant to our research questions.

In addition to how the collective entity is defined with respect to the digital environment, digital collectives are generally fluid with ill-defined boundaries and/or loosely defined criteria for inclusion. Digital collectives might, for example, be groups of individuals that are formally constituted and have a relatively stable (e.g., LinkedIn groups), or they might consist of multiple individuals that informally align themselves because they share a common interest (e.g., open source software developers). Groups of events might represent relatively unstructured processes/systems that are associated with transitional processes (e.g., grieving after the loss of a loved one), or more controlled processes/systems that are associated with everyday behaviours (e.g., selection and purchase of goods/services online). Groups can be relatively stable over time (e.g., commercial websites) or transitional in nature (e.g., disaster relief fundraising).

Focusing on interactions: Networks and connections

A key characteristic of the digital environment is its connectivity and the interactions that digital connectivity affords. Digital connectivity applies to people and is enacted through both words and images, using both directed (email, instant messaging) and less directed (social networking sites, blogs) communication. Connectivity between people can occur within a particular digital platform, but can also occur across platforms. Interactions may also, in the digital arena, include sharing others' messages via social media having altered or augmented the message. Interactions, for the purpose of sampling, are separate from the individuals that take part in those interactions, and when considered at the group level, connectivity/interactions can potentially become very complex as they can occur within the group, as well as across groups.

Digital connectivity also applies to things in terms of the ability of one device to be able to interact with another device, as in the internet of things (IoT), in addition to the digital connectivity that forms traces and patterns, which we as researchers can trace and try to make sense of. The digital connectivity and interactions create networks between individuals and groups but also between devices and platforms and these networks and connections can be visualised as research outputs. In many cases, as digital researchers, it is the interactions that connectivity allows that are the focus of our research. For example, a recent research study from one of the authors of this text was interested in understanding how people communicated the concept of innovation to each other through social media platforms. One stage of the research involved creating a semantic network map of the linked hashtag words used to denote the concept of innovation. This map illustrated how all the words used in the social media innovation content were linked together, the extent of those linkages and the strength of those linkages (Figure 1.2, Chapter 1).

Digital connectivity might be investigated through looking at the relationships between people or the connections between things. Research looking at connectivity/interactions might ask questions such as: How does the digital environment impact on the relationships between geographically dispersed social groups? What do these networks look like? For example, specific LinkedIn groups could be used as a sampling entity for researchers who may wish to research the extent of network reach within an industry or profession (see Quinton and Wilson, 2016). Alternatively, digital researchers might look at the choices that individuals and organisations make in relation to their connections, as entities can self-select which groups they wish to belong to on social networking sites or which feeds they wish to follow. Other questions might address more social aspects of digital interactions such as: What is cyberbullying? What is trolling? How does trust form in virtual organisations? How do digital interactions impact on an individual's health and wellbeing? For example, Veer's (2013) work looking at pro-ana website users, and Patterson's (2013) unpicking of texting, both explore the socio-cultural implications of digital connectivity through its impact on the relationships between people. Research projects that consider interactions might also be interested in how patients on forums communicate specific types of information, or the content of comments on different types of blogs. Research looking at interactions between things might ask questions such as: What are the relationships between different sources of news? How does money flow globally? Dorling (2016), for example, demonstrates how the global map can be redrawn by focusing on different population characteristics, while Hendricks and Denton (2010) have analysed Obama's use of social media during his 2008 presidential election campaign.

If a research question looks at digital interactions, then it implies the researcher needs to consider one or multiple aspects of that interaction as the sampling entity. Researchers may be interested in who are the main hub points in any network, the temporality of a network, the valence of the network, etc. Social network analysis (Scott 1991; Wellman and Berkowitz, 1988) and strength of ties and relationships in networks (Granovetter, 1983) now encompass social media networks (see the work of Klausen, 2015) not just of individuals but also of organisations. The traceability of digital data enables us as researchers to explore the connections between individuals and groups through their digital traces. Different aspects of a digital interaction can, nevertheless, be needed to explore particular research questions. These might include the starting point of the information exchange (the originator), the message itself, the medium through which the message is communicated, the receiver of the message, the response to the message and any further interactions between those parties along with new inter-actions and messages made by those who join in (the responses to the response), as well as all points between, such as how the message is impacted by the medium used in those interactions. A key question for digital researchers is whether the focus rests on who/what interacts, that is, the structure of digital communications, or on the con-tent/meaning of the interactions, that is, the semantics/semiotics of the interactions. Identifying exactly which part(s) of the interaction are of interest, and whether interest focuses on the interaction structure or meanings/consequences, will help us as research-ers identify our sampling entities.

Questions to ask when considering populations and sampling

Returning to the question at the beginning of this section of who/what can be accessed online, leads to four sets of sub-questions that we need to answer in order to identify a suitable population of interest and an appropriate sampling entity for our research.

First, we need to consider questions that are concerned with how populations of interest and sampling entities interact with the socio-cultural and digital context. These questions echo some of the more macro-issues identified in Chapter 2. For example, are national (geo-political) boundaries artificial when considering your research question? If so, what are the implications of this to the population of interest and with respect to the sampling entity? Are cultural (socio-ethnic) boundaries relevant to the population? If so, how? Are cultural (socio-ethnic) boundaries relevant to the sample? If so, why?

Second, questions concerned with the accessibility of samples in time and place/ space need to be addressed; again, these questions echo more general considera-tions raised in Chapter 2 concerning micro-factors that impact on digital research.

For example, are temporal boundaries more relevant than spatial boundaries when defining the population or the sampling entity? Which populations are accessible digitally? Is the whole population accessible digitally or will sampling digitally potentially introduce sampling bias? What types of populations (e.g., form and level) are more easily available digitally?

Third, questions related to the relationship between populations and sample entities (Table 5.1), and the research aims and objectives, need to be addressed. For example, what is the appropriate level at which to define the population? What is the appropriate level at which to define the sampling entity? What is the appropriate type/form of the population of interest? What is the appropriate type/form of the sampling entity? What are the opportunities and/or problems associated with using a different form (or level) of sampling entity in your research? How might digital populations/entities be biased when considering non-digital phenomena? (Based on how differences in samples impact on phenomena of interest – if at all.)

The final area that needs to be explored relates more to the practicalities of identifying digital populations and achieving sound samples. For instance, these include: How stable is the population of interest and the pool of sampling entities? Does it matter? What about population opportunities and issues surrounding access, anonymity, etc.? Do these change if the form of the sampling entity or its level is changed? How do samples relate to different data types? What is the relationship between data types/formats and samples? – anonymity and different sampling entities. How can my sample be reached (e.g., email, via forums, social media, banner advertising, through contacts/networks)?

MANAGING THE SAMPLING PROCESS

Once we have defined our population of interest and determined our sampling entities, we then have to work on how we will collect our data. Specifically, we have to decide on a suitable source of sample, and how to select each sampling entity from that source. The issues we, as digital researchers, need to consider here differ depending on whether we are looking to sample people (the 'who') or sample things (the 'what').

Digital sources of human samples are numerous. Researchers can source their participants digitally through, for example, partnering with relevant websites, placing online advertisements, engaging commercial online panels, posting requests on relevant social networking sites, and snowballing through online contacts. Researchers can also source participants for digital research through non-digital means, that is, source the sample offline to gain their participation in digital research (Patterson, 2013; Salmons, 2016). This section considers different aspects related to the digital sampling of human participants, before considering the automated sampling of things.

Sample source and researcher control

One of the major sampling differences between the use of digital tools to disseminate research instruments and non-digital research is the locus of control. The use of digital platforms to spread research instruments, and the recruitment of participants from more general digital platforms, requires us as researchers to loosen our control over the sample. If in non-digital research we choose to run a focus group, we will recruit a group of people who fit our criteria precisely. However, if we choose to gather data from an online community forum we cannot control who is active within that forum, who that forum is composed of, or indeed the interactions between community users. Consequently, the sample may not be stable, nor can we be confident that the pool of potential participants is clearly monitored. While researchers can identify a forum that has as its focus a specific issue or community of interest, such as the repopulation of birds of prey to rural Italy and ornithologists, we cannot control the individuals who may contribute to the interactions at the point in time in which we will be collecting our data. Indeed, newcomers to the community or fleeting comments made by irregular contributors may be included within our data, and these individuals may not be in our desired 'core' sample. However, it should be remembered that the extent to which 'irregular' contributions are an issue will depend on the research questions being asked and the underlying research paradigm.

Those critical of digital research often propose that it is hard to determine who is participating in the research and they cite the multiple identities possible for an individual as a reason to doubt the veracity of digital research outputs. We respond to this by questioning how is this different from a postal household survey, which could be answered, potentially, by one of several people. If those critics are also suggesting that one individual could be 'counted' multiple times or contribute several times over to a research project then, in the case of an online questionnaire, it can be designed to lockout more than one attempt from the same IP address. Furthermore, individuals who assume different identities or roles may actually be the population of interest in an ethnographic research study. One specific type of example of this would be the immersive world of virtual reality gaming such as Occulus Rift.

Two of the core characteristics of digital connectivity, reach and immediacy, can present additional challenges when sampling in the digital environment. While the opportunity to reach larger numbers of dispersed individuals and groups has never been higher, the instantaneous nature of digital formats may mean that those within the desired sampling frame may receive information, online questionnaires and recruitment messages on social media at local times, which are less likely to be effective in terms of response and interaction. The issue of timing can, to a certain extent, be overcome through the scheduling of Twitter requests, research blogs, etc. However, when the research requires synchronous interaction between disparate individuals or groups and involves Skype interviews, Google hangouts and similar digital communication tools, decisions will have to be made as to which of the participants will need to be inconvenienced and to what extent that may affect the sample.

Bearing these issues in mind, the specific type of digital samples can also present opportunities and challenges to the digital researcher. Digital samples can be recruited directly from participants online who are reached through digital advertising and/or by using participant platforms (unpaid and paid). Each of these is discussed below.

Direct recruitment of unpaid participants

Unpaid participant (i.e., volunteer) samples are common in digital research and can be accessed through the use of participant recruitment advertisements on different digital platforms; for example, social networks, blogs and online community groups. Recruitment for volunteers via digital advertising is useful in extending the reach of the research study, especially with geographically distant or disbursed populations of interest. Participants recruited in this way may also be more engaged with the research activity. However, if you wish to establish a probability sample from general digital advertising it can be extremely difficult as we are rarely able to identify the population of interest. As such, if the research question calls for a probability sample (as is sometimes the case in descriptive research) then recruiting via digital advertising may be inadvisable.

Digital samples can introduce bias into the research if there are differences between the population of interest and the proportion of that population available through digital sampling. The potential lack of representativeness of a volunteer sample should be considered in relation to the general type of research being conducted as well as the specific research questions asked. For example, if the research is causal, and volunteers are randomly assigned to an experimental group, then any sampling quirks should be minimised by the research design. However, if the research is descriptive, then using a volunteer sample may have serious consequences for the generalisability of the research results. One may well argue here that generalisability is not important to the study and its objectives and, if so, then a volunteer sample may well be appropriate. Inherent biases may or may not be present within volunteers, such as deeply held beliefs within the online gaming community or right to die advocates. Volunteer samples may have a greater tendency to demonstrate and support altruistic behaviour, and these could affect the findings of a research study. Researcher scepticism of research participant motivation can be overblown and while we might over recruit those people with strongly held views at polar ends of any spectrum, it is worth reflecting that most individuals do not have sinister motives when it comes to research participation. Indeed, as digital researchers, we should be embracing communities rather than questioning their members' motives. Crowdsourcing of research participants can also be considered as a contemporary snowballing technique to request volunteers who wish to actively engage in a research study. The accessing of these groups is likely to occur through digital communities of interest such as Facebook groups.

Some of the issues associated with the representativeness of volunteer samples can be mitigated by the sampling process. These measures include consideration of where, and when, volunteers are recruited, and the filtering of those that volunteer. Careful selection across a variety of relevant websites (e.g., online communities, commercial websites, blogs) where a call for participants is placed, and consideration of the timing (e.g., day of the week, time of the day) or trigger (e.g., in response to a relevant search, after completion of a purchase) of that digital advertisement appearing to potential participants, can help broaden the digital reach for participants – both in terms of ensuring that participants are likely to be members of the population of interest and that they are broadly representative of the population of interest that can be found digitally. In addition, the judicious placement of recruitment information on specific digital environments will help filter non-desired potential volunteer participants (Hewson et al., 2016). Indeed, if a portion of the population of interest is known to be less likely to be found digitally, then the sampling sources can be skewed towards where/when that under-represented portion of the population is likely to be found. For example, if older participants are less likely to be found online, then the sampling plan can include elements that deliberately focus on finding that element of the population of interest, such as direct offline recruitment from older person lunch clubs. Filtering questions can be also used to determine if the participant recruited fits the population of interest. For instance, asking potential participants 'How often do you use public transport?' rather than 'How often do you take the bus?' is less likely to be subject to the participant giving the answer they believe is 'right'. Thus, while the anonymity afforded by the digital environment might prevent us from evaluating some of the characteristics of our participants, it does not prevent us from asking questions that help us to understand those characteristics we need to know about.

Participant recruitment platforms

Obtaining a digital sample via online marketplaces (including participant recruitment platforms) is the digital equivalent of outsourcing participant recruitment to a contractor. In the non-digital environment, there is a well-established and regulated marketplace where participant recruitment can be outsourced. However, unlike offline panel providers that are generally regulated via bodies such as the European Society of Market Research (ESOMAR) and the Market Research Society (MRS), online marketplaces are not routinely scrutinised by external regulators. There are numerous 'marketplaces' online that allow individuals and companies to outsource tasks they wish completed. Participation in a research study could be defined as such a task. These marketplaces range from general websites where any task can be posted, through to more specific marketplaces such as CrowdSource that cater to people who have work for freelance editors and writers, to websites that specifically link researchers with online participants for a range of academic studies (e.g., prolific.com, findparticipants.com) or for studies in a particular discipline such as social psychology experiments, or low risk medical research. These websites provide a potentially valuable resource for digital researchers. However, as they are not subject to external oversight, it falls to us, as researchers, to exercise due diligence.

As obtaining digital (and non-digital) research participants becomes more difficult, these participant platforms (both paid and unpaid) are increasingly being used by digital researchers. There is no denying that the use of participant platforms can be effective as an approach to obtain a digital sample. However, the type of participant platform, whether participants are paid or not, and the underlying purpose of the platform needs careful scrutiny. As such, we need to consider two main questions before optioning to use a participant platform for our digital research. First, what is your institution's or university's policy with regard to the use of participant platforms for sample recruitment? If there is approval for their use, what are the criteria used to select its suitability? Second, what can be determined about the sampling frame on these platforms; are they a fair reflection of your population of interest or a distortion? For example, a non-commercially founded platform, that originates from a recognised university purely designed to facilitate research and endorsed by external research bodies such as www.callforparticipants.com may be preferable over the plethora of commercial platforms offering to solve your research recruitment challenges for a fee. Suggestions to help assess the suitability of a recruitment platform can be found in Table 5.3.

Table 5.3 Selection criteria for participant recruitment platforms for digital research

Sample quality criteria

- The suitability of the pool of registered potential participants
- The endorsement by external research bodies such as ESRC, RCUK, ESOMAR and BSI (British Standards Institution) to confirm compliance with ethical research policies
- The openness of access to previous studies and results, and live studies

Ethics-related criteria

- Disclosure of organisation ownership
- Disclosure of data storage and ownership and compliance with national and or international data protection regulations
- Statement of measures of quality control of both studies and participants
- Statement as to the type and level of incentives, if any, offered to participants
- Statement as to the type and level of referral incentive offered to grow pool of participants

Illustrative exemplar of participant platforms

An illustration of the importance of understanding the nuances of digital research and in particular sampling and ethics can be highlighted through examining the use of Mechanical Turk or Mturk as it is referred to. Mturk is an Amazon owned 'distributed workforce service' or crowdsourced data gathering platform, which has been frequently used for research studies across many subject areas such as social sciences, psychology, consumer studies, economics and medicine. Mturk functions on the basis that it connects those who wish to work or their employers anywhere in the world with tasks that can be completed online, very often online surveys and online experiments. Small payments are made to the 'Turkers' or workers who complete the tasks. The average payment is approximately $3 per hour (at the time of writing in 2016) but there is a lack of transparency in this owing to the piece payment system.

Several sampling issues are raised by this type of paid for participant platform. First, Turkers are frequently not one time participants in a single academic study. Second, sample criteria are answered to meet the profile required regardless of the real profile of the Turkers. Third, routine answering can and does occur without consideration of the questions as the Turkers become professional in responding to the questions/experiments set. In addition, important research ethics issues come to light. In developing economies there is frequently organised third party group involvement whereby payment goes to an intermediary company who then uses its workers to complete the tasks as a requirement of their employment for tiny financial gain. These people are not necessarily 'willing' or able to give 'informed consent' to participate in the research but Mturk and their equivalents are their main source of income. Worth noting is the increasing level of scrutiny now applied to research prepared for publication using Mturk data and several university research ethics boards in countries such as the USA, Australia and Canada no longer approve its use. Research grant bidding that incorporates this type of sampling may also be declined. Interestingly a notable marketing academic professor, Utpal Dholakia, who has published multiple studies using Mturk, changed his opinion of the mechanism after experiencing life as a Turker as a self-experiment. The new perspective he gained included the decision to use Mturk only for pre-testing studies and for exploratory research (Dholakia, 2015), suggestions which many researchers would find highly questionable.

Automated sampling

Within digital research, the sample may be influenced by technologies over which we as researchers have little or no control. The use of technology in research may impact upon sampling, for example: The use of Android or Apple mobile phones and their accompanying range of apps may impact the sample unit; or the range of beacons when conducting research relating to GPS locations may impact the completeness of a sample. The mapping of London underground users through Oyster card holders tagging in and out of stations may provide an incomplete picture of usage as some travellers may not use an Oyster card, thus the data are incomplete. Digital technologies also filter the sample that a researcher may receive, for example, the algorithms used by Google to collect and analyse internet searches are not known to researchers, so the data available may be pre-screened. The downloading of Twitter streams frequently results in incomplete collation of the Twitter firehose. These limitations of sampling should be acknowledged but should not deter researchers if the research question identifies that these types of sampling are necessary. Creative thinking about how to comple-ment the sample may be necessary. A further twist on automated sampling is the potential for automated respondents or participants. Artificial intelligence includes the use of Bots that are now able to interpret and answer online questionnaires, complete short phone interviews, and 'act' as informed respondents/participants; this advance in interactivity in research can thus muddy the water further in terms of obtaining a relevant sample.

CO-PRODUCTION AND CO-CREATION OF RESEARCH THROUGH A SAMPLE

The ability to share and augment digital artefacts such as text messages, photos, etc. has led to the greater interaction between individuals and groups. For example, crowdsourcing of new product ideas by commercial organisations has become increasingly common, such as new flavours of confectionery, with organisations becoming more customer focused (see for example C-space, www.cspace.com/). The involvement of people in the creative pro-cesses can be and is being transferred to the digital research environment. As a researcher you may wish to involve your sample in the creation of the questions asked in an online survey, and you may find insight from asking for feedback from a community modera-tor on how to improve your interactions with their members so as to elicit richer data. Furthermore, the co-production of research can include asking individuals to forward research instruments, such as email surveys, or to help recruit participants for a Skype group interview. There is evidence to suggest that a greater sense of involvement with a research project, including the design of the research and then the dissemination of the results, can encourage a deeper level of insight to be gained as those involved feel respon-sible for the outcome of the project (Burns et al., 2014; Caretta, 2015; Nierse et al., 2012).

If the nature of your research question encourages a greater level of involvement from your sample then you will need to consider the practical implications of this. The choice of your sample becomes of increased importance as these people are giving more than their focused contribution and responses to your questions. Your research design may take longer as there will be more discussion and the piloting may require several itera-tive stages. The greater involvement of others in the co-production of your research may include funding bodies or advisory panels that require you to include certain questions or formats in your research instrument. While the involvement of others can be seen as helpful it also requires the loosening of control of the project from the researcher. Other resource implications, beyond design time, include the potential for increased costs associated with the research project.

Data categorised as co-produced and co-created

The adoption of digital technologies by society has facilitated the potential greater involvement of people in research. If we take a simplified linear research process as an illustrative example, we can see how much more involved people can be in all aspects of research.

- Draft research ideas and thinking of potential research questions can be opened out to forums for comment, indeed the activity or interactions of online communities may spark the research question. Comments and scoping of the research project can now be gained quickly and from a wider range of actors than previously possible.
- The design of the data collection tools, be they online surveys, interview questions, or experiments can now be shared, piloted and developed by groups of individuals; this may improve the validity and reliability of the data collected.
- Participation in the research itself can be facilitated through digital recruitment and social media shout outs to gain a sufficient and appropriate sample.
- The analysis of the collected data can be undertaken, for some projects, by geographi-cally remote individuals, accessing data stored in the cloud.
- Dissemination of the results of a research project can be enhanced through individuals and organisations using their social media networks to promote findings and the implica-tions of those findings to a far wider audience than in the pre-digital environment.

The empowerment of people through digital technologies to become active in research, or as Marres (2012) describes it, 'the redistribution of research', provides the opportunity for us as researchers to consider what our role is as we reconsider the contribution that can be made by research participants. So participants can now take a more active role in research, and become co-producers, through this re-distribution afforded by the digitalisation of society. As co-creators of research, participants share ownership of and responsibility for the resulting research data. There exists ongoing academic contention over the differ-ences between co-production and co-creation (for a full explanation see Vargo and Lusch, 2008; Vargo et al., 2008) and whether any distinction is in fact necessary at all. For the purpose of this book we define co-production as the combining of researcher and research participant effort in the processes involved in the development, design and execution of research whereas co-creation is considered as the value created as a result of co-production. Research data that are co-produced may require explicit acknowledgement of those participants who have been involved in the data production; we would suggest that this is good practice and should be encouraged wherever possible on submitted theses, published papers and research project websites to recognise the contribution of others.

SUMMARY

This chapter has provided multiple different ways to consider data sources when conducting digital research and has clearly outlined the who, and the what, that might be accessed through digital research. Explicit linkages have been made to populations and

Table 5.4 Key considerations for justifying a digital sampling strategy

Step	Questions
Identify your population	1) Clearly define the phenomenon that is relevant to your research question, including whether it is a digital phenomenon.
	2) Based on the literature concerning the phenomenon itself, or closely related phenomenon, define your population. If the resulting population is too broad, restrict it using:
	a) criteria derived from the literature and your research question
	b) temporal constraints – e.g., recency or duration.
Identify your sampling entity	3) Consider how your phenomenon occurs.
	a) Is the phenomenon objective (i.e., behaviour) or more subjective (e.g., attitude), or can it be both? If there are multiple possibilities, revisit your research question (and the literature) to identify the most appropriate combination to consider.
	b) Who or what 'holds' the phenomenon – individual, interaction, group, process, event? If there are multiple possibilities, revisit your research question (and the literature) to identify the most appropriate combination to consider.
	4) Who or what manifest the phenomenon (or can report on those manifestations) as you have defined them?
	a) Consider both digital and non-digital possibilities. If there are multiple possibilities, revisit your research question (and the literature) to identify the most appropriate combination to consider.
Select a sample	5) Where can you access the occurrences of the phenomenon as you have described them?
	6) For your research question, do you need to be able to draw a probability sample?
	a) If so, have you identified the manifestations of the phenomenon in such a way as to allow this to happen?
	b) If not, how are you going to select your sampling units?
	7) For your research question, what is an appropriate number of occurrences of the phenomenon you need to be able to answer your research question?

sampling as they relate to digital research. In addition, this chapter has demonstrated that populations of interest, sampling and the sampling process, whether as part of the investigation of the digital phenomenon, or when considered as one part of the research design in the digital environment, are perceived as differing in several ways from what is already known about sampling. While the digital environment presents many opportunities to reach new samples because of characteristics such as anonymity, reduced cost and geographic spread, it also presents challenges related to the sampling. Table 5.4 provides a set of key considerations to reflect on issues related to digital data sources.

The 3Es

Consideration of digital data sources brings to the fore a number of issues related to ethics, expectations and expertise. When considering the ethical issues related to digital data sources, we have to return to the underlying principle of 'doing no harm' and how that may be achieved. If we consider what makes a participant vulnerable to harm, we have to consider multiple factors. Physical harm might come about because the research exposes a participant to danger through the views they express or the behaviour they reveal. However, if the digital environment protects the anonymity of the participant, such that even the researcher is unable to identify the individuals that take part, then using a digital data source might be more protective of participants than a non-digital means of collecting the data. For example, in research looking at the impact of living in high stress environments (e.g., domestic abuse victims, gang members) participants might be safer from physical harm if research is done digitally. Those individuals or groups susceptible to social harm might also benefit from the anonymity afforded by the digital environment as it can provide a protective barrier (e.g., research into views on abortion or euthanasia might be easier to express digitally). Protecting participants from psychological harm, however, may be more difficult in the digital environment. The cues that can be picked up through non-verbal communication in face-to-face interviews, for example, are not available when conversing with a participant through many digital platforms. Consequently, when researchers are considering the ethics of digital data sources, one key point they will need to consider is what 'type' of harm makes potential participants vulnerable and whether the characteristics of the digital environment mitigate or exaggerate the identified vulnerability.

The expertise we develop about populations, samples and sampling from established social science research training focuses on issues such as representativeness, sampling for differences, sampling procedures (strengths and weaknesses, impact on analysis), and sample size. When using established research methods, it is unlikely that we will encounter problems associated with, for example, too much data, unplanned research participants, non-human participants, or many of the issues that can arise with digital data sources. As such, we need to develop a different set of skills to enable us to use digital data sources effectively. For example, if we want to restrict survey participants to one completed questionnaire, we might consider restricting participation by IP address, or creating unique electronic invitations to that survey that can only be used from one IP address. However, if we undertake this type of control, then we need to understand, for example, how many potential participants might share an IP address, or consider whether potential participants might complete a single survey over time from different locations (and as such, potentially different IP addresses). Overall, given the differences between the non-digital and digital environments, we have to question how the expertise derived from established methods can translate into the methods that are emerging in the digital context.

Our expectations of the digital environment as a repository of almost unlimited data are also challenged by the reality of the digital context. Barriers to accessing data sources exist at multiple levels. Some of these barriers are technical, such as the ability to scrape data from websites, and can be overcome by developing our skills and expertise. However, other barriers exist in the form of proprietary ownership of the repository where the data are held, and/or restricted access to that data. Websites, whether commercial or not, whether due to legal reasons or because of promises they have made to their users (in the terms and conditions), do not allow unrestricted access to their data. Twitter does not allow researchers to freely sample its system, but rather provides authorised researchers with a sample based on undisclosed selection criteria. Access might also be restricted due to login requirements for particular websites and the associated ethical questions concerning whether data produced on platforms requiring users to login are public/private (even ignoring the questions posed elsewhere in this book concerning when data are public/private). Consequently, any naïve expectations we might hold concerning exploiting the data storage capacity of the digital environment for research can quickly be destroyed by the vested interests that control much of that data, and the reality of digital research.

Questions

1. Can you identify your sample for your digital research and how does it relate to your research question?
2. Does your sample focus on people or events and how will this impact on your data?
3. What, if any, specific digital challenges does your sample present?
4. How might you access any new individuals or groups that you wish to interact with digitally in your research that were not previously possible?

FURTHER READING

Bryman, A. (2015). *Social Research Methods* (5th edn). Oxford: Oxford University Press.

Bryman, A. and Bell, E. (2015). *Business Research Methods* (4th edn). Oxford: Oxford University Press.

Sloan, L. and Quuan-Haase, A. (2017). *The Sage Handbook of Social Media Research Methods*. London: Sage.

REFERENCES

Anderson, C. (2008). *The Long Tail: Why the Future of Business Is Selling Less of More*. New York: Hachette Books.

Burns, D., Hyde, P., Killett, A., Poland, F. and Gray, R. (2014). Participatory organizational research: Examining voice in the co-production of knowledge. *British Journal of Management, 25* (1), 133–144.

Caretta, M.A. (2015). Situated knowledge in cross-cultural, cross-language research: A collaborative reflexive analysis of researcher, assistant and participant subjectivities. *Qualitative Research, 15* (4), 489–505.

Carrigan, M. (2014). *The Social Life of Methods*. Available from: https://markcarrigan. net/2014/11/02/the-social-life-of-methods/ (accessed 14 April 2017).

Colleoni, E. (2013). New forms of digital marketing research. In R.W. Belk and R. Llamas (eds), *The Routledge Companion to Digital Consumption*. Abingdon: Routledge, pp. 124–134.

Davies, H., Eynon, R. and Wilkin, S. (2017). Neoliberal gremlins? How a scheme to help disadvantaged young people thrive online fell short of its ambitions. *Information, Communication & Society*, 1–16.

Dholakia, U. (2015). My experience as an Amazon Mechanical Turk (MTurk) Worker. Personal blog available from: www.linkedin.com/pulse/my-experience-amazon-mechanical-turk-mturk-worker-utpal-dholakia (accessed 19 September 2017).

Dorling, D. (2016). Maps that show us who we are (not just where we are). TEDxExeter. Available from: www.ted.com/talks/danny_dorling_maps_that_show_us_who_we_are_not_just_where_we_are (accessed 19 September 2017).

Farrell, D. and Petersen, J.C. (2010). The growth of internet research methods and the reluctant sociologist. *Sociological Inquiry, 80*, 114–125.

Geser, H. (2007). A very real virtual society: Some macrosociological reflections on 'Second Life'. Sociology in Switzerland: Towards Cybersociety and Vireal Social Relations. Available from: http://socio.ch/intcom/t_hgeser18.htm (accessed 19 September 2017).

Granovetter, M. (1983). The strength of weak ties: A network theory revisited. *Sociological Theory, 1*: 201–233.

Hendricks, J.A. and Denton, R.E. (Jr.) (2010). *Communicator-in-Chief: How Barack Obama Used New Media Technology to Win the White House*. Lanham, MD: Lexington Books.

Hewson, C., Vogel, C. and Laurent, D. (2016). *Internet Research Methods* (2nd edn). London: Sage.

Iphofen, R. (2011). *Ethical Decision Making in Social Research*. New York: Palgrave.

Jankowski, N.W. and van Selm, M. (2005). Epilogue: Methodological concerns and innovations in internet research. In C. Hine (ed.), *Virtual Methods: Issues in Social Science on the Internet*. Oxford: Berg, pp. 199–208.

Klausen, J. (2015). Tweeting the Jihad: Social media networks of Western foreign fighters in Syria and Iraq. *Studies in Conflict & Terrorism, 38* (1), 1–22.

Marres, N. (2012). The redistribution of methods: On intervention in digital social research, broadly conceived. *The Sociological Review, 60* (51), 139–165.

Molesworth, M. and Denegri-Knott, J. (2013). Digital virtual consumption as a transformative space. In R.W. Belk and R. Llamas (eds), *The Routledge Companion to Digital Consumption*. Abingdon: Routledge, pp. 223–234.

Nichols, W. (2013). Advertising analytics 2.0. *Harvard Business Review*, March. Available from: https://hbr.org/2013/03/advertising-analytics-20 (accessed 16 April 2017).

Nierse, C.J., Schipper, K., van Zadelhoff, E., van de Griendt, J. and Abma, T.A. (2012). Collaboration and co-ownership in research: Dynamics and dialogues between patient research partners and professional researchers in a research team. *Health Expectations, 15* (3), 242–254.

Patterson, A. (2013). Digital youth, mobile phones and text messaging: Assessing the profound impact of a technological afterthought. In R.W. Belk and R. Llamas (eds), *The Routledge Companion to Digital Consumption*. Abingdon: Routledge, pp. 83–92.

Quinton, S. and Wilson, D. (2016). Tensions and ties in social media networks: Towards a model of understanding business relationship development and performance enhancement through the use of LinkedIn. *Industrial Marketing Management, 54*, 15–24.

Salim, A. (2017). Data, old-school metrics and walled gardens: Measuring ROI can be a tricky business. Available from: www.thedrum.com/news/2017/01/30/data-old-school-metrics-and-walled-gardens-measuring-roi-can-be-tricky-business (accessed 16 April 2017).

Salmons, J. (2016). *Doing Qualitative Research Online*. Thousand Oaks, CA: Sage.

Scott, J. (1991). *Social Network Analysis: A Handbook*. Thousand Oaks, CA: Sage.

Tufekci, Z. (2014). Big questions for social media big data: Representativeness, validity and other methodological pitfalls. In *ICWSM '14: Proceedings of the 8th International AAAI Conference on Weblogs and Social Media*. Available from: www.aaai.org/Press/Proceedings/icwsm14.php (accessed 19 September 2017).

Vargo, S.L. and Lusch, R.F. (2008). Service-dominant logic: Continuing the evolution. *Journal of the Academy of Marketing Science, 36* (1), 1–10.

Vargo, S.L., Maglio, P.P. and Akaka, M.A. (2008). On value and value co-creation: A service systems and service logic perspective. *European Management Journal, 26* (3), 145–152.

Veer, E. (2013). Virtually 'secret' lives in 'hidden' communities. In R.W. Belk and R. Llamas (eds), *The Routledge Companion to Digital Consumption*. Abingdon: Routledge, pp. 148–158.

Wellman, B. and Berkowitz, S.D. (1988). *Social Structures: A Network Approach. Structural Analysis in the Social Sciences*. Cambridge: Cambridge University Press.

Wolinsky, R. (2007). WTF!?: The 8 strangest communities on the web. Cracked, 27 July. Available from: www.cracked.com/article_15250_wtf21-8-strangest-communities-web.html (accessed 19 September 2017).

Xun, J. and Reynolds, J.J. (2010). Applying netnography to market research: The case of the online forum. *Journal of Targeting, Measurement and Analysis for Marketing, 18* (1), 17–31.

6

RESEARCH PROCESSES AND THE HUMAN/ TECHNOLOGY INTERFACE

In this chapter we will:

- explore what is meant by active and passive in relation to digital research
- identify the opportunities and challenges in active digital data collection
- identify the opportunities and challenges surrounding passive digital data collection
- outline some of the arguments surrounding covert or disclosed data collection
- discuss the impact of automation on research design and analysis
- explore issues surrounding 'big data'
- provide insight into data sufficiency and data saturation
- explain aspects of validity, reliability and triangulation in relation to digital research.

INTRODUCTION

The preceding chapters have outlined and discussed the what (data), the when (temporality), and the who/what (sample entities) of digital research. In this chapter our focus turns to the 'how' of digital research, that is, the digital processes that may constitute new phenomena and/or be used as part of digital research. This chapter considers both active and passive modes of data collection, and the automation of data and the implications arising from automation for digital researchers. The emergence of 'big data' and the challenges for researchers that accompany big data are outlined and reflections are made as to the evaluation of digital research data to enhance the quality of digital research.

Data collection in the digital environment can be active or passive. With active data collection using methods such as pop-up surveys, warranty registrations, health app monitoring, the patient/citizen/consumer is aware that data are being collected. Digital technologies also provide opportunities for the hidden collection of data where the patient/citizen/consumer is passive (e.g., CCTV, GPS location); the digital data user is neither actively involved nor consciously aware of data being collected. The use of both passive and active data collection will be considered and examples outlined to provide some broad guidance for using both types of data collection. The contentious issues of disclosure and covert data collection will also be discussed with suggestions made for how to defend the research design choices needed where these issues may arise. This book does not intend to provide a definitive response to the contentious issue of disclosed/covert data collection but it will highlight the core questions that researchers should consider before making decisions concerning researcher visibility in data collection.

The automation of data has been facilitated by digital technology innovations and includes algorithms, processes of data capture and analysis software. These automations are digital phenomena that can be explored in their own right as well as potential innovations in research methods. It should be noted that when we speak of research design we are taking into consideration the whole life cycle of the research project. From the starting focal point of the research question, it is the research design that enables data to be collected, analysed and results disseminated. Commercial partners may enable access to much larger quantities of data and support the research through the use of proprietary analytical tools. However, at the time of writing this text it is perfectly possible to produce a doctoral thesis or internationally ranked academic journal article without commercial partnership or access to costly digital tools, although as digital research becomes more technical this may not be the case in years to come.

This chapter also considers 'big data'. The technology and analysis tools associated with big data, rather than its mythology (boyd and Crawford, 2012), have become increasingly spoken about in the social sciences and other areas of research. A common question asked across different research projects, at different levels (Masters' degrees, PhD studies or grant funded research), and across different social science disciplines, concerns data sufficiency and 'how much is enough'. We will provide reflections on this, and other phenomenological and methodological issues with big data, in light of the immense quantity of digital data now being collected and archived, partially for research purposes.

Throughout this chapter consideration will be given to digital data quality (e.g., validity, reliability and triangulation), irrespective of whether the research may be conceptualised and implemented as a deductive or inductive study.

ACTIVE OR PASSIVE DIGITAL RESEARCH

Researchers, participants and data in digital research design can be considered along a continuum related to the degree of available conscious choice that can be exercised, and/or the extent to which actions taken change what is happening in the environment: from active (i.e., related to choice or connected with a specific purpose) to passive (i.e., not knowingly impacting on what would occur anyway and/or not acting through choice). As researchers we can be more passive by confining our activity to observing digital phenomena to see what occurs (akin to an inductive approach), or we can actively engage with digital phenomena by, for example, exploring them through competing perspectives, or asking specific research questions (akin to a deductive approach). Participants in digital research can also be active in different ways. Participants may exert themselves by knowingly choosing to engage in research (active participation) or participation may occur without their knowledge if they are unknowingly included in a digital research project (passive participation), for example, due to their activity on a particular website. Data can also be considered active or passive. With data the division between active and passive is not focused on exerting conscious effort (as data are inanimate), but is about whether the data are 'naturally' occurring within the digital environment. If the data are 'naturally occurring', such as website navigation data, these are passive data. If, however, the data are specifically collected as a result of some intervention in the digital environment, these are active data, such as data from an online survey questionnaire or results from a live experiment.

These three elements of digital research design (researcher, participant and data) are presented below in Table 6.1 as dichotomies for simplicity. However, as will be seen as we progress through this chapter, in digital research we cannot neatly place researchers, participants and/or data into either the active or passive 'box'. Nevertheless, thinking about digital research design in terms of the active/passive nature of these three elements helps us to identify the opportunities and challenges available when researching digital

Table 6.1 The active and passive elements in digital research

	Active	Passive
Researcher	Has specific ideas or concepts or constructs to identify, investigate or measure	Observing to see what occurs, without pre-set objectives, the research question emerges from what is collected
Participant	• Knowingly exerts a conscious effort • Transparency of research • Consent can be gained, information can be distributed • Participant may retain the right to withdraw • Participant may impact on what is researched and how it is researched • Participant may change behaviour (including 'attitudes' as expressed through digital manifestations)	• No conscious effort exerted by the participant • Research opaque to participant • Consent cannot be gained, information cannot be distributed • Participant cannot provide clarifying information or withdraw from the research • Participant is 'done unto', may be unwilling to be studied • Participant behaviour (or expressed attitudes) unaffected by research
Data	• Visible/transparent data collection process • Includes both self-reported behavioural and attitudinal data • Occurs in the particular form only as a result of a specific interaction (e.g., mobile phone customer service pop-up survey, warranty registration) • May be subject to response-bias/demand characteristics • Data set collected can be tailored to specific research requirements • Data collected are determined by and restricted to clear research requirements	• Hidden/opaque (aspects of) data collection process • Includes both behavioural and (naturally expressed) attitudinal data • Occurs naturally without a specific intervention taking place (e.g., GPS location, posts on social media sites) • Unlikely to be subject to response-bias/demand characteristics • Data set collected likely to include a large number of variables that are superfluous to the research requirements • Data collected likely to include information that is superfluous to research requirements

phenomena and engaging in research through digital methods. We need to consider how and when researchers, participants and data exhibit more (or less) of the characteristics that would mark them as active or passive, and then consider the implications of this on research design choices, and research findings. We also need to consider how one element's degree of activity impacts on the digital activity levels of the other elements as the different aspects of digital research design are not wholly independent.

The remainder of this section explores the implications of active/passive processes in digital research. It looks first at the researcher, as digital researchers, through their positions as research designer, data collector, analysts and writer, have more choice as to whether they act in an active or passive way in relation to digital research. Next, the research participant is considered. The impact of the digital environment on the role of the research participant has been considered earlier (Chapter 5), so here we will concentrate on the implications of how our decisions as researchers make the participant active or passive. The final area addressed under active/passive is data. However, when discussing the implications of active/passive data, we do not include issues associated with automation, as these are covered separately.

The researcher

When considering active or passive in relation to ourselves as researchers, it is important to understand any value judgements we may make with respect to the factors that characterise an 'active' or a 'passive' approach to research. It is also important to not pre-suppose that a researcher possessing one of the characteristics of an active research approach will automatically possess other aspects of that approach. With these two provisos in mind, this section considers three factors that can be used to characterise our approach as researchers. The extent to which we:

- acknowledge the impact of socio-cultural and technological context on our choices
- intervene in the digital environment to collect data
- are aware of the characteristics of digital technologies, platforms, techniques and tools.

Socio-cultural and technological context

Being active as a researcher includes acknowledging what influences how we make our research choices. The choices we make are not unrestricted. As researchers we can be confined in obvious and visible ways, for example, what is ethically responsible or legal? As well as more initially unobtrusive constraints, for example, what is known about what or who is accessible? We are all confined within our socio-cultural context and by disciplinary norms. Disciplinary norms operate at all stages of our research from initial choices concerning what we consider interesting/appropriate as a research project, to how we write up our research. The extent to which we are expected to acknowledge what has influenced our choices is largely determined by our disciplinary norms and the norms of the research paradigm that we subscribe to.

Those researchers who are working within a positivist paradigm are likely to frame their choices not as a conscious effort, but as a logical deduction given their research objectives and context. The 'objective' stance taken within this paradigm means that the researcher's choices are not acknowledged (whether they are conducting digital or non-digital research) as being contingent on the socio-cultural technological context they are working in. That is, the research is passive in relation to the socio-cultural and techno-logical context. The characteristics of the digital environment, particularly its dynamic nature and the speed of evolution of technologies and platforms, mean, however, that research choices framed within a process of logical deduction in a given context, may not remain the 'logical' choice when those conditions change. As such, if we are working within the positivist paradigm, taking a more active stance, and acknowledging the general and specific context in which our choices were made, will both help us justify those choices and enable the reader to more appropriately interpret our research. For instance, when digital is the method of research, pre-existing websites might be chosen as they allow participants to perform particular tasks under particular conditions (e.g., product or information searches). However, a change in a website's design between a project's data collection phase and the completion of the research may impact both the appropriate-ness of the choice of website and the value of the subsequent results. Unless the purpose of the research was to prompt change in that particular website (this type of action-based research is more common in commercial research, where websites are frequently changed and the impact on search behaviour and interaction by consumers with those changes are then tracked, but it is unlikely to be an appropriate aim for an academic project), changes in a website for an academic study are likely to invalidate the research findings. However, acknowledging the change could provide support for recommendations in a research publication (Reynolds and Ruiz de Maya, 2013), if those changes overcome issues highlighted in the research results.

In contrast to more positivist research, those working within more constructivist par-adigms are used to framing their choices, as a minimum, within socio-cultural contexts, and acknowledging their personal influences. These paradigms expect researchers to actively consider what influences their choices. Personal interests, our disciplinary norms and socio-cultural background may have all contributed to our interest in research-ing digital phenomena or using digital methods. Unlike more positivistic researchers, it is relatively more straightforward for those of us working within more constructivist traditions to include the technological context as a situating factor when undertaking research.

Intervention associated with digital research and data collection

As digital researchers we may intervene in the digital environment and/or observe what is happening in the digital environment. We are being more active as research-ers when we intervene (Table 6.2), though intervention or non-intervention can take multiple forms and may be with or without the participant's knowledge (discussed in the section on the participant, below). Intervention for the purposes of this text refers to deliberate and planned interaction with either the digital phenomenon, or the use of digital research tools, or both, to conduct research in order to answer the research objectives. This intervention could be directly related to the research design used, and could, for example, include inserting a questionnaire into the online digital environ-ment, developing multiple websites to use as comparisons in an online experiment, convening a focus group in a dedicated chat room, or creating an avatar to become immersed in a virtual environment. In contrast, non-intervention as a more passive approach, attempts to understand the digital (or non-digital) phenomenon without venturing into the digital space. Non-intervention might take the form of observing virtual worlds as a lurker (someone who visits online communities to learn or observe for either personal or professional reasons but who does not interact with a commu-nity; see Kozinets' work for various roles that can be adopted online). Furthermore tracking how a hashtag is used on social media platforms, collecting and categorising the characteristics of online book reviews, or creating social media network images of #Iammyownguardian (the collection of social media images and comments related to the Saudi Arabian women's expressions of independence), for example, may prove insightful.

Table 6.2 Examples of researcher intervention and participant knowledge in digital research

		Researcher's impact on digital environment	
		Intervention	Non-intervention
Participants' knowledge of research	Clear awareness of the specific research taking place	• Online questionnaire • Focus group in chat room • Avatar creation and participation in virtual immersive environment	• Observation of vloggers (with permission) • Observation of interactions between online community members
	Lack of awareness of the specific research taking place	• Live-experiments with website designs • Question, or any other stimulus material, posted on an open forum	• Analysis of website social media posts/trending hashtags • Observation of closed forums (possibly with moderator's knowledge)

Digital researchers who actively intervene in the digital environment may deliberately want to change something in the environment to see how that impacts on the digital (or non-digital) phenomenon they are interested in. For example, researchers who set up live experiments to compare the effectiveness of different website design are actively intervening in the digital environment and observing the changes that take place in the website users' behaviours as a result of the changes they make; researchers who post a question on an open forum do so in order to elicit responses from other participants, such as questions posed on expat forums that might ask about the challenges of integration for workers in another country. Depending on how the research is set up, the research participants may, or may not, be aware that research is taking place. This non-disclosure/covert research removes the participants' choice, making them more passive, and as such is considered in more detail when discussing the active/passive research participant.

Digital researchers may actively intervene in the digital environment solely for the purpose of data collection; that is, they may use the digital sphere as a method of research. Here, the purpose of the research is not to change the phenomenon, but rather to collect data that are 'true' to, or reflective of, the phenomenon. Researchers are using their intervention as a means to gain information about a phenomenon and the digital environment is the means through which that information is gained. With this type of intervention the researcher needs to evaluate the extent to which the intervention might impact on what they are able to observe/measure concerning the phenomenon they are interested in. This might be considered similar to researchers considering the possibility of respondent bias when contemplating the use of questionnaires or personal interviews. Does the digital researcher change the nature of interactions in a community? Does asking questions about a particular product via an online questionnaire, for example, prompt participants to make concrete attitudes/opinions about that product that were not fully formed? Does taking part in an online focus group 'force' someone to express their own opinion, when if they had not taken part they would not have felt the need to articulate an opinion? In addition, researchers should consider the potential ethical implications of active intervention. Essentially, the researcher needs to consider whether active intervention in the digital context has the potential to cause harm to the community as a whole, or to individuals within that community. When digital research is used as a way of accessing research information, the participant is more likely to be aware that they are taking part in research, so consideration should also be given to the potential for changing the balance or environment of that community in which research is taking place (Langer and Beckman, 2005).

As digital researchers we can also choose not to intervene in the digital environment, that is, to be passive. Non-intervention research would generally be classified as observation, and in the non-digital environment this is generally restricted to behaviours. However, because of the archival nature of the digital environment, we can also explore the natural discourses found in that environment (e.g., posts on social media sites, personal blogs, tweets). As such, digital researchers are able, without intervention, to explore abstract digital phenomena (e.g., trending hashtags), behavioural traces of individuals' (and groups') actions (e.g., online shopping behaviour, interactions within and between forums), and internal characteristics of individuals and groups through their expressed attitudes, opinions and beliefs (e.g., political views, individual and societal values). These studies may be done with or without the knowledge of those leaving the data in the digital environment, and they may or may not require collaboration with the digital entity that either stores or owns the data, for example, Google or Facebook. As the digital researcher is a remote presence, it is not likely that the digital user that generates the research data will have considered the potential for their actions being studied in the future. Even if made explicitly aware of possible future research, we, as digital users, soon forget that someone else might have access to the digital footprints we leave behind.

Knowledge of the digital environment

As researchers working in the digital environment we vary in the depth and breadth of our knowledge of that environment at both a general level, and at a more specific level. Our knowledge of digital technologies and platforms also varies, as well as the digital research tools and techniques that are available to us and how to best use these. Even if, at a particular moment in time, we could claim complete knowledge of digital technologies and platforms, as well as digital research tools and techniques, the rate of change in the digital environment is such that it is impossible for any one individual to remain fully conversant with the research opportunities and issues in the environment. The problem of maintaining up-to-date knowledge is compounded when we consider that some of that knowledge is competitively sensitive – Google is not going to release its search algorithms, Amazon is not going to reveal how it makes recommendations, and Facebook is not going to let us select all the material from someone's wall.

Despite the impossibility of keeping up with all the changes in the digital environment, as digital researchers we cannot passively abdicate our responsibility to understand how we are obtaining, and using, data from that environment. We cannot assume that previous justifications for examining a particular digital technology or platform, or using particular tools or techniques, will hold in this changing, fluid environment. We need to actively evaluate previous assumptions within the digital environment we are researching to determine whether those assumptions still hold. We need to actively consider how the changes to the digital environment, and the digital tools/techniques we use, might impact on the data we collect. For instance, if our research question looks at trending hashtags in tweets, we might need to consider a number of questions including:

- What is the impact of us not understanding the algorithm that Twitter uses to sample tweets?
- How might we explore the implications of not knowing this algorithm?
- How might that exploration impact on how we approach our research question and/or interpret our data?
- How can we then provide a sound rationale for our research decisions?

The active digital researcher who exposes and examines, as far as is reasonably possible, their own and others assumptions about digital technologies and platforms, and digital research tools and techniques, will be better able to justify their research choices to others. They will be more able to defend their choices than the passive researcher who relies on others' justifications and assumes others' justifications can be transferred, without reflection, to a different socio-cultural and technological context.

The participant

Similar to the offline research environment the digital environment provides opportunities for data to be collected actively from participants who engage in the process of providing data to organisations and researchers, or passively. Pop-up surveys on social media platforms, warranty registrations on e-commerce sites, or experiments involving reactions to YouTube video clips all involve active engagement on the part of the participants. Participants can now have a much more active role in research (as discussed in Chapter 5), so this section is more concerned with what makes participation passive and why research of this type occurs. An underlying key issue is the extent to which the participant is made aware that research is occurring. In active digital data collection participants knowingly choose to participate in providing information to a research project. Their engagement with the research requires active involvement and implicit agreement to contribute to active data collection. When active participation occurs, data collection is a disclosed activity. In contrast, with passive participation, data collection is not disclosed, it is covert.

Before embarking on a discussion of covert or disclosed data collection, we need to acknowledge two issues: 1) the ongoing debate concerning whether and which data are public/private; and, 2) the language used to describe some digital activity. Disclosure is a contentious aspect of digital research that is closely linked to the ongoing debate and blurred division between what may be considered as public and private data. The concept of public versus private can be viewed from several perspectives as technology facilitates unknown others' entering people's lives. Within a digital platform, the originator of the content (data) may themselves believe that the data are public or private, the platform, and sometimes legal owner, hosting the content may hold a shared or opposing view of the status of the data, while the intended recipient of the content (data) and any third party involved in the interaction will also have viewpoints on the data's status. Indeed the perception of the data's status may change as the interactions occur and as the interactions change in nature. Generalised statements of 'if it is on a publicly accessible website it is public data' are overly simplistic and as researchers we need to think about the sensitivity of the subject we might be researching as well as the level of vulnerability of the research participants. Likewise does having to register to participate in an online community mean that any data within that environment are private and not usable for research purposes?

Social science researchers such as Huw Davies and Lisa Sugiura, among others, suggest reflecting on the intentions of the people who created and shared the data as one approach to determining the public/private conundrum. Celebrities who blog require optimal numbers of followers and interactions to maintain their commercial contracts with brands, therefore it is reasonable to assume that they desire their content to be disseminated and also commented upon, which includes the analysis of their content as a data source for research. Greater sensitivity may be necessary over research that incorporates data from the Tumblr site talkmentalhealth (http://talkmentalhealth.tumblr.com/), even though that site is open, and thus could be 'categorised' as public and many contributors are named. The site and its contents have been used by journalists (Cresci, 2015) to highlight how opening up the discussion of socially sensitive subjects through digital media can be valuable.

The established language used to describe the activities of a researcher in gathering research can be misleading. Terms such as 'covert' and 'disclosure' and 'lurking' contain socially laden meaning and are often used pejoratively, bringing up images of undercover police investigations or undesirable activity. Having acknowledged this potentially 'leading' language and while we wish to neutralise these established associations surrounding the terminology, we will continue to use these terms here for clarity and shared understanding. However, we would urge digital researchers to carefully consider the language they use to describe and justify their research activities and to make explicit the weighting given to these terms. By outlining the nuances and the slant given to the choice of terminology in research we can further stimulate the debate on research terminology development within social science research. As researchers involved in an emerging arena it is important to raise awareness not just of our research outputs but also how any digital research is framed, and language is one of the most valuable framing tools currently available to us.

Disclosure and non-disclosure

As researchers involved in digital research, whether as the focus and site of the research, or whether as a series of tools to be used in the answering of a research question, decisions have to be made as to where you as the researcher stand in how you collect your digital data. Depending on the nature of your research question, the level of sensitivity of your topic and the vulnerability of your research participants you may decide to announce yourself as a researcher within the digital spaces from which you are collecting data or you may choose to collect data while not disclosing your presence. Consequently, as digital researchers, we are making design choices that will result in active (informed) or passive (uninformed) participants.

There are strongly held views within subject areas on what is considered 'normal practice', on whether to disclose or not. Individual authors and researchers can also hold very different, potentially opposing, views. Helpful suggestions have been made by Mckee and Porter (2009) on whether digital spaces such as online communities should be viewed primarily as text or people in order to decide whether disclosure and gaining informed consent are required from potential participants or not. Kozinets, the originator of netnography (2002), proposes a more ethnographic approach to making decisions about disclosure and in his published work advocates disclosure of researcher presence to participants. However, Paccagnella (1997) and Langer and Beckman (2005) do not support disclosure of the researcher to participants. They are proponents of observing digital interactions to collect naturalistic research data without disturbing the natural ebb and flow of groups, networks and communities. Research conducted on chat room users' views on being observed found that users were less hostile to researchers not disclosing their presence than when researchers did disclose their presence (Hudson and Bruckman, 2004), which adds another layer of complexity. Both disclosure and non-disclosure will require justification to strengthen the validity and credibility of the research design, so both options are discussed below.

Non-disclosure

The nature of the research project may lend itself to the collection of data where the researcher does not disclose their presence. For example, research conducted in public places such as filming a street scene to observe citizens' movement and use of public spaces may be part of an architectural study. Filmed observational data are also often used by commercial organisations to look at the flow and physical behaviour of people in retail environments to make best use of the floor space in store. In both cases the research activity is not disclosed to the people going about their daily lives. Within the digital context and bearing in mind the nature of the research, the sensitivity of the topic and the vulnerability of the participants, non-disclosure of researchers is also possible. Research involving low level risk to participants and low level sensitivity, which has provided new insight into business behaviour includes Quinton and Wilson (2016) and their study of interactions within LinkedIn wine business groups and the formation of new contacts as well as new business contracts through these groups. By 'low level risk' we mean no more risk than would be considered normal in someone's daily life and by low level 'sensitivity' we mean research topics that are not contentious and those which would not cause distress to anyone by being discussed. Having said that it is worth remembering that sensitivity is a subjective matter and each of us will have particular issues to which we are sensitive, and researchers need to consider carefully any potential sensitivity within a proposed research project.

A sensitive research topic may still be pursued without disclosure, though design justification will need to be clear to gain ethics approval. A key factor might be the need to maintain 'normal' behaviour in a particular digital community/study, for example, accessing sensitive material via non-disclosed observing of online communities from potentially vulnerable groups such as individuals wishing to lose weight (Sugiura et al., 2012), and more controversially the use of message data obtained from a publicly accessible support group for those considering suicide (Barak and Miron, 2005). Within the social sciences there may be many worthwhile research topics that require entering into online communities or observing social media interactions without disclosing the researcher presence. Research ethics committees at institutions may feel uncomfortable with non-disclosure, as on the face of it, non-disclosure does not conform to obtaining 'informed consent' of participants in research. However, it can be argued that disclosing your presence as a researcher could cause harm and unbalance the social structures within the digital groups (Hewson et al., 2016), such as the suicide support group in the example above.

A more extreme version of non-disclosure, and one that the authors would be reluctant to endorse, is that of assuming an identity to 'become a participant'. This action involves actively deceiving individuals and/or digital communities. Certain journalists have, for instance, taken on the persona of an anorexic young woman in order to participate in pro-anorexia forums so that they can research the phenomenon. This type of activity is ethically questionable and, in the academic environment, would be difficult to support. On the other hand, taking on a persona or avatar in virtual world research would be considered within the norms of the virtual environment where all participants in these immersive 'other worlds' take on an avatar character.

In order to decide whether or not researcher disclosure is warranted, that is, whether it is acceptable to make our participants passive, we suggest reflecting on the previous points. This reflection will help determine whether a defendable research design is possible. Specifically, we suggest asking:

- What is the level of sensitivity of your chosen topic?
- Can you access data directly from a publicly available source?
- Can you determine the norms of behaviour within the online/digital activity you wish to research?
- Is there a stated policy on the use of gathering digital data for research purposes and if so what does it state?

- Has precedent been established by other digital researchers who have also researched your topic in a similar way?
- Is there a potential for negative consequences for the digital community if you disclose your presence?
- What is the level of vulnerability of the sample from which you wish to gather data?

Disclosure

The opportunities to engage with, and elicit rich data from, research participants have never been greater for researchers, largely due to the digital technologies that encourage connectivity and interaction. However, disclosing that research is being conducted, gaining informed consent and fully familiarising potential participants of the nature and details of the research is more complicated than for offline research. The remoteness of the researcher in digital research adds to the potential for misunderstanding of questions and data collection processes by the participants. While online questionnaires may be designed to contain a front page scoping the study, giving an ethics committee approval number (if possible) and requirements with an 'I consent' button, it becomes more complex when gaining consent from individuals or groups within online communities, or social media networks.

While various options exist for the clear and explicit disclosure of the researcher across different digital research platforms, some are more practical than others. A common suggestion for those interested in accessing online communities and forums is to seek permission through the moderator of the community or forum. In the early years of internet research many communities were happy to be part of research projects but as the volume of online research activity has increased and more concerns over the privacy of data have emerged, many communities and their moderators are sceptical about participating in research. Indeed this has led to some communities, such as YouTube channel HelloOctoberxo, a popular fashion and cosmetics vlogger with approximately 380,000 subscribers, giving an explicit statement in the 'about' section that no assistance with dissertation, educational projects or research through posting questions to the vlogger or asking for questions to be posted to the community will be permitted. The role of the moderator in this environment is hugely influential, they may function as the nominated spokesperson or they may make unilateral decisions about which research projects, if any, to endorse. The email contact details of the moderator are usually but not always available either by name, pseudonym or by title within the forum.

Many researchers are active across various social media platforms and in online communities as part of their own personal and professional interest groups. If some of these groups are relevant to the research being undertaken then already being established as a participative member is more likely to gain you access to these groups for a research project. This is quite common for PhD students who may have an ongoing interest in a particular subject area. In this instance declaring your research intentions within a group where trust is previously established should be fairly straightforward as long as it is made explicit how and when data will be collected. The data collection will start from a forward point in time. Data should not generally be collected retrospectively, unless there is a strong justification for doing so (e.g., a historical comparison study of discussion content), and permission to collect retrospective data is given. Occasionally supervisors might caution against 'advertising' your research intent as it discloses to a wider community your own research idea and plans to some extent. We would disagree with this overly cautious approach as the recruitment of participants and the dissemination of current research is important in order to obtain a suitable sample and also to facilitate the exchange of research-based ideas and extend interactions within the research community.

For some research projects it may be possible to contact individuals directly to outline the research project, disclose the intent of the researcher and ask for permission to use their digital data. For example, it is possible to contact those individuals who create or comment on a YouTube video by replying to them via the YouTube channel. Disclosing information about the research project and the researcher may be possible via a hypertext link to a detailed webpage or research project page (if funds and time permit the development of one) in order to strengthen the credibility of the research. These links can be shortened to send out via Twitter messages or equivalent platforms that have restricted message size.

A final thought should be given to the safety of the researcher who discloses their research intention and identity. Certain sensitive subject areas, such as political extremism, child neglect and ethnicity, can elicit very strong and negative responses from potential participants as well as others on social media. Abuse directed towards researchers can and does occur and can consist of rude messages and offensive material being sent and also attempted hacking of research websites or email accounts. More threatening behaviours can include doxxing, which is the publishing online of identifying personal details such as addresses or phone numbers of a person with whom someone disagrees with, or trolling to cause disruption by deliberately posting or contributing inflammatory remarks, in extreme cases proposing physical harm to people. It is worth considering whether disclosing your identity as a researcher, within the context of your research, could create personal safety issues or psychological harm to yourself.

As we have seen from the discussions above there is significant complexity in the disclosure or non-disclosure of researcher identity and research intention. Digital researchers need to contextualise their choices regarding disclosure, balancing the need to address their research question with consideration of the interests of the individuals and/or digital communities they are considering.

The data

The volume of digital data collected and archived every day is now exceeding our ability to make use of it (Meyer and Schroeder, 2015). For purposes of simplicity we have broken data into two main categories, passive and active data, both of which present specific opportunities and challenges. In the digital environment, data can be collected without our awareness or conscious participation. Passive data can be defined as data that are gleaned from individuals and organisations without participants' awareness or specific consent. Passively collected data tend to be behavioural data, the actual physical actions taken by individuals, though attitudes and opinions can be scraped from social network sites and other digital sources. Internet search history, hospital appointments missed, home energy use, loyalty card use are just some examples of behavioural data that are collected passively. Data are collected by government and non-commercial organisations as well as by employers, retailers and market research firms. For example, closed circuit television is commonly used in the UK to monitor and record the movement of individuals and groups with the justification provided of enhancing public safety. Other European countries also use CCTV, but to a lesser extent, to observe their citizens. Digital technologies have also created the opportunity to passively monitor individuals' health and fitness levels via the use of fitness wearables as part of the social phenomenon of self-tracking. As people wear these devices or download certain apps to their smartphone, so data are recorded and uploaded to software providers to be aggregated with others' data. While people are aware that they have chosen to wear and record their own body functions, many, we would argue, are unaware of the use made of the data by businesses such as insurance companies, sportswear brands, etc.

In addition, GPS and location-based passive data are increasingly being used by commercial organisations to pinpoint and then market specific promotional messages to targeted individuals via their smartphones. An example of 'proximity' marketing can be seen in the Regent Street retailers in London working with a technology firm to actively encourage consumers to engage with retailers along that shopping street (Nelson, 2014). Proximity marketing requires the user of the phone to actively switch on the location enabling setting within the function setting. So, it could be argued that the individual is actively, to some extent, engaging with and knowingly allowing location data to be made available. However, many smartphone users are unaware of how to switch the location setting on or off and furthermore, as service providers change settings regularly previously private information becomes more publicly accessible inadvertently, including location data. Even if the digital user knows how to block their location, those that chose not to may be unaware of the uses (other than the immediate, real-time location-based marketing) that their data may be put to. If one of these additional uses is research, then passive research data have been collected.

The research design required for macro-level passive data collection at country level is not within the scope of this text (though 'big data' are discussed more generally in the next section), except to say that many government departments will be involved as well as research bodies such as the ESRC or the RCUK, to collate the data extracted from digital archived data, and following that, statistical analysis will be conducted by teams of researchers in order to report back the findings, which may feed into government policy documents, charity reports, etc. An individual researcher at postgraduate or PhD level who wishes to investigate passive data is more likely to access pre-existing digital data sets from an open source repository. For example, the Web Observatory at Southampton University allows researchers to request access to certain digital data sets. The provenance of previously collected passive data needs to be scrutinised before inclusion in your own research projects (see the following discussion on algorithms). Consideration of these already existing data sets should include:

- investigation of the sample size and representativeness of the population
- examination of the extent to which, and how, the data set has been cleaned
- determining the age of the data set
- consideration of the original intention for which the data were collected
- exploration of who else has used the data set and for what purpose.

While there is obvious appeal in the use of digital archived data sets, which can be expediently used for research, and while it is easy to become beguiled by large ready-made data sets as a researcher, it is important to consider the quality of the data set as this is a cornerstone of a research project.

Finally, researchers can create their own passive data, for example, by filming or recording certain behaviours. The movement of people in a shopping street and the patterns shown of how these citizens enter certain shops, and in fact, which shops they enter, may be of interest to town planning researchers, human geographers and sociologists. Individual researchers can capture such activity easily through smart enabled phones, or inconspicuous video cameras including even the general soundscape of urban noise if required. Public street filming for the purpose of individual academic research in the UK requires no specific licence (as long as the street is public and not within a private estate or privately owned shopping mall). These types of passively collected data can provide great insight and can be uploaded and analysed through software such as NVivo, but the issues concerning participant knowledge remain.

Digital automation and algorithms

Algorithms play an increasingly influential role in all our lives. As citizens algorithms dictate our Google search results, the price charged when we take an Uber taxi, the credit rating we may have with our banks and even our likelihood of securing a particular job. The digitalised society is currently thought by many researchers to be over-trusting of these mathematically created and programmed algorithms. Algorithms are written as computer code by individuals or groups of people and tested using machine learning on existing data sets; concern is increasing at the consumer rights level, the government level and the international level about the lack of transparency and oversight of these powerful tools. The use of algorithms is often outside the scope of self-funded research unless you have the technical skills to write your own computer code to create one. A consideration here is the reductionist approach to data that can occur when using algorithms for data analysis, so that some data may not be included in the data set which is analysed or that the data which are included are analysed through a particular lens, which we as researchers may not have required.

The automation of data collection also means that third parties (e.g., Google, Twitter, Baidu in China) are allowing access to data that they have collected and stored. While there is significant potential in the adoption and use, where appropriate, of third party digital data, the impact of the use of commercial platforms for research and analysis should be acknowledged. Organisations that share data, and develop platforms and/or proprietary tools, have their own commercial or ideological objectives, which manifest themselves in the features offered, for example, the scraping of micro-blog content, or the tracking of social media exchanges. A key issue for researchers to be aware of is the influence that the design of these tools might have on the interactions detected and the limitations that might be present in the data collected. While consumers, citizens and patients are increasingly operating in an environment of accelerating change, algorithms that look to the past and recent past behaviour are increasingly being used to understand and predict future behaviour.

Digital tools can bring analytical efficiency to their users, business and public sector owners. However, naïve usage is common as the owners of the algorithms do not encourage questioning of this form of artificial intelligence. Indeed, danah boyd as the Chair of the Data and Society Foundation has suggested that there is a distinct lack of governance over such influential technology, and that a one fit solution to scoring or rating consumers and citizens that most algorithms employ is not a sound strategy. Currently any human oversight of algorithms is limited to a very few, usually technically expert, individuals inside a few commercial firms. These algorithms are seen as company assets and as such there is a strategic effort to safeguard any perceived competitive advantage created by them. These firms closely guard the code, change the algorithms frequently, and expect citizens to accept the outputs passively. Yet these algorithms can and do impact our lives and shape our life experiences.

Greater accountability and transparent processes for auditing these algorithms are now being called for by various consumer activist lobbying groups in America. Evaluating these algorithms should involve processes that include social and legal factors as well as the technical aspects of the created computer code. It is not necessary to know or unpick the code itself, rather the methodology of the code creation and a clear understanding of how the results of an algorithm are produced may be sufficient. Critics propose that more consideration should be given to the consequences for the social and legal impact of the algorithm during the design stage, as the code once written is replicated again and again. The 'front end' stage of the initial writing is of critical importance, as amendments should be made at this early stage, following transparent testing. A further point made by computer scientists themselves is that the algorithms are tested and 'learn' from previously created data sets, thus relying heavily on the completeness and validity of those previous data sets. So for example, if census data of a country are used but contain under-representation of certain groups of people, by ethnicity, employment type, etc., and are combined with other data sets then there is potential for these groups to continue to be under-represented and also evaluated as higher risk by algorithms for, say, financial services providers.

A first step towards the regulatory enforcement of greater transparency of algorithmic outputs has been made via the General Data Protection Regulation Act 2018 (GDPR 2018) by the European parliament. From May 2018 all European citizens will be entitled to request an explanation of any algorithmic decision. How this will be implemented and shown on our search results, credit scores. etc. remains unclear; a pop-up button could be added to each search engine query or next to each set of 'personalised' promotions now shown to us on our technology devices. The UK's decision to leave the EU will apparently not impact upon the adoption by the UK of the GDPR act (ICO.org.uk, 2016). The discussion above is relevant to digital research and digital researchers as both are impacted by algorithms and as researchers we need to understand the tensions that technology is creating.

Impact of automation on research design

The automation of data collection is a key characteristic of some digital research. Data collection and analysis algorithms allow huge volumes of data to be processed without direct human intervention. However, there are several issues of concern when this is examined in detail. One such issue is that algorithms, no matter how sophisticated, empirically reach back to define what is likely to happen in the future. Consequently, the more stable the past has been, the less flexible/responsive the algorithm used to predict the future is likely to be. In addition, there is a danger that researchers' questions will become empirically driven and theoretical explanations of phenomena downgraded. In addition, while data collection algorithms are akin to data collection instruments such as questionnaires or interview guides, researchers rarely have the skills to design or program algorithms. Indeed, these algorithms might not be transparent to researchers. The issue of the epistemological relevance and consequences of automated data collection also need to be addressed, thus how data collection is conducted relates to both the researcher's perspective and also the understanding surrounding the framings of digital tools. Two areas are considered here in more detail – research rigour and ethics.

Research rigour

While digital technologies have the ability to reconfigure our notions of research, the underlying premise of the requirement to produce rigorous research does not alter. When we choose to use data provided via the API of a social media platform, we need to understand and acknowledge that the data set is incomplete. Likewise when we use analytical software we need to appreciate that we do not understand the algorithm used to write that software nor its level of completeness. As such, we do not always have all of the information we need to confidently judge whether data or software are actually suitable for our specific research purpose. So although we may design and pilot our research to strengthen its rigour we are not in a position to confirm the rigour of the algorithm, the software, the data set, or possibly the sample in our research. The increasingly complex technologies involved in the production of research lessen our ability as individual researchers to tell a complete research narrative as the technologies are bound in commercial sensitivity and frequently undergo internal variations. Furthermore the potential for variability in digital research when replicated stems in part from these shifting technologies. One relevant question here is whether our research participant is, in fact, human.

The focus of our research may require us to question where the balance of human/technology interaction should lie. Consider, for example, Bots within the digital environment. Bots on patient portal websites can take on the role of humans to respond to patient questions. These responses are automatically generated via sophisticated computer programmes. The data resulting from these interactions may be highly relevant to a research project, so we need to ask whether (if we can identify the Bot generated responses) we should discard these responses just because they were not generated by humans. Here the answer, once again, lies in the research objective and the original focus of the research. If the original intention was to explore the speed and relevancy of response to specific questions, then whether or not the responder was human may not be important. However, if the intention was to understand the language used in response to questions asked, then the nature of the responder might be of significance. An interesting aside to this is that Bots could also be used to gather research data, to conduct online interviews, and ask rather than answer questions, in which case their design focus could have an impact on the research results.

An issue we also need to contend with in the digital environment is trust. Not only do we, as researchers, need to trust our data but we need our audiences to trust our data too, be they our peers, examiners or funding bodies. While automated processes used to scrape and/or clean data sets may add to time efficiency of a research project, an overdependence on automated processes may have the result of a lessening of trust in the results. Consequently, some human checking of completeness of the data set or random examination of the cleanliness of the data might be considered advisable. As researchers we may trust the data more if we can 'check' that they are complete and clean. Worth noting though, is the fact that, for multiple reasons discussed elsewhere in the text, much social media data and search engine data are not complete and this should be made explicit in our research writing.

Ethics

Digital technology allows us to collect data without being observed far more easily than in a pre-computer mediated environment. Authors within the virtual consumption environment have, for example, raised the issue of the extent to which avatars and virtual identities might have 'rights' as participants in research (Molesworth and Denegri-Knott, 2012). Overall, we need a set of considered operating practices to be established for the researcher with regard to how technology in research may impact ethics decisions. How the researcher will deal with ethics occurrences should, ideally, be made explicit in research planning and/or the execution of research, whether ethics issues arise in field notes or in the writing up of research results. While valuable overarching guidelines have been outlined by organisations such as the AoIR (Association of Internet Researchers, www.aoir. org) there are no set 'absolutes' or rules that govern the ethics of digital data. We agree with Hewson et al. (2016), among others, on taking a contextual approach to the disclosure or non-disclosure by researchers, depending on the nature of the topic and the level of vulnerability of those involved (see Chapter 3 for further discussion on vulnerability). However, there are a number of other ethics questions that also need to be considered surrounding issues such as how (if it is even possible or practical) to gain the consent from participants, and the notion of group as well as individual privacy. In addition, what are public and what are considered private data are now under scrutiny in the research community. We have to consider whether we can apply 'standard ethics procedures' (Brawley and Pury, 2016) in an environment that has changing socio-cultural norms of behaviour, and is so dynamic that new policies are quickly superseded by evolution in technology.

Technological replacement of human labour

One of the current topics within the social sciences is the extent to which automation may or may not endanger the established labour market (Chui et al., 2015), as well as the anxieties and concerns raised by the extent to which certain activities can now be automated (Whitney, 2016). Popular examples vary from the use of 'robots' as human look-a-like receptionists at Japanese hotels, through to self-service pay stations at retail shops, to online banking. This increase in, and potential for, automation is also apparent within the research context and raises interesting opportunities and challenges for us as digital researchers. The use of digital technology in the generation of knowledge and scholarship, and the discovery of a balance between human activity and endeavour, and technological data collection, collation, storage, analysis and dissemination can be complicated. The ability to make use of digital technologies, has, as stated before, changed the nature of how we as researchers undertake research (Meyer and Schroeder, 2015), but it should not abdicate our responsibilities as researchers in terms of research rigour or ethics. This section raises questions through these core themes that are pertinent to our new environment of digital technology enhanced research. Overall we propose that human oversight is always necessary in digital research.

BIG DATA

The term 'big data' has become an almost everyday item within the lexicon of mass media, yet the lack of understanding of what big data are, by citizens, consumers and/or patients, results in the inability to make informed decisions about it. Big data are understood to be about large data sets, but what is large? Understanding big data is less about knowing the size of the data set but more concerned with its complexity and the computational power required to manipulate and analyse it. As a very rough guide and one that is changing as the volume of digital data increases every day, a big data set might be the many terabytes of data contained in Wikipedia (1 terabyte = 1000^4). Big data are sometimes understood to be about the combination of different data sets. They are also known to have the ability to predict our behaviour, which makes them valuable to commercial organisations as well as in fields such as health. Big data are also associated with privacy concerns, as they create a vague belief that others know more about us than we know about ourselves. But none of these things that are 'known' about big data help us define what big data are, rather they indicate what their characteristics are or what they may, or may not, be able to do. The lack of understanding has significant implications for the notion of being able to give informed consent as a participant in research – a participant has to understand what they are consenting to, to be able to give informed consent. A lack of appreciation that their own data may end up as the components of big data is one issue; a lack of awareness that the overlaying of large data sets can inadvertently identify and profile previously anonymous participants is another.

Part of the problem understanding what big data are is their multifaceted nature. Big data, for example, rely on certain characteristics of the digital environment such as data storage capacity and analytical capabilities. How we understand big data is also tied up in the socio-cultural discourse about them. Boyd and Crawford (2012) capture these different elements of big data in their review stating:

Big Data is a cultural, technological and scholarly phenomenon that rests on the interplay of:

1. Technology: maximising computational power and algorithmic accuracy to gather, analyse, link, and compare large data sets.
2. Analysis: drawing on large data sets to identify patterns in order to make economic, social, technical, and legal claims.
3. Mythology: the widespread belief that large data sets offer a higher form of intelligence and knowledge that can generate insights that were previously impossible, with the aura of truth, objectivity, and accuracy. (2012: 663)

Using this perspective to understand the multifaceted nature of big data will help us to understand some of the research implications associated with big data as a phenomenon and as a research instrument.

As well as being multifaceted, big data can exist about many different things. Some big data do not involve humans (for instance, astronomy data sets involving star and planet information), so are not the concern of this text. However, there has been a proliferation of big data sets that now exist and include information about the human condition. The information held in big data sets about us includes almost everything about our lives. Big data sets exist that include, for example, shopping habits at particular stores, spending habits, sleep patterns (from apps), activity levels, contacts (e.g., texts and calls), social networks (e.g., Facebook friends), viewing habits, health records, driving patterns, financial information, work history, browsing history, social activities, travel habits and preferences, brand preferences, drinking habits, demographic characteristics, internet search history, family/household composition, complaint history, religious and political views, sexual preferences, preferred images, social security claims, driving licence/passport details, police record and educational achievements. The content of these data sets spans different levels of sensitivity, though what is sensitive can be greatly dependent on the individual concerned and how the data are combined. For example, information about my grocery shopping habits held by the grocery store I usually shop from and shared with the grocery brands that I purchase, gathered through a loyalty card scheme may seem relatively incongruous, even beneficial, if it is used to alert me to special offers in the store that I might be interested in. However, if information about my grocery shopping habits is combined with data from a fitness wearable app I use, and both are bought by a health insurance company to predict my health insurance premiums, then I might find that more invasive.

Any data set, indeed any data, has multiple stakeholders. Zwitter (2014) categorises three types of big data stakeholder: the generators, the collectors and the users of big data. The relationships between the three can be multi-layered and complex. For example, mobile phone usage data are generated by one user, are collected by the service provider who aggregates them with other users' data and which are then used by multiple commercial organisations to whom the collector makes the data available. To what extent the mobile phone user has knowledge of the use made by the collector and user is questionable, therefore making an informed decision is not possible. In digital research activity the notion of informed consent for the collection of data leading to the creation and then use of big data mirrors the example above. Participants are highly unlikely to be able to give informed consent as they do not have an understanding of the details of what they are giving informed consent to in terms of how their data may be used in the future.

Big data are both a social and a digital phenomenon, as well as an instrument through which digital research can be conducted. Drawing on boyd and Crawford's (2012) breakdown of big data into technology, analysis and mythology, social science researchers can explore the mythology of big data through both emerging digital and established research methods. Social scientists might, for example, explore the mythology of big data by exploring how different groups understand its potential implications, and/or how beliefs about privacy impact on behaviour. The analysis element of big data enables the exploration of both social science and digital phenomena. For example, if access to multiple data sets could be negotiated, then epidemiologists might use big data to explore how diet (using data from food purchasing data sets) impacts on health (using data from health insurers) in different populations (using data from census records). The analysis of social science problems using big data might be exploratory using broad data mining methods, or, if potential links are already known (e.g., links between specific dietary factors and specific diseases/conditions), more directed in its focus. Finally, big data as an emerging digital research instrument requires the researcher to maximise their understanding of the technological aspects of big data. These are discussed below.

Challenges of big data

Researchers considering big data are faced with a number of issues. One area that needs to be considered is privacy, which as a socio-cultural concept crosses all three elements of big data. In addition, digital researchers need to have sufficient technical expertise to at least understand how their big data set has come about, as well as understanding the analytical challenges that will allow them to provide research users with a fair representation of the data they are considering. The rise of unstructured as opposed to structured data within big data sets is also creating challenges for researchers and research organisations as the categorisation and managing of unstructured data are far more complicated. The irregularities of unstructured data mean that it is harder for computer programmes to sort and find patterns in the resulting data. Structured data have predetermined fields within relational databases making interrogation of the data by search engines or other tools straightforward. Structured data include spreadsheets; semi-structured data (in which certain aspects are categorised and searchable) include emails that can be categorised by sender, date and time but the content of which is more akin to unstructured data; and finally unstructured data include instant messaging text and image content.

Privacy issues in big data

The ability to collect and store large volumes of data and the decreasing costs associated with data storage and analysis have facilitated the reuse and re-purposing of big data sets. This reuse across a wide range of disciplines, previously unimagined nor planned, has implications for both informed consent (see section above) and privacy (Naughton, 2014). At the individual level privacy concerns might include individuals being identified by others as they go about their everyday lives. For example, the use of facial recognition technology by organisations such as Facebook is now also being used by Australian and American law enforcement agencies. This is only possible because the technology now exists in the form of facial recognition algorithms that can be combined with 'stock' images already held in a large data set. A greater concern could arise as information becomes even more pervasive. For example, it is not beyond the scope of the imagination to believe that data gathered through the 'internet of things' could eventually provide big data sets that allow others to determine when an individual is alone at home, or when a house and its immediate neighbours are empty. While most of the immediate stakeholders involved with big data are unlikely to have nefarious motives, the level of cybercrime already present in the digital environment should make us aware of the potential harm that might arise from big data technology and analysis.

While big data sets present the possibility that an individual can be identified from their data, the concept of group privacy violations has also been raised as a big data issue (Zwitter, 2014). Removing individual characteristics from a data set (i.e., de-individualising data) may make it harder to associate a particular individual with particular data, however, removing all individual characteristics could render the data set almost meaningless. An alternative approach might be to aggregate the characteristics, so, for instance, rather than using a street address and date of birth in an analysis, the block or zip code area and age group are used. Both de-individualisation and aggregation require manipulation of the data after data sets have been combined, and the level of each will depend on the skills and willingness of the data set users, their awareness of and concern for ethical considerations related to privacy, and the requirements of their research. Anonymisation of data is, according to Zwitter (2014: 4), 'a matter of degree of how many and which group attributes remain in the data set'.

The concept of group privacy also requires us to consider the level at which privacy concerns should surface. We imagine that we may agree that being able to predict how humans behave is not a violation of privacy, and we are also likely to agree that research that predicts how multiple different individuals will behave violates their privacy. It becomes problematic when we attempt to determine the point at which predicting behaviour becomes a violation of privacy. Is it a violation of privacy to be able to say with relative certainty that 75 out of 100 people will behave in a particular way? How about if we can say the same about 7,500 out of 10,000? In the commercial environment, for example, big data sets are being employed for a wide range of purposes. IBM's 'Personality Insights' is a powerful profile building tool gathering and linking a wide range of public and proprietary held data including how people write on social media and it has been designed to provide insight resulting in an enhanced understanding of customers for IBM business clients who purchase the tool.

The examples of the relationship between big data and privacy are relevant to us as digital researchers as they highlight what is possible through the use of big data yet also draw attention to the potential loss of the individual's privacy through big data. For an ongoing discussion of these issues see John Naughton, the UK *Guardian* newspaper's technology columnist, or the *New York Times* regular technology column.

Technological challenges of big data

As an individual researcher we are likely to be limited by our resources and our ability to handle and manage big data sets. The data storage requirements for downloading large files of data can, for example, cause many personal laptops to freeze or crash. Storing of either single large files or multiple large files can prove problematic, and extra storage capacity might be required. This extra storage capacity may be gained from your own institution or through a free or paid for cloud application. An additional requirement of big data research is that it is likely to include integrating different data sets. Integrating data sets that have originated from different sources can be extremely complex and time consuming. It is quite likely that time will need to be spent working out the algorithms that will allow, for example, matching of individuals across data sets, identification of missing data, and looking for data duplication. There may also be a need to work out how to identify and account for rogue data. The technical skills required to achieve these are generally beyond the standard training of social science researchers, creating a gap in skills between what we might, as digital researchers, desire to achieve, and our ability to achieve it. How we handle big data, both the big data we ourselves might have collected from digital behaviours and also the big data we might have accessed from other research, needs careful planning.

In many aspects evaluating the quality and fit-for-purposeness of big data is no different from evaluating the quality of smaller, less complex data sets, whether digital or offline data. If the data have not been collected by us as individual researchers or as part of a research team we will not know in detail how it was collected. Being removed from the data collection means that, where possible, we need to mitigate the lack of certainty by asking the provider of the data set questions about the origins and method of its creation. We also need to question the big data set's completeness and currency in relation to what data we need in order to be able to answer our research question. Many of the big data sets created and made available by national governments can be very dated, for example national census data, or national influenza data, and this 'old' data may then influence our findings. We should also reflect on the accuracy of the big data, as we are highly unlikely to be given the raw data in order to compare the raw data with the completed data set. In practical terms we can acknowledge the challenge of confirming accuracy of the data but there is little we can do beyond cross-referencing these data with others as a heuristic for accuracy. Furthermore, the samples used in the creation of big data may or may not be well defined, which in turn may bias the findings.

Analysis challenges of big data sets

Once we have a big data set that we are confident of, we need to analyse the data. The analysis of any data aims to identify patterns in order to provide a fair representation of that data. While there are multiple digital big data sets that we might refer to, one that all of us are likely to be familiar with is Twitter, so this will be used for the examples in this section. As digital researchers, the specific focus of our analysis will depend on our discipline, and the specific research question we are asking, but in all cases analysis can be considered at two levels: What do the data look like? And what do the data mean?

What the data look like itself has two aspects: What is the format of the data? And what is the content of the data set? The format of the data represents the structure of data found in individual data sets, and this structure is likely to contain biases (Tufekci, 2014). We need to be aware of the potential for biases in big data sets as biases can impact on the type of insights we can 'extract' from the data. For example, the detail or depth of data may be limited by character length or message size, which was until 2016 the case with Twitter. The second aspect, when considering what the data look like, lies in the problems associated with getting an overview of the huge volume of data that needs to be considered. While statistics might enable us to extract certain descriptors about the data, and frequency counts might allow us to identify dominant themes (e.g., trending hashtags), these methods will only show us what is most common, and this will not necessarily reflect what is most interesting. Even if we are interested in a phenomenon associated with a commonly found category of the data, the structure of search filtering through, for example, hashtags, which can be used on several social media platforms, will find exactly what is searched for. For example, a search for #Iammyownguardian (the social media movement questioning the male guardianship rules of women in Saudi Arabia) will scrape exactly that, and only that, hashtag. If the research questions relate to the broader questions concerning, for example, gender equality then anyone needing data around that subject needs to think more broadly about how to search, even if their purpose is only to find contributors who have used different, abbreviated or incorrectly spelt hashtags or even no hashtags at all.

With any study involving people and their behaviour, the meaning of the data is not always transparent. For example, while a researcher can note the particular hashtags used in tweets, the user's choice of hashtags is embedded in their socio-cultural and personal biases. So developing insights about a social phenomenon using big data is likely to require a critical evaluation of the findings within the socio-cultural context. For example, #guncontrol may appear neutral from its wording as it could represent someone who is for or against gun control, whereas #gaysagainstguns makes the stance taken explicit. A further challenge with the use of hashtag data sets is the self-tagging or self-selection aspect. A piece of data on social media is tagged with one or more hashtags by its creator and/or sharer, thus choosing how the data will be categorised. The act of selecting a hashtag in itself and attaching it to social media content thus creates a filter, which the creator and/or sharer has chosen, not one which the researcher might choose to categorise or filter by. In rudimentary terms, the creator or sharer has pre-coded the data, which may or may not be helpful to a digital researcher, but which will certainly limit the connections possible between different pieces of social media content. A simple illustration could be given by someone visiting a restaurant, photographing their meal and posting it on Instagram with the following hashtags: #deliciousfood #sopretty #salmonandspinach, but not including the restaurant's name. Here the person posting to Instagram has categorised their post and pre-coded it using those three hashtags. These hashtags are useful to a researcher who is searching under those terms (see earlier point) in English to gain insight into the descriptions used by restaurant goers. However, if a researcher was interested in the interactions and relationships between consumers and restaurants through social media, this post without the restaurant's name would be highly likely to be overlooked and, as such, of limited value to the research.

When considering meaning, we also need to consider that popular hashtags which are spread and used widely create very large data sets, which potentially only reflect one perspective, albeit a possibly overwhelming one. The 'other' perspective, the 'missing data' (Allison, 2001), may be less visible on social media, and potentially less easy to capture as data, but may be important in order to reflect the phenomenon being researched. Pursuant to the size and popularity of certain hashtags is the deliberate manipulation of algorithms by people with vested interests to encourage certain hashtags to 'trend' and thus become even more widely spread and even more popular. Those vested interests may be political, such as raising awareness of a politician's illegal behaviour prior to an election, or those interests could be public service information based, such as earthquake information. Digital researchers should recognise this type of forced amplification of a topic and determine, based on their own research objectives and the research context, whether the data sets created can be justifiably used.

Macro and micro big data issues

At a macro-level, in an effort to raise awareness and education about the potential and the challenges of big data and their use in society, various pressure groups, lobbyists and non-politically aligned organisations have begun to ask questions at national and international levels. For example, during the Obama administration's Big Data Review, starting in 2012, the following questions were posed and comments requested from a diverse range of stakeholders, including members of the American public (EPIC, 2014).

> What potential harms arise from big data collection and how are these risks currently addressed?

> What are the legal frameworks currently governing big data, and are they adequate?

> How could companies and government agencies be more transparent in the use of big data, for example, by publishing algorithms?

> What technical measures could promote the benefits of big data while minimising the privacy risks?

> What experience have other countries had trying to address the challenges of big data?

> What future trends concerning big data could inform the current debate?

At a more micro, individual research project level, Tufekci (2014) suggests looking at the individual behind the big data, not a single digital footprint, in essence following the user of hashtags rather than the hashtag itself. Whether this strategy is suitable, or course, depends on your research objectives. Despite the limitations outlined above, big data can provide valuable insight into the human condition. For example, hashtag data sets can provide insights into language use, valence of expressed views, networks created, topical issues, etc. Some of the problems of individual big data sets might be addressed by looking at the same issue across multiple platforms. For example, a variety of social media platforms could be used within one research project. Indeed the data sets created by social media could also be combined with other complementary methods, to enhance the rigour of the research (Felt, 2016). Ultimately we would agree with Tufekci that the context is important and that researchers should sensitise themselves to the context in which their research is situated.

ASSESSING DIGITAL DATA QUALITY

Despite increasing digitalisation in people's lives, countries and global economies, we are aware that digital research is still an emerging research method. As such, researchers who incorporate digital research either as a peripheral, supporting mechanism in their research, or as the core method of investigation, will be required to justify and defend their research choices explicitly in order for the research to be deemed valuable and credible. The terminology used to demonstrate value in research stems from pre-digital research but we are using the broadly accepted terms for ease of reference rather than as an acceptance of the values carried by those terms. Whether we as researchers come from the positivist or constructivist school of thinking we need to demonstrate rigour in our research in order for it to be credible to others. Overall, what appears to be emerging is that when digital is employed as a data collection tool the pre-existing norms of data quantity apply (the established questions, emerging methods quadrant and also the emerging questions, established method quadrant of Figure 1.1 in Chapter 1). So the accepted heuristics for survey numbers, interview numbers, observations undertaken, etc. remain apparently appropriate when transferred to the digital arena. However, when research is on the digital phenomenon itself the context becomes increasingly relevant (emerging questions, emerging method quadrant), which currently might require higher and more explicitly described standards than non-digital norms to produce believable insights to quell any scepticism of the value of the research.

Part of the process of any research project involves assessing the quality of the data and how that impacts on achieving research objectives. In previous sections we considered specific aspects of data quality in relation to research objectives (e.g., how spelling errors might impact on big data searches); here, we consider more general issues such as data sufficiency, validity and reliability of data. While some of these terms have generally been associated with a specific type of data collection, in this text, unless specifically stated, they are used in their broadest sense. That is, sufficiency refers to whether we have enough data to have confidence that we are accurately representing the phenomenon of interest, validity is concerned with how well we are able to show that we are achieving what we claim to be achieving, and reliability addresses our ability to show that our findings are consistent.

Data sufficiency

In all research, data sufficiency has a technical and a perceptual element. Data sufficiency has been achieved when both technical and perceptual minimum requirements are met. The perceptual element is, simply put, whether your research users believe you have sufficient data for the insights you gain from the data to be believable. Identifying what is sufficient for the perceptual element of data sufficiency is usually achieved through looking at historic requirements within the disciplinary context of the research being conducted. As with non-digital research, identifying precedents in previous research within your subject domain will be helpful as a baseline. We suggest searching the relevant academic journal databases (e.g., Business Source Premier, for Business and Management, PsycINFO for Psychology, etc.) and focusing on the method rather than the specific content of a paper in order to determine what quantity of data other researchers have used and how they have justified this amount of data. However, as the digital context is less established than the non-digital context, perceptual data sufficiency is likely to be on the high side of disciplinary/paradigm norms, rather than at the low end.

The technical requirements for data sufficiency depend on the type of research that is being conducted. With more exploratory research, the aim is likely to be related to achieving data saturation. It is hard to definitely determine when data saturation will be reached prior to data collection, and with digital research this might be even more difficult as the data are not necessarily analysed as they are collected. For example, when a researcher has scraped social network content data or Instagram hashtags, it may be that the data have to be collected in stages, or that a larger volume of data than is needed is downloaded, and then that is analysed in stages. The dynamic nature of digital data might mean that what is collected may be representative of that time period's topics across various digital platforms, so careful thought is needed concerning how an appropriate sample can be gained.

In contrast to more exploratory research projects, the data sufficiency requirements related to research projects that determine what a population looks like (descriptive) or whether one thing leads to another (causal) tend to be associated with the analysis procedures used. Statistical analysis tools and techniques, for example, each have 'rules' concerning the technical requirements for the method to be robust. Many of these rules are specific to the technique used, but they often depend on population characteristics and/or research design. For example, sufficient data to be confident of the insights gained about a highly variable population will be greater than what is considered sufficient for a population with little variation. More data will be required to understand the causal relationships between six variables than will be required to understand the relationships between three variables. Overall, data sufficiency in quantitative analysis is not just a case of more data points, but also closely related to how those data points were collected (i.e., the research design). While the digital environment tends to allow access to vast quantities of data, verifying the way in which the data were collected can be more challenging.

For example, if considering conducting a study to explore the relationships created within LinkedIn, using a netnographic approach (for an overview of netnography and netnographic approaches see Kozinets, 2010), the following questions could be asked.

- Which other researchers have used netnography, and where has their work been published?
- How many online communities were incorporated in research designs of this type?
- Within the communities how many conversation threads were followed; how many exchanges were required in each thread?

This information could then be overlaid by the period of time data were collected for: a week, a month, a year, etc. In an example of business relationship development within LinkedIn (adapted from Quinton and Wilson, 2016), eight online wine communities were identified as per Kozinets's (2006) selection criteria, and 186 threads, determined as having a minimum of three exchanges each, were followed for a period of four months, so a total 558 interactions were analysed. These data were then complemented by 12 in-depth Skype enabled interviews with experts from within the chosen industry who were members of those online communities. This number may initially appear to be quite 'low' in relation to the immense volume of digital data generated globally every day. However, as researchers we have to remember the importance of the relevance of the data we need and the ability to access that digital data. So while there may be far more LinkedIn data generated, much of the data are not relevant to the focus of the study and in addition may not be accessible to academic researchers as the data are situated within closed membership groups.

Validity

Validity, put simply, is the extent to which the researcher can demonstrate that they achieved what they set out to achieve. Validity is a measure of trustworthiness and authenticity of the research undertaken (Guba and Lincoln, 1994). Demonstrating validity involves all aspects of the research process, so to demonstrate validity we need to show that there is theoretical congruence between what your research has found and what previous researchers have found; that the methods employed are appropriate to the research questions asked; that the humans or their footprints we examine as part of the research are able to provide data that will contribute to insights in the research area; and that the data analysis used fits with all of the previous elements of the research. That is, in its broadest sense, validity refers to how well the different elements of the research fit together (McGrath and Brinberg, 1983).

Demonstrating validity in digital research requires us to ensure that the different elements of our research design and theorisation fit with our data collection and analysis. This can be problematic when we are using emerging methods that are not fully understood and/or investigating phenomena in a rapidly changing environment. As digital research develops, a greater repository of work will become available. This will provide us, as digital researchers, with the opportunity to see how others have overcome research problems and/or justified their research decisions. This also prompts us to take a more critical stance towards our own digital research and potentially to re-evaluate the value of early studies.

Reliability

Reliability infers consistency. In descriptive and causal research this implies that replication should be possible; in more exploratory research reliability might be related to whether a model can be applied in other contexts. When reliability is considered, it is worth thinking about the level at which consistency is needed. More exploratory research might look at consistency at the model level, descriptive research might be interested in consistency within certain parameters (e.g., confidence intervals), whereas experimental research might want to show how the results can be consistent over time, or across different populations. These types of consistency apply whether or not the research is digital; what is particularly problematic in the digital environment is the dynamic nature of the environment. So, for instance, descriptive research might be hampered because new users on a digital platform (e.g., Twitter users) have substantially changed the population; exploratory research models and experimental findings might become out of date because of changes in the technological environment that change behaviour.

The dynamic nature of the digital environment means that we, to some extent, have to look at our research findings at different levels – that is contextualise them in the socio-technological environment. As the environment changes we are able to identify which aspects of change might have impacted on our insights, and which might not. Because there are so many variables that could change we offer some suggestions for improving reliability in digital research. As digital researchers we can:

- Collect data from multiple data sources – whether these data sources are defined by the human that generated the data or the footprints they leave behind will depend on specific objectives of the research project. For example, you might access core social media influencers working within political activism, then add interview data from elected politicians and layer these data again by adding information from politics journalists.
- Use multiple data collection tools/techniques – by combining non-digital with digital data collection tools you may manage criticism from sceptics who are unused to dealing with digital research. The use of established collection tools as complementary to the 'new' digital tools may help in the persuasion of the reliability of the research.
- Collect data at different time points or over time. This suggestion is to assist in ironing out the 'atypical' data that may have arisen based on an event, such as social media content reporting on civil unrest, and the accompanying trending hashtags or e-commerce activity in the pre and post-Christmas sale period.
- Transfer an established theory to a new subject or context. By taking an established and recognised theory, you are at least starting with a strong foundation, though some critics might argue that the digital environment in and of itself is a new world and that much previously established theory no longer is applicable. For example, you could decide to apply models of face-to-face communication to the social media environment, or the Technology Acceptance Model to the use of wearables by older people to track their health.

Another way of ensuring the quality of the insights derived from digital research is to use methodological triangulation. Indeed, many of the methods used to increase reliability are related to producing a stronger body of evidence, which any reviewer, examiner or supervisor can then evaluate. Triangulation, which may also include mixed methods approaches to research, can help in reinforcing your findings. However, triangulation/ mixed methods research may also bring to light core differences between results generated from different sources or different data collection tools. These differences can form the base for further study or can lead to the redesign or amendments of the current study in order to clarify the research insights.

SUMMARY

In this chapter we have explored what constitutes passive and active digital research and identified the core opportunities and challenges of both. Importantly we have outlined arguments for contextually dependent, non-disclosed data collection and have provided a set of questions that will be valuable for researchers in determining a justifiable research design when deciding whether or not to disclose themselves. In addition, we have highlighted when disclosure is important within social science research. Our discussion has extended to the increasing use of automation in research design and analysis and has proposed the need for human oversight as digital research becomes more technology driven. Big data as a concept has been outlined in the context of digital research with its attendant challenges. Suggestions have been provided as a guiding measure to assist with the issues of achieving data sufficiency within the digital research realm. Finally we have explored the concepts of validity and reliability in relation to digital research.

The 3Es

Ethics issues are abundant when considering research sampling. A crucial challenge is the decision on whether or not to undertake research in a particular research environment, considering, for example, participant vulnerability, topic sensitivity and the potential for participants to retain their anonymity in the digital environment. If the decision is made to go ahead with research, then ethics considerations continue and include when, indeed if, and how, the research is disclosed to the participants. More broadly, digital researchers have to consider ethics issues related to how we view research participants and their 'ownership' of the data they provide, whether passive data collection is desirable, for example, and how disaggregated research findings need to be to constitute an invasion of privacy.

Learning how to identify the 'who' or 'what' that is researched in the digital context is a crucial skill for researchers to master. However, it has become apparent that many of the skills required of social science researchers working in the digital domain are not consistently developed within social science methods training. The consequences of this are that social science researchers may need to look outside their disciplines for the expertise required to undertake truly ground-breaking digital research. For example, the complexities and increasing automation of the digital environment challenges us to develop the knowledge and skills necessary to manage research within this increasingly algorithm driven environment. Is it desirable or even necessary to understand these algorithms and the potential impact they have on digital research?

As researchers we may expect to be able to collect and/or access large digital data sets. This idealistic expectation is rarely realised as many digital data sets have high commercial value, and the proprietorial interests mean commercial owners of the databases are unwilling to provide access. Furthermore, digital researchers encounter the obsolescence of much of the data held in open data sets, which necessitates them altering their expectations to be able to work with incomplete data. Digital research also challenges our expectations in relation to the resources required to undertake research projects. Institutional resources such as computing power, as well as the time and effort required to develop the skills necessary to undertake digital research, need to be considered when planning digital research. More seriously, our expectations that establishing validity and reliability will ensure research longevity do not always hold because of the rapidly changing digital context.

Questions

1. Have you reflected on the implications of disclosed or non-disclosed data collection and made that explicit in your writing up?
2. If algorithms are involved in any aspect of your research, what provisions have you made to justify their usage?
3. What steps can you take and then explain to enhance the validity of your digital research?

FURTHER READING

John Naughton's ongoing observations on big data, society and privacy can be found in the *Guardian* newspaper.

Crawford, K. (2013). The hidden biases in big data. *Harvard Business Review*, 1 April. Available from: https://hbr.org/2013/04/the-hidden-biases-in-big-data (accessed 28 November 2016).

Perry, W.L., McInnis, B., Price, C.C., Smith, S.C. and Hollywood, J.S. (2013). *Predictive Policing: The Role of Crime Forecasting in Law Enforcement Operations*. Santa Monica, CA: RAND Corporation. Available from: www.rand.org/content/dam/rand/pubs/research_reports/RR200/RR233/RAND_RR233.pdf (accessed 19 September 2017).

REFERENCES

Allison, P.D. (2001). *Missing Data*. Thousand Oaks, CA: Sage.

Barak, A. and Miron, O. (2005). Writing characteristics of suicidal people on the internet: A psychological investigation of emerging social environments. *Suicide and Life Threatening Behaviour*, *35* (5), 507–524.

Boyd, D. and Crawford, K. (2012). Critical questions for big data: Provocations for a cultural, technological, and scholarly phenomenon. *Information, Communication & Society*, *15* (5), 662–679.

Brawley, A.M. and Pury, C.L. (2016). Work experiences on MTurk: Job satisfaction, turnover, and information sharing. *Computers in Human Behavior*, *54*, 531–546.

Chui, M., Manyika, J. and Miremadi, M. (2015). Four fundamentals of workplace automation. *McKinsey Quarterly*, November. Available from: www.mckinsey.com/business-functions/digital-mckinsey/our-insights/four-fundamentals-of-workplace-automation (accessed 19 September 2017).

Cresci, E. (2015). #timetotalk: Is social media helping people talk about mental health? The *Guardian*, 5 February. Available from: www.theguardian.com/technology/2015/feb/05/timetotalk-is-social-media-helping-people-talk-about-mental-health (accessed 27 June 2016).

EPIC (2014). Big Data and the future of privacy. Economic Privacy Information Center. Available from: https://epic.org/privacy/big-data (accessed 26 January 2017).

Felt, M. (2016). Social media and the social sciences: How researchers employ big data. *Big Data & Society*, Jan–June, 1–15.

Guba, E. and Lincoln, Y. (1994). Competing paradigms in qualitative research. In N.K. Denzin and Y.S. Lincoln (eds), *Handbook of Qualitative Research*. Thousand Oaks, CA: Sage, pp. 163–194.

Hewson, C., Vogel, C. and Laurent, D. (2016). *Internet Research Methods* (2nd edn). London: Sage.

Hudson, J.M. and Bruckman, A. (2004). Go away: Participant objections to being studied and the ethics of chatroom research. *Information Society*, *20* (2), 127–139.

Kozinets, R.V. (2002). The field behind the screen: Using netnography for marketing research in online communities. *Journal of Marketing Research*, *39* (February), 61–72.

Kozinets, R.V. (2006). Click to connect: Netnography and tribal advertising. *Journal of Advertising Research*, *46* (3), 279–288.

Kozinets, R.V. (2010). *Netnography: Doing Ethnographic Research Online*. Thousand Oaks, CA: Sage.

Langer, R. and Beckman, S.C. (2005). Sensitive research topics: Netnography revisited. *Qualitative Market Research: An International Journal*, *8* (2), 189–203.

McGrath, J.E. and Brinberg, D. (1983). External validity and the research process: A comment on the Calder/Lynch dialogue. *Journal of Consumer Research*, *10* (1), 115–124.

Mckee, H.A. and Porter, J.E. (2009). *The Ethics of Internet Research: A Rhetorical Case-Based Process*. New York: Peter Lang Publishing Inc.

Meyer, E.T. and Schroeder, R. (2015). *Knowledge Machines: Digital Transformations of the Sciences and Humanities*. Cambridge, MA: MIT Press.

Molesworth, M. and Denegri-Knott, J. (2012). *Digital Virtual Consumption*. London: Routledge.

Naughton, J. (2014). We are all being mined for data but who are the real winners? The *Guardian*, 8 June. Available from: www.theguardian.com/technology/2014/jun/08/big-data-mined-real-winners-nsa-gchq-surveillance (accessed 5 November 2016).

Nelson, L. (2014). Proximity marketing in retail – Regent Street. Airspace, 30 June. Available from: http://airspace.cc/proximity-marketing-in-retail-regent-street/ (accessed 19 September 2017).

Paccagnella, L. (1997). Getting the seats of your pants dirty: Strategies for ethnographic research on virtual communities. *Journal of Computer-Mediated Communication, 3* (1).

Quinton, S. and Wilson, D. (2016). Tensions and ties in social media networks: Towards a model of understanding business relationship development and performance enhancement through the use of LinkedIn. *Industrial Marketing Management, 54*, 15–24.

Reynolds, N. and Ruiz de Maya, S. (2013). The impact of complexity and perceived difficulty on consumer revisit intentions. *Journal of Marketing Management, 29* (5–6), 625–645.

Sugiura, L., Pope, C. and Webber, C. (2012). Buying unlicensed slimming drugs from the Web: A virtual ethnography. In *Proceedings of the 4th Annual ACM Web Science Conference*. ACM, June, pp. 284–287.

Tufekci, Z. (2014). Big questions for social media big data: Representativeness, validity and other methodological pitfalls. In *ICWSM '14: Proceedings of the 8th International AAAI Conference on Weblogs and Social Media*. Available from: www.aaai.org/Press/Proceedings/icwsm14.php (accessed 19 September 2017).

Whitney, J. (2016). The cultural anxieties of automation. The Digital Cultures Research Centre, 25 February. Available from: https://rhystranter.com/2016/02/29/robots-technology-automation-anxiety-cultural-history/ (accessed 04 January 2018).

Zwitter, A. (2014). Big data ethics. *Big Data & Society*, July–Dec, 1–6. DOI: 10.1177/2053951714559253

PART 3
Moving Forward with Digital Research

This part moves the text beyond the discussion focusing on specific aspects of digital research into the more applied and practical realms of actually doing digital research. Having unpicked the complex and often integrated concepts concerning both the phenomenon and the methods of digital research, including outlining how ethics, expectations and expertise related to each area, our attention now turns to practical aspects in Chapter 7 before drawing the ideas together and closing the book in Chapter 8.

In Chapter 7 we consider the practice of digital research. Managing practical aspects of digital research can be intimidating and so we have included insight into the public/private data blurring, temporality and the questions researchers should ask, in addition to how to manage and avoid some of the more common digital research pitfalls. Acknowledging the dynamic digital environment, we draw attention to the ongoing dilemmas for digital research and researchers. The three Es of ethics, expertise and expectations are embedded within Chapter 7 rather than considered in its summary. Ethics aspects of designing and executing digital research are foregrounded in Chapter 7 with guidelines to act as a foundation for good practice in what is becoming a significant topic within digital research. Issues of expertise include the increasing need for a researcher to develop a portfolio of skills to be competent as a digital researcher both in terms of executing rigorously designed research as it becomes increasingly technical, and also as a knowledgeable appraiser of other researchers' digital research. Expectations of research stakeholders include the consideration that must be given to participants who are the core constituents of digital research.

Chapter 8 revisits what has already been covered. It opens by briefly considering how this book has contributed to digital research before recapping the three Es. While the three Es have been treated separately previously, here we provide an extended illustration to show how they might be encountered within a particular digital research issue. We started the book with a simplistic summary of digital research from two interacting perspectives – phenomenon and method/instrument. We close by presenting a more nuanced view of how these two perspectives interact, providing a summarising tool researchers can use in their own research.

7

THE PRACTICALITIES OF DOING DIGITAL RESEARCH

In this chapter we will:

- outline the different ways the digital context might contribute to research
- highlight key ethics issues that arise in digital research
- foreground the practical aspects of digital research
- suggest the skills required by the digital researcher
- discuss key pitfalls and provide advice for digital researchers.

INTRODUCTION

This chapter melds the previously discussed re-conceptualisations of research that have been outlined across the book into a set of pragmatic guidelines and suggestions to make the previous abstract discussion more concrete for those researchers engaging with digital research in the social sciences. The core themes of context and temporality will be returned to and the skills required to be a digital researcher will be explicated. We will illustrate how to defend your digital research ideas through providing models and frameworks in this chapter and we will offer practical advice on designing your research. Importantly this chapter will also contribute a guide to conducting ethical digital research.

Having established in Chapter 2 that the boundaries of research have become increasingly blurred by digitalisation and the adoption of digital and social media by society, in this chapter we offer suggestions for researchers who are trying to refocus the blurred boundaries. The boundaries between qualitative versus quantitative research have altered, the division between public and private data has been smeared, and digital technologies have irrevocably changed what we can research within the social sciences and how we can conduct research. The implications of this extended research horizon means that with so much choice for researchers, clarity and congruity becomes increasingly important as a way to establish rigour and internal validity in our research.

As we have frequently stated in this text, digital research is an emerging area and, as such, it is having to earn its place in both the research methods lexicon and through its adoption by social science researchers. Early digital research often used digital methods in a supporting role, as a complementary but very much junior research partner; for example, transferring an offline questionnaire about people's musical preferences to an online questionnaire alongside expert interviews. Incrementally we have seen digital research methods become used as part of a mixed methods approach to research in the social sciences. Indeed the *Journal of Mixed Methods Research* frequently contains research combining digital and non-digital methods (e.g., Hesse-Biber and Griffin, 2012) and now research papers are published that use digital research methods as a stand-alone research approach;

see, for example, Stefanidis and co-authors (2013) in geography, Maire and colleagues (2017) in computing and statistics, and Xiang et al. (2017) in tourism management.

HOW CAN DIGITAL FORM PART OF MY RESEARCH?

As you are reading this book you may be considering the ways in which digital could be used in research or how it could form part of a research project. To assist in shaping your thinking, a non-exhaustive list of how digital might be used in social science research is shown in Table 7.1. This list is intended to spark your own further thinking.

Table 7.1 The potential uses of digital in social science research

Digital as

- phenomenon
- a research process
- data sets to examine
- recruitment tool for participants
- dissemination tool for research instruments
- research instrument
- complementary research tool
- part of analysis process
- communication tool for research outputs

First, digital has potential for research as a social science phenomenon. Here it forms the basis of the research question. Second, digital can be considered as the basis for the research process, forming a stand-alone methodology or used in conjunction with non-digital methods as part of a mixed methods approach. Both of these possibilities have been discussed throughout this book. Third, digital can be the source of the data sets we examine. Digital might provide you with already collected data sets, which can be ana-lysed as secondary data, for example, the Web Observatory at Southampton University, and open source data sets such as SOTORN in Australia. Digital might be able to pro-vide an avenue for the collection of primary data through the use of digital tools, for example, the design and implementation of online questionnaires or the vlogging inter-actions of vintage car restoration enthusiasts. Historic primary data can also be digital, such as scraping an online community forum on post-natal depression for a project focusing on post-natal depression. Fourth, digital might be used as a recruitment tool for researchers to access potential participants in research projects such as requests via Facebook social media or posting a request to special interest online community groups, such as gardening groups, for a project interested in understanding the role of physical activity in the wellbeing of older citizens.

Fifth, digital communication can be used as a dissemination tool for research instruments. Social media and digital tools such as email and Twitter messages can assist in spreading the research instrument, distributing an online questionnaire, to a wider, non-geographically limited audience, for example, exploratory research focusing on sustainable fashion purchasers may be spread easily across countries/borders. Sixth, digital platforms might host the research instrument, for example, a straightforward online questionnaire, or using Skype for interviewing. Seventh, digital platforms might be used as complementary research tools. If the disciplinary or institutional norms are not fully accepting of the potential value of having a purely digital focus to how data might be collected and/or analysed, then we suggest using digital as a complementary tool, where appropriate, in a research project. For example, interviews with workers in a firm could be combined with observation and tracking of website usage in a project investigating information searching within an organisational capacity. Alternatively health wearable data could be combined with face-to-face focus group data to determine the influences on the purchase of fitness wearables and the subsequent usage of the product.

Eighth, digital processing may be used as part of the analysis. Collected data can be drawn from a wide range of established or digital data collection tools then uploaded into software analysis packages. For example, NodeXL, which has been built on the Excel platform, can import Flickr, Twitter, Instagram and Facebook data and illustrate relationships between the content of posts as well as the links between the posters and commenters etc., through semantic network visualisations. The ninth way in which digital can be used as part of research is as a digital communication tool that can be used for research dissemination. Good practice in research requires us to disseminate our results as broadly as possible and certainly to the stakeholders of our research, be they participants, organisations which granted us permission, research funders, or the wider local community. Digital can be a vital tool in this dissemination of research outputs. Activities such as writing a research blog, creating a podcast of your main findings and uploading this to a research project website, or posting a conference paper you have written or providing slides to Slideshare after a presentation for the benefit of the wider academic community, can all be used to disseminate research digitally. While these activities take time, they are very low cost, and will increase the awareness of your research and your research results.

Socio-cultural context of digital research

Within the social sciences, different disciplines have different research norms, different institutions differ in their level of acceptance of novel research methods, and different countries have different laws that might apply to research in the digital environment.

These all contribute to the socio-cultural context of the digital researcher themselves. Layered onto the digital researcher's socio-cultural context we have the socio-cultural context of the research participants. While there are claims that social media and digitalisation are 'globalising' the world and producing more homophilic behaviours, the influence of socio-cultural norms and behaviours that may be disparate remains prevalent. Human behaviours and attitudes found in the digital context reflect the lives as lived in particular socio-cultural contexts; for example, attitudes towards gay marriage in Australia or what constitutes modest dress in different parts of the world. The digital environment is not separate from the interactions, attitudes and prevailing patterns of behaviour across groups of people, indeed, in some instances these are magnified by the digital environment. Some behaviours have been facilitated by the advent and adoption of digital communication and social media platforms, such that behaviours that would be considered unacceptable offline are not uncommon online. Think, for example, of flaming and trolling on social media and the need for moderator or community interventions when people post abusive content that would rarely if ever be said face-to-face. New socio-cultural groupings can also emerge via digitalisation. These can cross previously established socio-cultural boundaries of age, geography, economic status. These homophilic groups are based on common interests, be it carers of people suffering from a particular disease, students on the same MBA course, or Spanish guitar players. None of these groups are bounded by where people live, how much money they earn or demographic factors such as gender or age. The digital context has rendered irrelevant previously applied segmentation variables, so as a digital researcher the consideration of context of the sample remains important. Nevertheless, the increased spread and reach of digital and social media does create the potential for large data sets which may transcend specific contexts, and may encourage the belief that results are generalisable. However, combining culturally different data sets can create issues as not all social concepts and beliefs are universal. The socio-cultural context will help guide our research choices both in terms of what is likely to be accepted within the particular academic context we operate in, and in terms of what makes sense for our particular research questions.

Temporality in digital research

As outlined in Chapter 4, temporality within digital research creates opportunities and challenges for researchers across a number of areas. When considering how temporality can impact on how digital contributes to research, different aspects of temporality have to be considered. Research into unpredictable events and the speed of digital responses to those events can result in data collection occurring after the event itself. For example, analysing the speed of the spread and reach of the communication of the Boston marathon bombing in America would involve collecting the digital data across multiple social media platforms, alongside mainstream news and media channels, potentially in more than one language, to create insight. When, for how long, and how data were collected could, among other factors, impact on the insights gained into the phenomenon, influence the choices concerning how the data sets were accessed, and affect how participants were 'recruited'. Slower moving events such as the rise of awareness of online gambling addiction in young adults through mainstream media journalism and social media content, present different temporal problems. Temporal research decisions, such as at what point in time these relatively slow moving changes are studied and for how long, need to be considered as these research decisions will relate to the insights gained. Overall, as researchers working in the digital environment we need to be aware of the limitations and the influence of temporality in relation to our digital research.

Taking a practical view of temporality, the following questions need to be answered when we scope our research project.

- What socio-cultural perspective are we talking about with regard to time as a concept, and will that have implications for our research?
- What perspectives on temporality and time do our intended participants hold (if we know this)? The latter point may be pertinent if we are intending to conduct multi-national research and/or a project that includes participants from non-Western backgrounds as values and notions concerning time and temporality can be very different.
- What time frames and in what time period are we intending to research and why?
- Which technologies and/or platforms will assist in facilitating our data collection in relation to whether synchronous, near synchronous or asynchronous data or a mixture of data are required?
- Should we include non-digital approaches to data collection in addition to or instead of digital technologies if they will contribute a more temporally complete data set with which to answer our research objectives?

DIGITAL RESEARCH ETHICS

Navigating the digital research ethics terrain can be complex and, at the time of writing, there is limited concrete advice for those undertaking research using digital tools or research encompassing the digital phenomenon. The Association of Internet Researchers (AoIR), based in the USA, does provide a helpful overview, which is updated periodically (http://aoir.org/). The association includes 'digital' within its definition of internet research and so for consistency we will use 'internet' when referring to the AoIR's guidelines.

The AoIR outlines current tensions and the resulting research challenges within internet/digital research. It separates these tensions/challenges into aspects concerned with 1) human subjects, 2) public/private, and 3) data both as text and people. Human subjects and their consideration as the central point of research ethics may be problematic when internet research does not necessarily directly involve humans. The term 'subject' also creates issues for researchers in relation to the passivity associated with the term and its origination stemming from laboratory based science research in which humans were 'subjected' to tests etc. The AoIR guidelines recognise that the previously binary division between what is private and what is public has now been significantly and irrevocably blurred by the advent of internet/digital research. Importantly, the perceptions and expectations of individuals in regard to whether their data are public or private is socially constructed across different cultural and/or geographical barriers. The aggregation of data into big data sets can exacerbate problems as data may be combined from sources with different notions of what is public/private. The fluidity creates a significant challenge for researchers. Data as text or as people is also problematic within the internet/digital sphere as people may or may not be part of the research. For example, digital researchers may be unaware that avatars, Bots and artificial intelligence units could either be involved in research or 'acting' as human participants in research. AoIR propose a detailed set of questions to ask ourselves, which will help to pinpoint research ethics issues. These are presented in Table 7.2.

Table 7.2 Ethics questions to consider (adapted from AoIR guidelines)

Research value

- What are the potential benefits associated with this study?
- What are the potential harms or risks associated with this study?

Context and focus

- How is context defined and conceptualised?
- How is context (venue/participants/data) being accessed?
- What is the primary object of the study?

People

- Who is involved in the study?
- How are we recognising the autonomy of others and acknowledging that they are of equal worth to ourselves and should be treated so?
- What particular issues might arise around the issue of minors or vulnerable persons?

Data analysis and findings

- How are data being managed, stored and represented?
- How are texts/persons/data being studied?
- How are findings presented?

In addition to the AoIR guidelines researchers can also look to more general principles, such as the 2015 Academy of Social Science (www.acss.org.uk) guidelines. Their five principles provide guidelines that are based on the underlying socio-cultural context in which the research work is taking place, and provide normative advice concerning how researchers should behave (see Table 7.3). Not surprisingly both organisations include evaluation of the contribution the research is expected to make, consider the relationship between methods and research questions, include explicit consideration of the research participants and also expect researchers to act responsibly.

Table 7.3   The ethics principles of the Academy of Social Science

Social science is fundamental to a democratic society and should be inclusive of different interests, values, funders, methods and perspectives

All social science should:

- respect the privacy, autonomy, diversity, values and dignity of individuals, groups and communities
- be conducted with integrity throughout, employing the most appropriate methods for the research purpose
- act with regard to their social responsibilities in conducting and disseminating their research
- aim to maximise benefit and minimise harm

How, then, can we ensure we make appropriate ethics decisions in the design and execution of our digital research? Two key areas are helpful to consider: How do we practise respect for research participants? How do we enact ethics in digital research?

Respect for research participants

When ensuring the respect of digital research participants by researchers, there are three key areas where the characteristics of the digital environment lead to additional consideration being required. These relate to consent, withdrawal and attachment to digital artefacts.

On-going consent

Aside from the difficulties of gaining consent associated with the identification of individual participants (see previous discussions), digital research may involve multi-layered data collection processes and outputs, for example, the production and analysis of digital images, the contents of which are not known at the outset of the research. In these cases, assuming participants can be identified, a process of on-going consent can be initiated at different stages of the research rather than the established one-off consent at the beginning of a research project. Consent might also be implied by the participant taking part in a particular stage, as long as this is made clear when participants are engaged in the relevant digital activity. We have transferred this idea from arts-based subjects such as social sculpture where research is often a series of progressing interventions, with unknown outputs at each stage. Through requesting consent at different stages of the research the element of trust may be enhanced between researchers and participants.

Whether consent is needed for digital research has also been questioned. A useful scale system created by Mckee and Porter and augmented by us can help in determining whether informed consent is advisable (Table 7.4). Using the scale you can determine whether or not you are likely to need informed consent; the higher your overall score is when you add all the individual scale items together, the more likely you are to require some level of informed consent from your participants.

Table 7.4 Scale to evaluate the need for informed consent

Sensitivity of the research topic	Low .... High
Vulnerability of person or community	Low .... High
Level of interaction required by researcher	Low .... High
Extent to which data are considered private	Low .... High
Potential risk/harm to participants of identifiable data	Low .... High
Extent to which images of people are involved	Low .... High

Withdrawal from digital research

Following good practice in offline research ethics, participants in digital research should be explicitly informed that they have the right to withdraw at any stage of the research and that any unprocessed data will be removed from the study. Furthermore participants should not be asked why they are withdrawing as this could be perceived as implied coercion. However, this is sometimes easier to achieve with established research methods as removing digital data can be complex and time consuming.

The participant's right to withdraw needs to be considered when the digital research design is developed. As all participants have the right to withdraw from research without being asked why, it is worth considering how explicit we make this right in the design of any digital research. How should this right be communicated? Is withdrawal implied when a participant ceases to engage with the research? For instance, do we design online questionnaires with a withdraw button at the end of every screen page as well as at the end of the questionnaire prior to submitting any responses (British Psychological Society, 2013), or do we assume that participants who have not completed the whole questionnaire have exercised their right to withdraw? Following this suggestion to make the option to withdrawal more explicit, the option to submit should also be very clearly communicated so that the participant is aware that by pressing a button the data they have provided will be uploaded to the research project. A confirmation should also be designed into the instrument, thanking the participant and confirming that the data have been submitted. Many online research instruments miss these stages.

The research design should also consider and have a strategy in place for any post submission data withdrawal requests (though this would need to be before the data analysis process has been undertaken). The research design ideally needs to consider the feasibility of a mechanism to link each participant to their original data, which may be difficult in the case of experiments and/or totally anonymised surveys where no IP addresses are logged etc. If the design does not allow a link between individual participants and their particular responses, then this should be made clear prior to submission of any data. However, if a participant can withdraw after submission of their data, then consideration should be given as to where and how they are made aware of this option. Regardless of whether withdrawal is technically possible after data have been submitted, it remains important for transparency and as part of good research practice that the researcher should be contactable by any participant.

Identification of research participants

Another consideration that digital researchers might need to think through is whether it is appropriate to ask participants for email addresses in order to disseminate the research results and how this may relate to any promises of anonymity that have been given to participants. Platforms such as Qualtrics have the ability to request and store email addresses separately from the main part of a questionnaire, for example, if participants wish to be entered into a prize draw as a response incentive. This may be helpful to researchers as a way to contact specific participants but will obviously not include all the participants.

Acknowledgement of participant attachment to artefacts

Digital research needs to recognise the extent and level of participant involvement in and with the digital context. Research participants, particularly those engaged with social media and visual-based platforms, may have a strong attachment to content that has been either self-generated or has strong connective associations for those participants (Gubrium et al., 2014). Insufficient consideration has been given in research about how people feel about digital, particularly visual, content and how it relates to their sense of self (Belk, 2013), for example, uploaded photographs and videos that might contain people, animals or places that those who created and/or shared care about, such as family members, domestic pets or family homes. An explicit statement acknowledging the value attached by people to visual and other digital artefacts can be included within any research design.

Enacting ethics in digital research

What is good research practice? How do we ensure that we develop projects that meet the ethical expectations of the research stakeholders? These questions are relevant to how we, as digital researchers, enact good research practice and are considered below.

Adopt good commercial research practice

A large volume of the digital research that occurs is undertaken outside the academic environment. These digital researchers design and execute research within the ethical guidelines of their professional bodies and their good practice may provide a source of how digital ethics challenges may be addressed. Although academic researchers may be initially doubtful of referring to the world of commerce, many of the innovations in digital research have originated in the commercial world of market research. Commercial researchers have access to more extensive resources that allow them to pilot newer forms of research, for example, marketing research firms using neuromarketing research which involves tracking brain activity in relation to promotional material and ecommerce websites. Looking towards how market research organisations and research foundations operationalise their digital research may provide valuable insight into good research practice such as the offering of summary reports by email to participants.

Unpacking collaborative research expectations

Explicitly recognising the expectations of the different stakeholders in digital research can contribute to ensuring that individual research projects avoid potential problems. Even as a solitary Masters' or PhD researcher working alone on a project your participants will have expectations. As research in the digital era becomes increasingly collaborative, explicit guidelines for managing this type of research should be written for each research project (Cox et al., 2014). An outline of the expectations of the different participants and collaborators in the research should be documented and shared. Where suitable, this document could even be placed on a research website for increased transparency. Improved clarity between researchers, funders of research and participants has also been highlighted in a report by Evans et al. (2015) for the UK policy research group Demos regarding social ethics and research as being increasingly important.

Dissemination of research results

Increasingly within Europe, the UK and beyond, good research practice includes the wide and appropriate dissemination of research findings. Researchers are increasingly being encouraged to reflect on the societal and cultural impact of their research as well as the development of scholarship within a subject area. Digital technologies can provide a real advantage in the dissemination of research results from individual small scale studies to larger international funded projects. The diverse platform opportunities facilitated by digital technologies means that it is easier than ever before to reach wider audiences and to interact with research stakeholder groups. It is, however, worth thinking carefully about how research dissemination is achieved – for example, consideration is needed of when it is appropriate to make different elements of the research public, and digital researchers should consider how digital dissemination of results, for instance, might impact on more traditional forms of academic dissemination (e.g., journal articles). Posting results of a research study onto a research blog before you have submitted a doctoral thesis or an article that contains the same data to a journal is not advised as accusations of self-plagiarism or academic misconduct can arise, based on a search engine's ability to find other, similar versions of your own work.

Digital dissemination can take many forms. Some of these are outlined in Table 7.5. The platforms and approaches to dissemination you take will depend on the context of the research project and your subject norms.

Table 7.5 Examples of digital dissemination of research

Blogs	Individual researchers can use blogs as researcher diaries and include interim results and summaries of findings as well as send web links to the participants of a study. Thus the participants can engage with different stages of the study and stay informed about the progress of the research.
Image-based social media platforms	Any research project that involves images as part of its analysis of results could use Instagram or Flickr to great effect to upload illustrations and/or visualisations, word clouds, charts, etc. to a chosen platform to exhibit the results of a project.
Text-based social media platforms	Research can be quickly disseminated to certain stakeholders via Twitter or LinkedIn with links to research reports, research websites, etc. embedded in the short messages. This form of dissemination can be effective in reaching key individuals in industries, commercial organisations, as well as social media influencers who might 'retweet' to a far wider audience that you could reach alone.
Research websites	Funded or sponsored research projects may decide to spend some resources on the design and content management of a dedicated research project website. These websites can act as a research hub with all the information in one place, including documents such as participant information sheets, consent forms, time lines as well as any background to the study and its funders. Interim reports and conference papers can also be uploaded and links to related projects and/or researcher profiles can also be included. Videos outlining key results can be embedded on these websites and used as a further resource for broadcasting the research to wider audiences. Links from research websites can be made to the relevant universities, non-profit organisations and research funders that may be partners in the project.

Ongoing ethics challenges in relation to digital research

Despite the best intention of ethics guidelines for digital researchers various ethical issues remain unclear in digital research including areas such as the use of closed groups on social media, autonomy of participants, and fair exchange for the co-creation of research by participants. As researchers in the social sciences, research ethics should remain uppermost in how we conceptualise and implement our research. The advent and evolution of digital research requires us to try to regain some focus on the blurred boundaries of research ethics that might have occurred. Key research ethics issues facing digital researchers include: the use and attribution of social media data; the use and ownership of visual image data; the desirable levels of anonymity of social media data; the lack of transparency in algorithms both in data collection and analysis, and in participant platforms and sampling.

Issues associated with research design and implementation

A continuing challenge in the digital context arises from the researcher having less control over sampling. Characteristics of the digital environment such as the relationship between physical identity and individual accounts on a particular platform (see Table 5.2 in Chapter 5), as well as user ability to separate their digital and physical identities, contribute to this lack of control. Lijadi and van Schalkwyk (2015) among others have proposed the use of secret groups on social media platforms such as Facebook to help regain some control of the sample. Recruitment using secret groups can ensure that the participants are not able to identify each other, even though the researcher can actively manage the constituents of the group through their invitation to the group. However, these secret groups have been misused by those wishing to share and discuss illegal and/or socially unacceptable activity such as paedophilia, and we suggest caution is used when considering the suitability of these type of closed social media groups.

Non-digital established research ethics principles remain the baseline for responsible digital research, and one aspect of digital research – data and their storage – clearly falls within the remit of research ethics. While some universities sign storage arrangements with organisations such as Google (e.g., using of Google Drive as a 'safe' storage facility), sceptics might point out that Google then has all that research data – across formats and levels of de-identification and what such organisations might do with that research data is not transparent. In our experience, large organisations sign these types of agreements without understanding the issues of data ownership, potential misappropriation and the commercial value of data. Careful scrutiny of these agreements is needed to ensure that the data concerned cannot be accessed, sold and/or used by other parties. Another potential danger if data ownership is not clear is whether data sets can be combined to create profiles and thus the likely identities of the research participants as a result. Safer cloud storage is offered by organisations such as the French service Cozy or the German service T-Systems, which remove the risks associated with Amazon and Google services.

Alternatively we can seek more controllable environments for our research data, whether through a different set of tools or storage facilities. These alternatives have developed from certain European countries that are concerned about digital data storage, specifically Germany and Denmark. For example Xing is a German equivalent of LinkedIn where all data are stored on servers in Germany that fully comply with strict data protection laws in Germany. Smaller organisations and charities often use Facebook as a cheap approach to sharing information, even health related information, yet Facebook's terms and conditions mean that they have access to those highly personal data. Groupcare is a Danish-based alternative to Facebook groups, on which the individual retains all rights to the data that they share. These groups are hosted by servers in Denmark. For research students with specific concerns or an interest in data ethics, www.dataethics.eu is an apolitically independent think tank based in Denmark, which acts as a resource hub for those thinking about data and the ethical implications arising from the collection and storage of digital data.

Considering research participants and other stakeholders

Ensuring the autonomy, privacy and dignity of potential participants also remains a complex issue. As digital researchers we have an ever greater ability to research a variety of phenomena and work with different individuals and groups. Nevertheless, this does not necessarily mean that we should undertake research into some phenomenon and/or participants. Some individuals and groups choose digital methods of interaction in order to remain inconspicuous and unknown to the wider population. These people have the right to privacy and autonomy in deciding not to be involved in any research, though this presupposes they are aware of any research being conducted in the first place.

Fair exchange for research participants is an area that has been largely disregarded by academic research across the social sciences. While some studies include token incentives for participation, or the possibility of receiving a summary report of findings, full consideration has yet to be made of the value provided by research participants in their contributions to research. We recognise that full financial payment to a research participant may not be possible owing to a lack of research funding. We also recognise that financial payment might be counterproductive when the motivations of participants are considered – think, for example, of the motivations of people who contribute to open source software development, or share their knowledge via platforms such as Wikipedia. Consequently, full financial reimbursement may not be desirable as most research in the social sciences is founded on the basis of voluntary, unpaid participation and this norm should be maintained. However, greater explicit acknowledgement of participants and other stakeholders who inform our research should be given. This acknowledgement could be in the form of written thanks, distribution of summary reports of the results, or acknowledging generally the participants in the foreword of a thesis (though not necessarily by name).

Furthermore and importantly, ethics issues can arise in not understanding the cultural norms of the groups with which we engage digitally or through social media. Different norms exist within different online communities and across international groups. Prior to commencing any research project it is worthwhile sensitising yourself to the norms of your intended research participants. Sensitising can take the form of reading others' work on the same types of groups, it can also include lurking at the peripheries of these groups to learn their use of language, communication interactions and expected behaviours, so as to design strengthened and contextually nuanced research (Kozinets, 2010). Socio-cultural group norms can be nuanced and implicit, or more explicit and guided by a moderator or key influencers in the group, so it is worth noting which approach appears to dominate in an online community. It is also advisable to elicit support for the research by approaching any key individuals. Unless, of course, you believe that the interactions and subject material would be fundamentally changed by doing so and thus alter the research data collected (see Chapter 6 on disclosure/nondisclosure).

As researchers we consider the pre-eminent principle of doing no harm to our research participants but within the digital domain we need to extend this to doing no harm to any digital community we may wish to involve or use in our research. Collaborative interactions can impact on the ownership or perceived ownership of content that may be collected and used for research. Mckee and Porter (2009) discuss whether communities and online interactions should be considered as spaces made up of people or spaces as text. If the former then even greater care is required not to disturb the balance of the ecosystem, if the space is considered text then possibly informed consent is not required but attention should be paid to any legal copyright or ownership of material.

SOME PRACTICALITIES OF DIGITAL RESEARCH

There are many practicalities associated with particular digital research projects, and the section below considers some commonly encountered issues that need to be reflected upon in relation to digital research.

Digital platforms, protocols and packages

An increasing amount of digital research involves access to and use of various types of technology, from social media platforms, through software packages, to API protocols. These require not only the specific skills needed to maximise the effective use of the specific technologies (see section on skills required below) but also the expertise to be able to assess the suitability of the technologies now available for research. Practically speaking, researchers may find it helpful to use the set of questions in Table 7.6 as criteria for assessing potential technologies for a digital research project.

Table 7.6 Questions to assess the usefulness of digital research technologies

What does the technology do?

- Might this technology assist in finding answers to my research question?

How has this technology previously been used?

- Who else has used this technology and for what purpose has it been used?
- How has it been used? As a data collection tool, as an analytical tool, as a visualisation of findings tool?

How does this technology apply to my research project now and in the future?

- What is my unit of analysis and how might this digital technology help me with accessing the individual/small group/organisation or larger societal grouping?
- Is this technology open source or proprietary and are there constraints or limits on its use?
- Is this technology likely to be still available in the future or is it a short term fad?

What is required to use this technology?

- What are the resource requirements for this technology? The financial cost, the technical support offered by the firm, the compatibility with other technologies that you might be using, the time required to install, run and manage the technology, the level of institutional support available should all be considered.
- Will I be able to access an expert user of this technology when I need to?
- If working in a research group can this technology be shared by members of the group effectively?

One area of digital research that is heavily dependent on digital technologies is digital data collection. Figure 1.1 identified how digital research might use established or emerging methods/instruments. This simplistic representation did not explore the blurred boundary between established and emerging methods that exists in the form of established methods that are implemented by or through digital tools. For example, is an online questionnaire an established or an emerging instrument? Is interviewing via a Skype connection using an established or emerging method? As digital researchers, we have to consider how the characteristics of the digital environment both enhance and diminish established research methods/instruments as well as examining the usefulness of emerging research methods/instruments in relation to how well they provide data that help us address our research questions. For example, does the ability to search for information online impact on how people answer questionnaires? What is the impact of synchronicity on the responses gained from participants taking part in interviews? How does the lack of access to non-verbal communication cues impact online group discussions? How might the choice of device impact on participants' responses to experiments or interactions with the researcher?

Public or private?

When undertaking digital research reflection on whether our research data might be designated as public or private or indeed somewhere between the two, and how and why that matters, requires careful contemplation. Examiners and supervisors of research work, and indeed editors of journals, can become very uncomfortable with where data sit on this once simple categorisation. In the digital context rather than consider whether data are public or private, we have to consider *how* data are public or private. The binary divide between public and private that existed with non-digital research more closely resembles a continuum in the digital context.

For example, is a post to an open discussion board public because anyone can see it, or is it private, because it was written 'in the moment' and represents a fleeting response that in the non-digital context would disappear with that moment? If your social media profile is set to 'friends only', and a friend reposts one of your comments for everyone to see, is that public or private data? We propose that the purpose of much data created in the digital sphere is to be shared and as such may be considered for inclusion as research data, but this comes with caveats as we have outlined earlier in this book, related, for instance, to participant confidentiality (Bruckman et al., 2015).

In practical terms determining whether the data you wish to use in digital research are public or private can be daunting. As researchers we should adopt and practise responsible behaviour and be mindful of our duty to embrace appropriate ethics standards such as the Academy of Social Science's 2015 call that we 'should respect the privacy, autonomy, diversity, values, and dignity of individuals, groups and communities'. From that starting position we recommend considering three core components of the research when deciding where data fall on the public/private continuum: participant vulnerability, topic sensitivity and the original intention of the author.

First, how vulnerable are your proposed participants (remembering that participants are of higher importance than your research topic when it comes to ethics principles)? Your proposed participants may self-categorise as 'vulnerable'; previous researchers in your area may have termed them as 'vulnerable' or you may have decided they are vulnerable. Their level of vulnerability has a direct influence on whether you should consider the data they generate as public or private in the digital environment. For example, even if data were posted on a publicly available website or forum, were not sensitive in nature but were posted by someone who was 'vulnerable' (e.g., a pre-teen), we need to be very cautious about using such data. The person's vulnerability may mean that they are not aware of the ramifications of posting data online. Obviously if we gain permission with fully informed consent to use the data for our research then we can use that data.

Second, the research topic sensitivity may require us to reappraise the use of even public data. Discussions on public forums, and Q and A information sites, can include fairly personal and private information around specific subjects, for example, personal debt advice forums. The use of these data, even though they are publicly available, should be treated with caution by us as digital researchers. In these cases, careful anonymisation of the data may be a way forward. This includes not just anonymising the contributor but also ensuring that the content is not trackable through a search engine, for example, by re-ordering or removing certain parts of the content.

Third, we need to make an informed decision about the original intention of the data that were shared by the digital user. So Facebook posts of holiday destination images or tweets written and posted by recognised film stars, professional sportsmen and women, can, with some certainty, be deemed to be posted with the intent that others will view them. The original intent was likely to be for the digital data to be shared and spread across networks of both those known to the posters and those not known. Thus the original intention of the data was to be shared and can be diligently and responsibly used for research purposes. If, however, the photos were sent privately via email to one or more individuals without any indication that forwarding to others was expected, then as researchers we would have to consider whether that material was intended to be shared. Equally, if someone posted a photograph on Facebook and restricted its distribution, that should alert us to its less public nature.

Digital research resources

Digital research will require resources beyond just that of the researcher's time, for example, at a very basic level, a consistent internet connection with a good level of bandwidth may be the bare minimum to undertake digital research. At the other end of the spectrum, large scale social media data scraping, analysis and presentation of results are likely to require significant memory capacity on computing hardware, alongside specialist software for analysis possibly combined with visualisation software. In some cases projects may require access to coding resources – which may require time to acquire, or financial resources to pay for, the service. Projects may require incorporating different types of data and will consequently need consideration of data compatibility and the resources needed to manage these data. One caution is particularly important here – be aware of any limitations of 'free' resources available via the web. Free resources can be unstable and you might find yourself halfway through a project with a resource package that no longer works, has been removed from the web, and/or is not reliable. Free resources may have terms and conditions related to rights to use data within their system, which could violate ethics policies related to confidentiality. Data storage and the resources required also need to be considered. Cloud storage, for example, can be useful if you are using a lot of image data as image data tend to have large files sizes, but use of cloud storage should comply with your institution's policies on support for any online resources as well as policies governing research data storage.

SKILLS REQUIRED TO BE A DIGITAL RESEARCHER

Just as the digital context has dramatically changed the research landscape, especially in terms of what can be researched and how social science research is conducted, so have the skills necessary for researchers changed to reflect the dynamic digital research environment. To be a competent researcher producing meaningful research now requires a greater understanding of technical tools in the conducting and analysing of research data, and the ability to critique data and communication to multiple audiences. These core skills are now discussed below.

Conducting and analysing digital research

Engaging in digital research is not for the faint hearted. Both using digital as a tool or set of tools to enable a research project, and researching the phenomenon of digital, are likely to require you to tackle new techniques/tools, or unpick novel behaviours. A bank of knowledge and experience has yet to be built up to be passed on within the research community in relation to digital research. Certain researchers, such as Robert Kozinets, Christine Hine and John Postill, have provided invaluable transparency in their own approaches to digital research, which has enabled others to follow in their footsteps. Being prepared to try something new, and being open in terms of what data may be collected, or what the data might reveal, may well provide you with novel and meaningful insight and enable you to make a valuable contribution to your discipline.

Having collected data digitally, such as social media data or YouTube video material, certain skills are required in order to optimise the potential insight that can be gained through the various and growing analytical software packages that are available. The excitement of using new software to expedite the process of analysis can, however, turn to disenchantment. Asking the advice of other experienced researchers about the benefits and drawbacks of various tools, including your own university's technical support department, will help limit some of the time wasted. Training via short face-to-face courses, remote webinars and YouTube tutorials, is commonly available across a wide range of analytical tools. We suggest that trialling software once you have data is more helpful than deciding at the outset which package fits best. Unless you are extremely proficient in computer coding we do not suggest you create your own programme or algorithm for analysis as it will take hundreds of hours and require extensive testing before you would be able to use it on your own data. In addition, whichever software you may decide to use it will require justification in your final thesis/dissertation/project report.

As supervisors we are aware of an increase in the use of third parties to assist in the technical aspects of a research project in order to overcome deficiencies in researcher's skills. Different institutions and research groups will have different views on whether this is appropriate, so do ascertain what the prevailing and accepted norm is within your place of research. We urge caution in contracting out core aspects of your research, particularly if it is self-funded, for several reasons. First, for example, there is a risk that the web designer of your interactive game designed to test motor skills or brand awareness of in-game brand placement fails to deliver a useable game. There is a need to consider the potential impact of any failure to deliver on your research project and any deadlines you need to meet. Second, if someone else has constructed an element of your research, are you confident that you can explain and justify this design in detail to your examiner? Third, if the web designer or contractor decides to share your research results with others in their network, how detrimental will that be to the perceived value of your research? Fourth, if you have used participant platforms, such as Mturk or callforparticipants.com, in order to obtain participants to what extent can you rely on the sample and therefore the results?

As individual researchers we do not possess the complete set of skills required to design, conduct and analyse many digital research projects at the outset of that research. We can learn some skills as they are relatively straightforward (e.g., designing online questionnaires), and we may be able to purchase other tools and then learn them as we use them (the use of Qualtrics as a questionnaire platform, dissemination tool and data repository). Many of our skills as digital researchers will be learned by doing and practising. Becoming a competent digital researcher is an iterative process, which is why asking colleagues and supervisors about their own digital research experiences will enhance your learning.

Critiquing the data

As previously discussed in this text, the volume of data now generated that can be used for research in the social sciences is far beyond our ability to analyse that data. Quantity of data should not be misinterpreted for quality, or indeed relevance, of data. As researchers we need to question our assumptions about the data we are using, whether the data are secondary, such as social media interactions about political unrest in a country such as Syria, or whether we have collected primary data using an online questionnaire. Being able to reflect on and critique the data relates directly to issues of reliability and validity (see Chapter 6). The skills required for undertaking this critique involve an appreciation for where the data come from and how they originated. This critique is becoming increasingly technical. To illustrate, a researcher needs to understand the process of social media data scraping before they can evaluate whether the data set before them is sufficient and makes sense within the context of the research. Questions to ask would include: From where (which platform, which person) did these data originate? When do these data date from (the date and timing of day of collection)? Was the API released to the researcher to scrape the data or was this conducted by a third party? How complete are the data? Have we acknowledged that the results from a social media scraping may differ when replicated? What do we know about any algorithms that are associated with the data collection? These questions are important and yet little discussed in research methods classes. In a similar vein, the same level of reflection is needed on online questionnaire data: Has the structure provided sufficient scope for you to collect the data you need? If a recruitment platform was used, how can you be sure of your sample? How did you identify duplicate responses? Can you identify duplicate URLs or IP addresses? If using an automated, simplified analytical tool such as the one offered by SurveyMonkey, did it provide you with sufficient depth of analysis and appropriate visualisation beyond pie charts and descriptive statistics?

Communicating research digitally

As a digital researcher you may wish to consider how you communicate with research participants either during or after the research. The creation of a research blog or website may prove useful to you in terms of acting as a repository for important research information such as project outlines, results updates that you may wish to share, and/or calls for further participants. A research blog is straightforward to set up via simple platforms such as www.wordpress.com. A website requires more, but not significant, resources including hosting costs, but would be an option for any funded research project.

As a digital researcher you may want to master the art of writing succinctly for an internet-based audience. Research blog updates of approximately 300–400 words with an image or two will engage and inform your participants and/or sponsoring organisations. These blog posts can and should be linked to any professional social media presence you have (e.g., LinkedIn) so as to maximise potential readership. Non-academic writing skills and simple digital-based communication skills are, we believe, increasingly important for researchers. Beyond keeping your research participants informed, which is an element of good research practice, these platforms can and should be used to disseminate your research results (post viva if a doctoral student). Sharing your contribution to knowledge broadly will enhance your professional academic profile, as well as add credibility to other work you may undertake. Spending a day learning the skills associated with how to design, use and populate a research blog site is likely to be productive in the long term.

MANAGING DIGITAL RESEARCH PITFALLS

Based on our own experience and that of colleagues and research students, as well as issues cited in the research methods literature, we outline below some of the main pitfalls encountered in digital research.

Over-reliance on technology and equipment

The increasingly complex nature of the digital research environment and the sophisticated computer programmes used in the design and implementation of digital research are creating a situation where there are a relatively small number of people with the technical skills required to conduct some types of digital research and/or to help rescue it when aspects of the technology fail. Furthermore, the more complex research instruments that require downloading of apps, or voice activated responses by individual participants, the smaller the number of 'ordinary' people who will be able to participate in the research. Compatibility can also be an issue when research has been conducted on different digital platforms and then requires integration for analysis. Software updates, plugins and patches when 'holes' are found in analytical software can also be time consuming and may be imperfect quick fixes to larger underlying issues. Unless your research project is well funded and/or you have highly advanced technical computing skills, we would advise you to embrace digital technologies where relevant for your research but be aware of their imperfections. Novel approaches and methods are important to trial as otherwise we will not make advances in digital research methods scholarship, but plan to spend more time than you imagined if you decide to use tools that you are not familiar with or new tools that have a limited track record in research.

Hacking and/or viruses and other device issues

Whatever type of research we undertake as social scientists, be it digitally based or not, our use of computer technology even if only for writing up our research will leave us vulnerable to exposure to computer viruses and/or hacking attempts. This vulnerability is increased as we use more and different types of technology and computer software, as is the case when we engage in digital research. Malware and ransomware (a virus that demands money to be paid for the restoration of a computer's functionality) have been used against academic researchers including PhD students, and although we might feel individually targeted this is highly unlikely to be the case. In order to minimise the risks to your data and your work you need to ensure that you have up-to-date virus protection on all the devices you use in conjunction with your research. Many institutions have their own preferred software and may even assist you by making it freely available. You should also be aware that sometimes updates to devices including smartphones can wipe or alter information stored on those devices. So digitally stored interview data, for example, can be distorted or found to be incomplete after a version update. We recommend uploading all data and research material, field notes, etc. on a daily basis from devices onto a secure storage facility to minimise the impact of any virus, ransomware demand and/or version update destabilisation. Backup versions of research work and a separate master copy of the raw data set should be maintained on either secure university servers or a reputable paid-for storage provider that has a technical support team function.

Causing disharmony in an online community

As researchers, following an ecological metaphor, we would like to leave as faint a digital footprint of our presence as possible. We should endeavour to 'tread lightly' on the digital planet as far as we are able. We should aim to minimise or avoid disruption to communities in which we are interested or with whom we are researching. Having said that, there may be times when disharmony in an online community is perceived by one or more members of that community to be the responsibility of a researcher or a research project. Whether or not the researcher has been a cause of destabilisation is not the point, if the community feels that this is the case then apologies of a formal nature should be undertaken and amends offered. For example, a statement could be written by the researcher and posted on the community forum via the moderator, or a video made and posted, not just apologising but perhaps offering an overview of the value of the research and the results.

Having spent a significant part of this chapter deliberating issues associated with ethics in the practice of digital research, we shall not dwell on it further, suffice to state that useful heuristic guidelines are available from the AoIR website. The E of expertise is important to reflect on in both the skills that are required to design and undertake rigorous research but also the expertise and skills necessary to make the most of disseminating the results of the completed research. Dissemination is an important but often overlooked aspect of good research practice and we encourage this activity wherever possible and particularly when aimed towards those who have assisted in the research itself, such as participants, gatekeepers and other stakeholders. As researchers we have expectations that our research will go to plan but this is rarely the case. We need to make provision for issues such as low recruitment to the study, more time than planned for data cleaning, identifying back-up sources of data, frustrations over data analysis and software issues, etc., etc. We need to expect some level of unforeseen challenges and plan for the 'unknowable' to avoid missing research deadlines for paper or thesis submissions.

SUMMARY

This chapter has taken a more applied stance than the earlier chapters of the text in order to provide actionable assistance to digital researchers. The chapter has reiterated the blurred boundaries of researching in the digital environment and the centrality of the role of context in digital research decision-making. How digital may be incorporated into research in the social sciences has been suggested. Practical aspects of the private/public data debate and the use of these data in research have been outlined, along with the practical aspects of temporality, and technology and resources. The skills necessary to be a competent digital researcher have also been outlined and advice on how to manage digital research pitfalls given. Importantly, a significant part of this chapter has been devoted to good research ethics practice for digital researchers and sources of further information have been included.

FURTHER READING

Lewis, S.J. and Russell, A.J. (2011). Being embedded: A way forward for ethnographic research. *Ethnography, 12* (3), 398–416.

Marres, N. (2012). The redistribution of methods: On intervention in digital social research, broadly conceived. *The Sociological Review, 60* (S1), 139–165.

Paulus, T.M., Lester, J.N. and Dempster, P.G. (2014). *Digital Tools for Qualitative Research.* London: Sage.

Williams, S., Clausen, M.G., Robertson, A., Peacock, S. and McPherson, K. (2012). Methodological reflections on the use of asynchronous online focus groups in health research. *International Journal of Qualitative Methods, 11* (4), 368–383.

REFERENCES

Academy of Social Sciences (2015). General principles for social science research. Available from: www.acss.org.uk/developing-generic-ethics-principles-social-science/academy-adopts-five-ethical-principles-for-social-science-research/ (accessed 29 June 2016).

Belk, R.W. (2013). Extended self in a digital world. *Journal of Consumer Research, 40* (3), 477–500.

British Psychological Society (2013). *Ethics Guidelines for Internet-mediated Research.* INF206/1.2013. Available from: www.bps.org.uk/system/files/Public%20files/inf206-guidelines-for-internet-mediated-research.pdf (accessed 26 October 2017).

Bruckman, A., Luther, K. and Fiesler, C. (2015). When should we use real names in published accounts of internet research? In E. Hargittai and C. Sandvig (eds), *The Secrets of Studying Behaviour Online.* Cambridge, MA: MIT Press.

Cox, S., Drew, S., Guillemin, M., Howell, C., Warr, D. and Waycott, J. (2014). Guidelines for ethical visual research methods. The University of Melbourne, Melbourne, Australia. Available from: http://socialequity.unimelb.edu.au/__data/assets/pdf_file/0006/1981392/Ethical-Visual-Research-Methods-WEB.pdf (accessed 19 September 2017).

Evans, H., Ginnis, S. and Bartlett, J. (2015). *#SocialEthics: A Guide to Embedding Ethics in Social Media Research*. DEMOS/Ipsos MORI. Available from: www.ipsos.com/sites/default/files/migrations/en-uk/files/Assets/Docs/Publications/im-demos-social-ethics-in-social-media-research-summary.pdf (accessed 19 September 2017).

Gubrium, A., Hill, H. and Flicker, S. (2014). A situated practice of ethics for visual and digital methods in public health research and practice: A focus on digital storytelling. *American Journal of Public Health, 104* (9), 1606–1614.

Hesse-Biber, S. and Griffin, A.J. (2012). Internet mediated technologies and mixed methods research: Problems and prospects. *Journal of Mixed Methods Research, 7* (1), 43–61.

Kozinets, R.V. (2010). *Netnography: Doing Ethnographic Research Online*. Thousand Oaks, CA: Sage.

Lijadi, A.A. and van Schalkwyk, G.J. (2015). Online Facebook focus group research of hard-to-reach participants. *International Journal of Qualitative Methods, 14* (5), 1–9.

Maire, F., Moulines, E. and Lefebvre, S. (2017). Online EM for functional data. *Computational Statistics and Data Analysis, 111*, 27–47.

Mckee, H.A. and Porter, J.E. (2009). *The Ethics of Internet Research: A Rhetorical Case-Based Process*. New York: Peter Lang Publishing Inc.

Stefanidis, A., Crooks, A. and Radzikowski, J. (2013). Harvesting ambient geospatial information from social media feeds. *Geojournal, 78* (2), 319–338.

Xiang, Z., Du, Q., Ma, F. and Fan, W. (2017). A comparative analysis of major online review platforms: Implications for social media analytics in hospitality and tourism. *Tourism Management, 58*, 51–65.

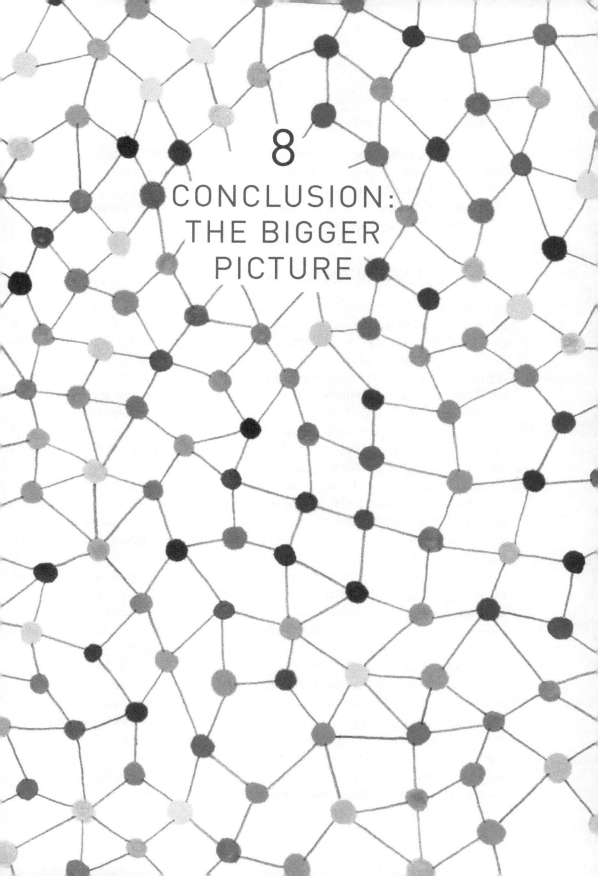

8

CONCLUSION: THE BIGGER PICTURE

In this chapter we will:

- draw together the key concepts from the preceding chapters
- review the emergence of digital research and its contribution to social science research
- suggest what the characteristics of rigorous and responsible digital research may look like.

INTRODUCTION AND REFLECTIONS

As a reader reaches the end of this text they would be forgiven for thinking that there are no clear answers to the dilemmas within digital research, and on this point they would be correct. The context of the research, however, remains a central guide to the research decisions made and so of course there cannot be a 'correct' way to do or think about digital research. The dynamic environment of the digitalised society means that even while this book was conceptualised, written and published, digital research had changed. The distinctiveness of digital research, its dynamic nature, its interdisciplinary and cross-disciplinary potential, the connectivity possible between researcher and participant but yet also the removal and detachment possible, makes digital research both fascinating and complex. Digital technologies have created multiple new social science phenomena for us to study, as well as having contributed methodological innovation in two ways. First, 'big leap' innovation through the creation and use of approaches such as netnography and data visualisations; second, 'small step' innovation through the incremental shift of data collection tools towards digital formats, such as online questionnaires and Skype interviews.

In our writing about digital research we have made no greater emphasis of the technical over the social nor the social over the technical, both elements are embedded within digital research and are interdependent. We do not consider one to be dominant over the other. Computer science, the creation of algorithms and the increasing automation of all aspects of data (data identification, collection, collation, analysis, dissemination, storage) have brought digital data within the grasp of many social science researchers. Similarly the socio-cultural changes in human interactions creating data, and in researchers working to make sense of the technology enabled research results, should not be underestimated.

Throughout this text we have given a broad range of digital research examples across the social sciences in order to help explicate the value of digital research. By encouraging reflection on digital research we have offered a way in which to clarify and hone subsequent research projects and outputs, be they Masters' projects, PhD theses, funding bids or research leading to publications. Both research conducted within the digital phenomenon as well as digital as a method/instrument have been delineated and the associated questions asked in our discussions.

This chapter brings together some of the ideas explored throughout the book. It starts by exploring the relevance and value of digital research, then considers how the digital environment presents us, as digital researchers, with a context that requires us to revisit research ethics, examine our expectations of research and the digital environment, and develop appropriate expertise. We then re-examine digital as a phenomenon and a method/instrument with a more nuanced view than was possible in Chapter 1, before presenting some concluding remarks.

DIGITAL RESEARCH VALUE AND OUR CONTRIBUTION

The value of digital research is currently underemphasised in the social sciences as current research activity does not reflect the impact digital has on the lives we now live. With greater visibility and acceptance through greater use and dissemination of digital research, this should change. More researchers should be encouraged to consider digital research in order to bring it from the peripheries of social science research to the centre stage. In order to achieve this, what is taught in research methods courses may need revision to include some of the tensions and solutions outlined in the earlier chapters of this book. Digitalisation is now embedded in everyday life; it has ceased to be just a separate activity. Social science researchers should at least consider embracing this digitalisation in how they approach their research.

The overarching aim of the book has been to fill a knowledge gap on the critical understanding of the relevance and value of digital research in the social sciences. Although it is up to the reader to determine whether or not the aim has been met and value created, we aimed to contribute to research methods and social science methodologies in the following ways. First, the breadth of examples included in the book has provided explicit illustrations of what is possible within digital research and has shown that new paths in the research landscape can be carved. These examples can be used to support and justify other innovative digital research. Second, the articulation of the tensions and challenges of conducting digital research and reflecting on these may encourage other researchers to be more reflexive in their own work. By encouraging greater reflexivity this may produce more rigorous digital research as reflecting on our own knowledge and practices is likely to improve the outcomes of our own research projects in the future and raise the general standard of digital research. Third, value has been created by this book by not over-hyping the potential of the 'new'. Newness and innovation in research and research methods are not to be feared but adopting something for the sake of 'newness' or lack or previous research is not, in and of itself, a justification for research in or with the digital phenomenon. Digital research is not a panacea, it places great demands on the research and the researcher. Digital research requires greater ethical consideration, and technical expertise, as well as demanding that we re-evaluate our underlying assumptions concerning both research methods and the digital context. Fourth, this book has contributed to scholarship by linking some of the 'harder to think about' more philosophical elements of research methods with the more practical 'how to do' digital research, providing an accessible yet well-founded source of information for digital researchers.

RECAPPING THE 3ES

In Chapter 1 we introduced the 3Es of ethics, expertise and expectations as a way of highlighting some of the issues encountered by digital researchers. We discussed the 3Es in relation to the content of each chapter. In this section we summarise what has been discussed elsewhere. We do not claim to have exhaustively addressed all the issues that might be encountered. Even if we had been able to achieve a comprehensive review in each area, the dynamic nature of the digital environment would have soon rendered any such effort out-of-date. Instead, we hope to have encouraged a mindset where you ask yourself three basic questions:

1. How can I ensure that I engage in ethically sound research within and through the digital context?
2. What are my expectations surrounding the digital context I am working in and, more specifically, my research project?
3. What expertise do I lack and how should I best ensure that this expertise is available for this digital research project?

Ethics

We maintain that ethics concerns in all research centre on an underlying principle of 'doing no harm'. While discussions concerning 'doing no harm' generally focus on the research participant, this principle also extends to protecting the researcher undertaking research as well as ensuring that we 'do no harm' to the research user by, for instance, over-claiming the relevance and/or usefulness of our research findings. Researchers working within the digital context cannot rely solely on established ethics guidelines as the characteristics of the digital environment have implications for what can and cannot be achieved by researchers. Instead, digital researchers often need to think through how their planned research adheres to underlying ethics principles.

In Chapter 2 we discussed how the socio-cultural environment impacts on what is considered ethical. What was not explicit here is that the dynamic nature of the digital environment means that we have to constantly refer back to the socio-cultural norms and values of all research stakeholders, and attempt to identify common ground and/or acceptable compromises. That is, we need to consider what participants may, or may not, consider acceptable, how research ethics committees might interpret ethical standards, and what our disciplinary norms are, as well as consider the standards of 'accuracy' needed to make our research findings usable by our intended audience(s). These socio-cultural norms are not static, they depend on changes in the cultural context and interact with technological possibilities.

Chapter 3 considered digital data characteristics. Here particular ethics challenges such as the extent to which digital data can or should be considered public or private were considered. Questions concerning what is public or private are well understood in non-digital research, but need to be revisited when considering digital data. We revisited the idea that a 'fixed' set of rules is difficult to develop in a dynamic environment. Other ethics challenges discussed in this chapter included the vulnerability of participants, the sensitivity of the research topic, management of third party data, and how to manage anonymity in digital research.

Chapter 4 considered temporal aspects of digital research. The ethics issues in this chapter were not as extensive as those encountered in other chapters. However, the broad consideration of research longevity does require some awareness of the usefulness of research for research users.

Chapter 5 considered sources of digital data and returned to issues of participant vulnerability and anonymity, as well as how research value might be impacted by the researcher potentially being unable to verify who research participants are. Ethics concerns around combining different data sources, and the potential to inadvertently identify research participants, were also raised, and ethics-related criteria for the selection of research participants were provided. This chapter considered what 'harm' might mean; specifically, psychological, social and physical harm were discussed.

Chapter 6 considered research processes. In this chapter the ethics implications of understanding (or not) digital research processes were raised. Many of the ethics challenges here were related to maintaining research users' confidence in the research quality rather than specific issues related to research participants. Though issues related to disclosure were covered.

Chapter 7 turned to the practicalities of research in the digital context, and in this spirit identified some specific guidelines/principles that are useful for digital researchers. Two specific areas – respect for research participants, and how ethics might be enacted by digital researchers – were considered in more detail.

Overall, this book has emphasised the central importance of assessing ethics by considering the underlying ethical principle of 'doing no harm'. Issues that might arise have been considered as different areas of digital research have been explored. The dynamic nature of the digital environment, different disciplinary and institutional norms, and varying knowledge of the digital tools and techniques available, are all factors that feed into the complexity of ethics in digital research. As digital researchers our responsibility to our participants, our research users and ourselves lies in remaining vigilant of socio-technological changes and their ethics implications. One key role for us as researchers in this context may be to ensure that we are conversant with digital research ethics debates and guidelines so that we can provide evidence for research ethics committees and internal review boards at universities and research institutions. We should have no expectation that non-digital researchers will be aware of either the specific ethics challenges the digital environment presents, or the potential solutions that have been developed.

Expertise

The digital environment is an emergent one so it should not be a surprise that long-established social science research training programmes do not develop all the skills necessary to successfully work and research in the digital context. Consequently, as digitalisation increases and spreads into the research environment, researchers need further technical skills in order to optimise the potential of their digital research. An individual may choose to develop their own technical skills or through building relationships with others who are proficient or indeed with organisations that may offer such skills and technologies for hire, in order to compensate for a gap in an individual's skill set. The evolution of the expertise required will continue to increase in velocity as well as an expansion in the different types of technical expertise. This section summarises some key capabilities identified where social science researchers may need to be aware that a potential knowledge gap exists.

Chapter 2 challenges our notion of what it means to be an expert digital researcher. What does it mean to be an 'expert' in an environment that is unstable and developing, where new technologies are constantly appearing, existing technologies are morphing or becoming obsolete, and no one individual can identify, never mind master, all the information that is available? What is an expert when specific knowledge quickly becomes useless? Maybe we have to redefine expertise around the process of acquiring and absorbing relevant information, recognising the potential of new tools/techniques, and being able to exploit those tools/techniques in a rapidly changing environment?

What does expertise mean then when we look at specific aspects of research in the digital environment? In Chapter 3 we talk about the characteristics of digital data. Across the social sciences expertise exists in the analysis and interpretation of many different data types. Some social scientists use advanced statistics, others are expert at interpreting images, yet within disciplines we tend to develop expertise with particular types of data and methods of analysis. In the digital environment, where different data types are often mixed, we have to question the usefulness of isolating one aspect of the data (e.g., text) from another (e.g., image). Consequently, we are much more likely to have to analyse and interpret novel (for our discipline) data. Acknowledging this lack of expertise allows us to identify collaborators (or specific training needs) to be able to develop appropriate expertise.

When considering temporality (Chapter 4) we have to consider how time and place impact on our ability to understand and interpret the digital context. We need to develop our temporal awareness to recognise the characteristics that are likely to impact on the research questions we are asking, as well as recognise and account for any temporal factors associated with our research methods (for example, when considering the time we are interviewing someone, should we look at their time or ours?). As non-digital researchers temporal factors are relatively straightforward to interpret in our, and others, research. As digital researchers, the temporal factors are associated with the platforms themselves, the socio-cultural context, and the methods we use. Consequently we need to develop our expertise by developing our ability to critically evaluate temporal aspects of digital research.

Our expertise related to data sources is also challenged by the digital environment and we explore this in Chapter 5. In contrast to temporality, which is not closely considered in established social science research training, data sources are addressed. As such, when we consider digital data sources we need to constantly evaluate whether, and how, established social science knowledge concerning topics like sampling processes, identifying participants and managing research participation, is applicable or even necessary. While the expertise we have acquired through established social science research training does not always apply in the digital research environment, we need to use that expertise to develop our justification for digital data sources as our research environment (e.g., research ethics committees) may still evaluate our research using those established norms.

Chapter 6 examines digital research processes. It points to the lack of expertise around issues such as building 'big data' sets and interpreting digital algorithms. Many of the technical aspects of digital research have not traditionally fallen within the expertise of social science researchers, but as digital researchers we cannot afford to remain ignorant of the technicalities. Nevertheless, just as we do not need to know how a telephone works to understand the benefits and constraints of telephone interviewing, as digital researchers we need to be able to clearly identify the benefits and constraints of the digital tools and techniques we use for research.

Chapter 7 addresses how we might investigate our lack of knowledge of digital tools and techniques as well as the digital environment by providing some questions that focus our attention on how we might, for instance, explore our level of knowledge concerning the topics discussed elsewhere (e.g., ethics, digital research tools). Indeed, the existence of this book is because, as digital researchers, we believe there is a need to develop digital research expertise in the social sciences. While much of this book presents you with more questions to ask about your digital research, we hope that bringing those questions to light helps you develop your digital research expertise.

Expectations

As researchers we all have expectations not just about the desirable outcomes of the research we are undertaking, the possible findings and the value of the digital research but also of how research should be conducted, what obstacles we might face doing research, and how many resources (time, effort, money) we will need to devote to our research. Recognition of our own biases, both positive and negative, concerning the digital context generally, and digital research more specifically, should, at the very least, be made explicit in our own notes. Indeed, sharing our biases with others, particularly when presenting our research findings, could help advance digital research more rapidly than if we hide them.

In Chapter 2, we explicitly stated some existing expectations of established research methods, before moving on to the impact of the dynamic digital environment on our socio-cultural expectations of both the digital context being 'always on, 24/7', and research within the digital context. Indeed, much of this chapter was devoted to questioning our macro- and micro-expectations of digital research in relation to time, place and space, as well as the socio-technological context of research.

When discussing digital data in Chapter 3, we touched on our socio-cultural/generational differences in relation to expectations of privacy, considering concepts such as 'oversharing' and disinhibition. This chapter also explicitly challenged us to consider the information that digital data can actually provide. Sometimes overly optimistic researchers can see the proliferation of digital data as an unfettered opportunity and so are naïve to constraints that do exist in the digital context such as access to digital data.

Chapter 4 discussed temporality. Temporality in the digital environment challenges our expectations on many levels as paradoxical conditions apply. For example, data are both fleeting with only 'now' being up-to-date, and yet also frozen with everything that has existed being available for inspection. Time does not degrade our 'memory' in the digital environment, yet we do not have the time to check what is, or is not, factually accurate. This chapter also addressed some of our expectations concerning the blurring of boundaries between different aspects of our lives (work/leisure).

In Chapter 5 we considered sources of digital data. Sampling in the digital context challenges our expectations concerning sampling processes, appropriate sample sizes as well as potential data sources. We asked you to unpick your expectations about: who/what your data source consists of and whether they/it can or should be accessed digitally; how the ethics of consent, which implies a need to identify participants, might in the digital context make that participant more vulnerable to harm; the extent to which we can control our sample; as well as our expectations concerning participants' roles and the accuracy of algorithms.

Digital research processes were considered in Chapter 6. Here our expectations of areas such as 'big data' and automation were explored. In many ways, developing our technological expertise leads us to lower our expectations of what can be done within a particular research study. The more naïve we are about digital research, the less constrained the possibilities seem. This is not to say that digital research does not open up numerous novel approaches and/or new research areas, just that, in common with all other types of research, it has weaknesses and well as strengths.

Chapter 7 focused on some of the practicalities of digital research. Here we asked you to examine your expectations of what your research participants might consider 'good' ethical practice, how you expect research collaborations to benefit your research and how you will manage those relationships, as well as consider what your expectations of the research are.

Overall, by raising issues concerning expectations that we might hold as researchers, we hope we have empowered you to examine any assumptions you are making about research in the digital context. Unpicking expectations is the first step towards examining any assumptions we are making about digital research and should be an ongoing exercise when undertaking research in a dynamic environment.

An illustrative example

While discussed separately in the chapters and above, ethics, expectations and expertise act interdependently. To illustrate this interdependence we have annotated a discussion between digital researchers concerning anonymising participants. Table 8.1 presents the discussion, some potential reflective questions that might be prompted from the thread contribution, and some thoughts on digital ethics challenges, ours and others, expectations of research and the digital context, and our and others, digital and non-digital expertise.

Table 8.1 Ethics, expectations and expertise – worked example

Illustrative scenario over anonymising tweets	Reflexive questions to ask as digital researchers	The 3Es
Hi Research Forum **I am attempting to get ethics approval for a study that involves the use of Twitter data and I have been told by my professor and the ethics committee of my university that I should anonymise the Twitter handles, how do I do this? Are there any software programmes to help with this? Thanks.**	• What is the purpose of the study? Do I have the most appropriate digital and/or non-digital data to help me answer my research questions? • What are my institution's policies on social media data use? • Where might I find expert help and guidance; are there official recommendations I can follow?	The researcher is recognising their own lack of *expertise* and is asking a research community for guidance. The question reveals the impact of the researcher's socio-cultural context, which is relevant to both research *ethics* and *expectations* concerning protecting participants' identities. The question also indicates that those guiding the research themselves appear to lack *expertise* with respect to digital research as they do not seem aware that anonymising the Twitter handles is insufficient to disguise the source of the tweet.
Response A **An interesting question but actually anonymising Twitter handles will not anonymise the data as the Twitter content will still be easily searchable through a search engine such as Google.**	• Do I understand the different levels of anonymity of author versus content that are possible, and to what extent does this matter to my research? • What am I trying to achieve by 'anonymising' the Twitter handles? Can it be achieved another way?	Here *expertise* in digital research is demonstrated. There is also an acknowledgement of the complexity of anonymity within social media and the digital context. The need for digital research to consider *ethics* is not questioned.
Response B **Have you considered if the context is important in your research? By detaching the username and thus the context you may lose meaning and depth to your data.**	• Does context and nuance matter to my research? If so, how much?	In this comment the responder questions the *expectations* of the researcher as to the purpose and nature of the research project as this will impact the subsequent design and data collection. They question how the socio-cultural context of the authors of the tweets might impact on research findings.

Response C

I don't agree with B, the removal of the user handle will not impact much on the context but removing the tweet from the conversation in which it was situated will lessen the value, it depends on what you are trying to achieve here.

- What am I trying to achieve through my use of social media data?
- What does context mean in relation to my research? Are there socio-cultural factors that might be identified via the Twitter handle, or is it more relevant to consider the conversation in which the tweet is embedded?

This respondent also connects the mechanics of the data collection and anonymising process to the *expectations* of the researcher and what is needed for the research project. Their point also raises points of (research) *expertise* – is it the Twitter handle that provides contextual information, or is it something else (e.g., Twitter profile, usage history) that matters. The discussion here has moved away from *ethics* and towards understanding the research study in question. These respondents are attempting to understand the context of the original question.

Response D

Are you undertaking qualitative or quantitative research? Quantitative research is less likely to create a problem regarding anonymity as you will be using large aggregated data sets of the Twitter content and it will be so much harder, though not impossible, to identify the individual user. You can replace the user name easily in SPSS or Excel by using a number instead of the name and then remove the user handles from the data set, don't forget to keep a secure master file somewhere with both the numbers and user handles just in case.

- What is the purpose of my research, will it be better served through the use of quantitative or qualitative approaches or should I use mixed methods?
- Do I have sufficient expertise to manage and use my data effectively?

In this response *expertise* and advice are offered, and an important question is raised about the type of research being undertaken as this may influence the level of anonymity required of the Twitter data. The *expectation* of how the data should be analysed (i.e., aggregation of data, versus examination of individual data points) in the research needs to be considered in relation to what the aims of the research are, and how *ethics* issues will be addressed.

Response E

Have you considered whether you will include deleted tweets in your research, there is a reason why they were deleted and you need to think about the ethical issues of including such material.

- What type of content am I looking for in my data?
- Is there material that may be relevant but that should not be used based on ethics grounds?

In this comment the participant in the forum reminds the researcher to consider whether or not it is ethically appropriate to include and use tweets that were posted and then deleted. This point is often overlooked. The original author of the tweet deleted that material (or possibly it was deleted by Twitter for being offensive etc.). *Ethics* based decisions need to be made through the balancing of the rights of the author of the tweet with the need of the researcher, but the former should take precedence. This also shows that *expertise* may be necessary to identify which tweets can and cannot be used: As data is deleted after data have been collected will that be detected by the researcher?

(Continued)

Table 8.1 (Continued)

Illustrative scenario over anonymising tweets	Reflexive questions to ask as digital researchers	The 3Es
Response F Hi. Don't forget that geographic indicators in user handles and/or tagging of certain content will make it easy to identify certain people, so you need to think about this too, particularly on a global community like Twitter.	• Do I understand the nature of identifiers and the impact that this could have on my research? • Have I considered the author's intent when posting the data? Would they consider it public or private? • What might the impact of exposing the author be within and out-with the digital environment?	This comment can be related to both *expertise* of understanding how identifiers can be used in social media and the original *expectations* of whether or not the author of the tweet would expect to be identified. This feeds directly into the first comment and the concerns about how the *ethics* of participant anonymity may (or may not) be achieved when using social media data.
Response G To add to this thread ... have you thought about whether you want to include any visual material, stuff like the images in links to the tweets you want to use ... this might cause ethics panels a problem, even though Twitter is a public platform.	• Do I want to include any visual material? If so how? • What contribution will it make to my research? • Do I have the ability to manage and use this type of data?	Again here is evidence of the *ethics* responsibility of the use of images: who do the images actually belong to and what content do they portray? The comment also relates to the *expectation* of the researcher in questioning what it is that the researcher might want or need to use. The *expectation* of the participant concerning the public/private nature of the data is directly addressed here, as are potential *expectations* found in the socio-cultural context the researcher is working in as the ethics panel is directly referred to.

REVISITING DIGITAL AS A PHENOMENON AND A METHOD

In Chapter 1 we discussed how digital research can comprise investigating digital phenomena or by using digital methods/instruments, or a combination of both. As we have moved through the discussions in this book, you are likely to have realised that the introduction on how digital might impact on social science research was too simplistic. Our introductory chapters began the discussion of the boundary spanning nature of the digital context. Some phenomena exist that are neither only digital bound nor just physically enacted, but rather they are boundary spanning. Some digital researchers use established methods that cross over the boundary into the digital context. In many cases the characteristics of these methods are so similar to their non-digital counterparts that it feels disingenuous to consider them as products of the digital environment. Figure 8.1 expands Figure 1.1 in

	PHENOMENON		
METHODS	***Physically enacted***	***Boundary spanning***	***Digitally bound***
Established	Physically enacted phenomenon explored using established physical methods *e.g., medical compliance behaviours explored through observation*	Boundary spanning phenomenon explored using established physical methods *e.g., motivation for participating in flash mobs examined using mall intercept survey*	Digitally bound phenomenon explored using established physical methods *e.g., geographically isolated online community members interviewed by telephone*
Adapted from established	Physically enacted phenomenon explored using established methods in a digital form *e.g., mental health explored through an email questionnaire*	Boundary spanning phenomenon explored using established methods in a digital form *e.g., purchasing decision-making examined using Skype interviews*	Digitally bound phenomenon explored using established methods in a digital form *e.g., website design factors investigated using online experiments*
Digitally enabled	Physically enacted phenomenon explored using digitally enabled methods *e.g., physical activity change examined through data uploaded to apps*	Boundary spanning phenomenon explored using digitally enabled methods *e.g., maintenance of social relationship explored via social network connections*	Digitally bound phenomenon explored using digitally enabled methods *e.g., viral spread of online videos investigated by looking at digital links*

Figure 8.1 A typology of research in the digital age

Chapter 1 to account for these boundary spanning/crossing research elements, providing typology which gives a more nuanced view of how the digital context may impact on digital research. Thus the two by two matrix has now been developed into a three by three typology, which allows the exploration of this more nuanced view.

Research that investigates physically enacted phenomena using established research methods contains all those research studies that are independent of the digital environment. These studies present the fewest novel problems for researchers, participants and other research stakeholders such as university ethics committees, as they are carried out in a research environment that is familiar to all stakeholders and where traditional research heuristics, and the majority of ethics guidelines, have been developed. Research studies that investigate physically enacted phenomena using established methods adapted for use in the digital environment are also relatively straightforward for those not familiar with digital research. Novel problems encountered with these studies may involve questions around whether the sample obtained digitally is 'suitable' to achieve the objectives of the research. For example, is a sample of internet shoppers 'typical' of all shoppers. Questions might also arise concerning how well a particular method/instrument can be transferred into the digital context. For example do you as a researcher understand the machanisms used to randomly assign participants to experimental groups.

Physically enacted phenomena can also be investigated using novel digital methods. These research studies commonly use the digital methods to try to gain new insights into relatively established phenomena. This may be because the data used were not previously available (e.g., sleep quality investigations using sleep monitoring mobile phone apps), because the data are more accurate (e.g., GPS distance and times for running/walking routes), or because the data are more detailed (e.g., heart and breathing rate apps monitoring day-to-day physiological data). Research studies intending to use these types of apps are essentially observing the details of their participants' behaviours. Digital researchers need to ensure they have gained the appropriate permission to research the participants, but they also need to consider how they will gain access and analyse the data. Researchers need to consider whether they have the expertise to build an appropriate 'app' to access the data, and if researchers are not building proprietary platforms to collect the desired data, they need to consider how they will gain access to the data from platforms that already exist.

Digitally bound phenomena are phenomena that would not exist if the digital context did not exist. While the digital environment that enables these phenomena is novel, academic researchers are familiar with the problems associated with studying a novel phenomenon. Researchers investigating a digitally bound phenomenon need to start by establishing how understanding this digitally bound phenomenon will make a contribution. What is the relevance of the phenomenon to the discipline? How does understanding the phenomenon help us to understand the lives we now live? Once the value of understanding the digitally bound phenomenon has been established to the satisfaction of research gatekeepers (e.g., funders, supervisors, ethics committees), the researcher can then unpick the different ways the phenomenon might be investigated. The methodological issues that need to be addressed will mirror many of those discussed earlier. However, it is unlikely that questions concerning the relevance of a digital sample will arise given the nature of the phenomenon. Indeed, it might be more difficult to justify a non-digital sample than a digital one.

Boundary spanning phenomena can exist independently of the digital environment, but are enhanced, extended, or changed by the digital context. For example, research into identity existed prior to the digital environment being commonly used, yet now the digital context allows people to explore their identities in novel ways. Extending this example, identity researchers may need to consider both digitally bound and physically enacted elements of identity, they might compare an individual's identity work across both digital and non-digital contexts, and/or look at the relevance of non-digital theories in the digital context. Other boundary spanning phenomena (e.g., online gaming, consumer purchasing processes, socialisation, and relationship maintenance) will encounter similar issues. The research methods appropriate to investigate boundary spanning phenomena will need to fit with the specific research objectives of the researcher. For example, a research study looking at online multiplayer gamers' behaviour might focus on game-play behaviour – a digitally bound aspect of the phenomenon – and consequently the research methods are likely to be digitally enabled. Another potential research focus might be on how online gaming impacts on gamers' health – a physically enacted phenomenon that might be researched through questionnaires (digital or otherwise) and physical observation. A third possibility is that the researcher might be interested in how socialisation occurs in the community of online multiplayer games. This research focus might suggest looking at the socialisation of characters within the online multiplayer game as well as the socialisation of the gamers in the digital environment. This focus would need to consider both the digitally bound and physically enacted aspects of socialisation, and the research methods used would have to account for the dual socialisation contexts.

CONCLUDING REMARKS

Our focus and discussion of digital research has excluded those people who cannot or do not participate in the digital environment, those people who have neither the access nor the expertise to interact digitally as well as those who choose to remain digitally 'off grid'. Obviously there are implications for individuals, groups and society of being digitally disenfranchised (Robinson et al., 2015) and although these issues extend beyond the scope of this book, they should not be forgotten. Likewise organisations and academics that do not engage at some level with digital research are exposing themselves to a loss of potential knowledge generation (Quinton and Simkin, 2016). Nevertheless, as we have proposed throughout the text, research, both in nature and in execution, is being transformed by digitalisation, and thus we echo the ideas of Meyer and Schroeder (2015). The considered use of digital research does, and will continue to, contribute to scholarship across the social sciences. Consequently, we need to ensure that the standards applied to digital research are appropriate to the digital context, as well as reflecting our established social science norms of research relevance, robustness and rigour. If we, as researchers, can achieve this then researching digital life as lived will be rewarding for everyone.

REFERENCES

Meyer, E.T. and Schroeder, R. (2015). *Knowledge Machines: Digital Transformations of the Sciences and Humanities*. Cambridge, MA: MIT Press.

Quinton, S. and Simkin, L. (2016). The digital journey: Reflected learning and emerging challenges. *International Journal of Management Reviews* (in press). DOI:10.1111/ijmr.1204

Robinson, L., Cotten, S.R., Ono, H., Quan-Haase, A., Mesch, G., Chen, W. and Stern, M.J. (2015). Digital inequalities and why they matter. *Information, Communication & Society*, *18* (5), 569–582.

INDEX